"We know that rivalries are a leading source of international conflict, and we know a great deal about the dynamics and consequences of international rivalries, but we know little about how international rivalries begin. Until now. In its exploration of the conditions and processes through which rivalries emerge, *Becoming Rivals* fills a glaring gap in our knowledge and makes an important contribution to the study of international conflict."
 —Jack S. Levy, *Rutgers University*

"*Becoming Rivals* tackles a theoretically important and understudied topic—the factors that increase the likelihood that two states will become rivals. This is a highly original study with new data and a theoretical analysis that increases our knowledge of interstate conflict. Scholars and students in political science and history interested in rivalry will find it a must read."
 —John A. Vasquez, *University of Illinois at Urbana-Champaign*

Becoming Rivals

Rivalries are a fundamental aspect of all international interactions. The concept of rivalry suggests that historic animosity may be the most fundamental variable in explaining and understanding why states commit international violence against each other. By understanding the historic factors behind the emergence of rivalry, the strategies employed by states to deal with potential threats, and the issues endemic to enemies, this book seeks to understand and predict why states become rivals.

The recent increase in the quantitative study of rivalry has largely identified who the rivals are, but not how they form and escalate. Questions about the escalation of rivalry are important if we are to understand the nature of conflictual interactions. This book addresses an important research gap in the field by directly tackling the question of rivalry formation. In addition to making new contributions to the literature, this book summarizes a cohesive model of how all interstate rivalries form by using both quantitative and qualitative methods and sources.

Brandon Valeriano is Lecturer at the School of Social and Political Sciences, University of Glasgow.

Foreign Policy Analysis

DOUGLAS A. VAN BELLE, *Series editor*

The Routledge series *Foreign Policy Analysis* examines the intersection of domestic and international politics with an emphasis on decision-making at both the individual and group levels. Research in this broadly defined and interdisciplinary field includes nearly all methodological approaches, encompasses the analysis of single nations as well as large-N comparative studies, and ranges from the psychology of leaders, to the effects of process, to the patterns created by specific dynamic or contextual influences on decision making.

The Unilateralist Temptation in American Foreign Policy
David G. Skidmore II

When Things Go Wrong
Foreign Policy Decision Making under Adverse Feedback
Charles F. Hermann

Prospect Theory and Foreign Policy Analysis in the Asia Pacific
Rational Leaders and Risky Behavior
Kai He and Huiyun Feng

Becoming Rivals
The Process of Interstate Rivalry Development
Brandon Valeriano

Becoming Rivals
The Process of Interstate Rivalry Development

Brandon Valeriano

LONDON AND NEW YORK

First published 2013
by Routledge
711 Third Avenue, New York, NY 10017

Simultaneously published in the UK
by Routledge
2 Park Square, Milton Park, Abingdon, Oxfordshire OX14 4RN

First issued in paperback 2014

*Routledge is an imprint of the Taylor and Francis Group,
an informa business*

© 2013 Taylor & Francis

The right of Brandon Valeriano to be identified as author of this work has been asserted by him in accordance with sections 77 and 78 of the Copyright, Designs and Patents Act 1988.

All rights reserved. No part of this book may be reprinted or reproduced or utilised in any form or by any electronic, mechanical, or other means, now known or hereafter invented, including photocopying and recording, or in any information storage or retrieval system, without permission in writing from the publishers.

Trademark Notice: Product or corporate names may be trademarks or registered trademarks, and are used only for identification and explanation without intent to infringe.

Library of Congress Cataloging-in-Publication Data
Valeriano, Brandon.
   Becoming rivals : the process of interstate rivalry development / Brandon Valeriano.
      p. cm. — (Foreign policy analysis)
   1. Balance of power.   2. International relations.   I. Title.
   JZ1313.V35 2012
   327.1'12—dc23
   2012030835

ISBN 978-0-415-53753-7 (hbk)
ISBN 978-1-138-91062-1 (pbk)
ISBN 978-0-203-10356-2 (ebk)

Typeset in Sabon
by IBT Global.

Dedicated to My Parents, Gil and Susan Valeriano

Contents

List of Figures		xi
List of Tables		xiii
Series Foreword		xv
Acknowledgments		xvii
1	Introduction: Rivalry and International Politics	1
2	The Steps-to-Rivalry Model	11
3	The Empirical Dynamics of the Steps-to-Rivalry Model	52
4	Timing and the Steps-to-Rivalry Model	65
5	The Complete Steps-to-Rivalry Model	92
6	The Rivalry Story: Iraq and the United States	103
7	What Do We Know about Rivalry Now?	138
	Notes	151
	References	155
	Index	163

Figures

4.1	United States and USSR (1947–1989).	75
4.2	United States and China (1949–1974).	77
4.3	United Kingdom and Germany (Prussia) (1887–1922).	78
4.4	United Kingdom and Russia (USSR) (1940–1985).	79
4.5	Russia (USSR) and Japan (1895–1984).	81
4.6	Russia (USSR) and China (1862–1986).	82
4.7	Germany and Italy (1914–1943).	83
4.8	France and Germany (Prussia) (1830–1887).	85
4.9	France and Germany (1911–1944).	86
4.10	China and Japan (1873–1958).	87
4.11	United Kingdom and Russia (1876–1923).	88

Tables

2.1	List of Rivalries	16
3.1	Rivalry and Relevant Alliances 2x2	58
3.2	Relevant Alliances and Rivalry Coefficient Estimates, Logit Model for Rivalry Type	59
3.3	Predicted Probabilities for Alliance and Rivalry	60
3.4	Rivalry and Horn Mutual Military Buildups 2x2	61
3.5	Rivalry and Valeriano et al. Mutual Military Buildups 2x2	61
3.6	Horn Mutual Military Buildups and Rivalry Coefficient Estimates, Logit Model for Rivalry Type	62
3.7	Valeriano et al. Mutual Military Buildups and Rivalry Coefficient Estimates, Logit Model for Rivalry Type	63
3.8	Predicted Probabilities for Horn Buildup and Rivalry	63
3.9	Predicted Probabilities for Valeriano et al. Military Buildup and Rivalry	64
4.1	Alliance Timing Distribution	69
4.2	Mutual Military Buildup Timing Distribution	71
4.3	War and Mutual Military Buildups at the Early Conflict Stage	72
5.1	Rivalry and Territorial Disputes 2x2	95
5.2	Territorial Disputes and Rivalry Coefficient Estimates, Logit Model for Rivalry Type	95
5.3	Complete Rivalry Model Coefficient Estimates, Logit Model for Rivalry	96
5.4	Predicted Probabilities for Complete Rivalry Model	98
5.5	Complete Rivalry Model by Rivalry Type Coefficient Estimates, Multinomial Logit Model for Rivalry Type	99
5.6	Complete Strategic Rivalry Model Coefficient Estimates, Logit Model for Rivalry	100
5.7	Predicted Probabilities for Thompson Model	101
5.8	Paths to Rivalry: Rank Order of Predicted Probabilities	102
6.1	Military Expenditures in Iraq and the United States, 1985–2003	132

Series Foreword

We seldom refer to linkage politics anymore. Many, if not most of the studies that we think of as part of a Foreign Policy Analysis (FPA) research program could use the term and refer back to those early studies from the 1960s but rarely do. It's a shame in many ways because often if we made the linkages between domestic and international a little more explicit, and put a little more effort into exploring how they shape foreign policy we would probably see a fair bit more progress. It is also likely that invoking the conceptual frameworks of linkage politics would help FPA scholars communicate more effectively with scholars working with other theoretical perspectives or engage with topics that are seldom considered as part of the FPA rubric. *Becoming Rivals* is a case in point, and as the Foreign Policy Analysis series editor I considered (but decided not to) insisting that this study should be reframed and presented in terms of linkage politics.

In the end I decided to approve the manuscript without asking for any significant changes to the presentation and there were two simple but compelling pragmatic reasons for doing so. First, the language of the rivalry literature is heavily imbued with power-politics focused empirical social science terminology and concept presentations that quickly become unwieldy if you put too much effort into translating them into a discussion that prioritizes the mechanisms and forces linking the international and domestic levels of politics.

Second, I decided that I could get the best of both worlds by leaving the manuscript in the language of the rivalry literature and simply drawing attention to the linkage politics here in the Foreword. Scholars of rivalry will see what they find familiar and will be encouraged to add a linkage politics dimension to their thinking. Those more fully immersed in the FPA perspective can read this from the linkage politics foundation that pervades so much of that sub-field and find the same value had I insisted on reframing the presentation.

In the end, this book adds a critical new dimension to our understanding of rivalry because it adds the linkage politics perspectives that are needed to start engaging the emergence of rivalries. Existing or enduring rivalries seldom make sense from a purely rational, international politics perspective and their beginnings are even harder to fathom by focusing on alliances, power, and threats in the international system. It is only as the domestic political side of the equation is brought to bear that we really see that it makes sense for the leaders to engage in rivalries even if it does not make sense for the country as a whole. As Valeriano notes at the beginning of the book, conflicts that grow into rivalries have a foundation in the domestic national psyche that appears to trap leaders in the rivalry. This comes to the fore in the latter stages of the book and makes for some interesting analysis.

—Douglas A. Van Belle

Acknowledgments

This book has been in the making for a long time. I am glad I finally returned to this project and the examination of rivalry, my first academic love. Even after starting this project early on in my career, the importance of rivalry as a unit of analysis, a concept, and a factor of interest has endured. I now see it everywhere in social life. In some ways I dedicate this book to rivals, enemies, and competitors worldwide. Rivals make life interesting, complicated, and dangerous all at the same time.

Most of this book was written while house-sitting, while sitting in tea shops, at various sandwich shops, and in secluded offices. Research is a tough process that requires concentration and seclusion in some cases (clearly sandwiches are also required). My parents have always been particularly supportive, even though they seem to have no idea what I do from day to day. As a family of immigrants, there is no greater goal or dream than education, and I thank my parents for helping me achieve that. Early drafts of this manuscript were produced during intense debates over the status of immigrants in Arizona and other states. Certainly the rule of law is important, but so are the potential contributions of those excluded from the American system. The United States changes, and it does so largely due to the strength and contributions of migrants. I do what I can to play my part as a Latino scholar, but in the end all I can do is be an example to a community.

I thank the people who have been in my life since I moved to Chicago and have helped me focus on this project. None more so than Megan Preusker, who provided distractions and made me a foodie. Big thanks also to Sasa Krsitic, Walter Porras, Kate Pothoven, Jaime Dominguez, and Andrew Bauer. I would thank the University of Illinois at Chicago, but that experience has just been too traumatic. I do thank Whan Choi, Yoram Haftel, Barry Rudquist, Dennis Judd, and Even Mckenzie for their support. Chicago has been fun, now on to Scotland.

In the field of international relations, I have to thank my two main mentors, John Vasquez and Patrick James. John Vasquez adopted me early on at Vanderbilt University and has given me a career and an example to follow.

xviii *Acknowledgments*

The questions that I seek to answer in this volume in many ways flow from his original contributions to the field. Pat James has always been supportive in helping me navigate this field. I could not be more grateful. I also cannot leave out Fred Bergerson, my mentor at Whittier College so many years ago. I am lucky to have so many mentors. Other academics who have provided support, advice, or general shenanigans include James Lee Ray, Katherine Barbieri, Jack Levy, Jacob Bercovitch (RIP), Frank Wayman, J. David Singer (RIP), Dan Geller, Paul Hensel, Sara Mitchell, Rickard Tucker, Donna Bahry, Laura Sjoberg, Steve Saideman, Norrin Ripsman, Kyle Beardsley, Jon Dicicco, Tom Walker, Susan Sample, Sam Whitt, Dennis Foster, Kwang Teo, Chris Leskiw, Dave Sobek, and Erik Gartzke. I would like to particularly thank the early rivalry scholars Paul Diehl, Gary Goertz, Jim Klien, Michael Colaresi, and Bill Thompson for their help through the years. Their data have been critical to this project, and I thank them for advancing the notion of rivalry. The two Dougs, Van Belle and Gibler, also deserve particular thanks for their support, kind words, and blunt honesty that I sorely needed.

Choong-Nam Kang helped me recreate the data set used in this project and deserves great thanks for figuring out how to utilize the updated rivalry data. Shareefa Al-Adwani provided extensive comments on Chapter 6. Matt Powers helped greatly with Chapters 3 and 5 and provided some great advice on the interpretation of results. John Van Benthuysen and Anahit Gomstian edited various parts of the manuscript. As always, all errors are mine alone.

Most of all I thank my students. Their interesting and probing questions have always motivated me to rethink my assumptions, ideas, and goals. They have proved to be an important sounding board for much of what is presented here, particularly my early classes at Vanderbilt and my international rivalry seminars at UIC. The classes at Vanderbilt taught me to be precise and exact about historical processes. Empirical and statistical work matters little if these ideas do not translate to concepts that are easily digestible to students and practitioners. The various graduate students I have worked with throughout my time have been important: Victor Marin, Vitaliy Voznyak, Matt Powers, Anahit Gomtsian, John Van Benthuysen, Ryan Maness, and my undergraduate research team of Hugh Vondracek and Michele Zetek. Thank you all.

"When two elephants fight, it is the grass that suffers."

—African Proverb

Brandon Valeriano
Chicago, Illinois, USA
July 2012

1 Introduction
Rivalry and International Politics

INTRODUCTION

On May 24, 2010, South Korea declared North Korea its archenemy in response to a sinking of a South Korean ship by a North Korean torpedo.[1] The term *archenemy* might be new in diplomatic parlance, but it is not a new concept in international affairs. Archenemies in international history have long been the source and focus of conflict in the international system. This book is an exploration of the beginnings of mutual long-standing hostility. Call the situation what you will—enemies, archenemies, protracted conflict, or foes—the conclusion is almost always the same: rivals in the international system represent a dangerous situation that should be a prominent factor of study for scholars and peace activists.

The key to peace lies in the elimination of persistent historical animosity expressed between states or actors in the international system. The roots and direct causes of violence can be found in the accounts of why relations between two international actors develop into hatred and rivalry. Rivalries are a fundamental aspect of conflictual international interactions. Rivalry is endemic to social relations of all shapes and forms. Rarely can an international news event occur without mentioning the important context of rivalry as an influential factor. The concept of rivalry suggests that long-standing, mutual hatred may be the most fundamental factor in explaining and understanding why nation-states commit violent international acts.

By understanding the historic and diplomatic factors behind the emergence of rivalry, the strategies employed by states to deal with potential threats, and the issues critical to long-standing enemies, we can attempt to find solutions to the scourge of international violence. This study explains the process through which states develop into rivals so that in the future we can predict and prevent rivalries from occurring. Intervention can only occur once the causes to the problem are understood. The goal here is to scientifically explain the process of becoming rivals. Only by understanding how something comes about can we take measures to end its existence in the international community. By ending rivalry, the deadliest wars in the system could be eliminated.

2 Becoming Rivals

The unintended consequences of war, which include violence within the state after conflict, degradation of population health, and loss of minority rights, tend to far outweigh any benefits that conflict operations may provide. Even wars begun for the right reasons, with the right intention, tend to fail to achieve the lofty goals of stability and progress suggested by those who push wars to start. Yet, why are there still international wars? Why did the United States and Iraq fight (again) in 2003? Why did India and Pakistan fight (again) in 1999? Why did Somalia and Ethiopia fight (again) in 2006?

Rivalry provides the answer to these questions and many other puzzles posed by international relations scholars.[2] Rivalry can help explain much of what occurs in the realm of interstate conflict. In the last two decades, rivalry as a concept has become ascendant in international relations as an explanation for escalation of tensions and war. Rivalry can explain who fights whom, when, and where (Bremer 2000).[3] Rivalry is simply a situation of long-standing, historical animosity between two entities with a high probability of serious conflict or crisis. During rivalry, relative positions matter, and rivals will fight about anything and everything.

A simple question needs to be answered about interstate rivalry, and the quest for this answer is the purpose of this book. If states engaged in a rivalry can account for the majority of wars and disputes (Diehl and Goertz 2000; Thompson 2001) that have occurred since 1815, why have scholars generally failed to explain the beginnings of this important event? Research has uncovered little about why and how pairs of states become rivals. There should be no more pressing concern in international affairs than uncovering why pairs of states become rivals. Even in the era of globalization, climate change, and economic collapse, scholars still have failed to deal with perhaps the most pressing problem in the international community: repeated violence and historic animosity. Interstate violence has not withered away like many thought after the Cold War. War and conflict continue to be a reality of international life. This is because nation-states continue to cultivate rivalries and hatreds.

The recent increase in the quantitative study of rivalry has largely identified who the rivals are (Diehl and Goertz 2000; Thompson 2001; Hewitt 2005), but not how they form and escalate. Questions about the development of rivalry are important if we are to understand the nature of conflictual interactions. These questions are also important if we are to understand why states would even think of fighting each other in the first place. This book addresses an important research gap in the field by directly tackling the question of interstate rivalry formation and development. In addition to my own contributions to the literature, this book will summarize a cohesive model of how all interstate rivalries form by using both quantitative and qualitative methods that can account for the onset of rivalry. The fields of international relations and peace studies can hardly move forward without explaining why two or more states would focus their collective national plans and efforts on exterminating an enemy.[4]

Many scholars and observers take rivalry as a given. The point of this book is to explain how the situation of rivalry develops before serious conflict erupts. Rivalry cannot be assumed as a normal function of international life. In fact, rivalry is a critical factor that needs an explanation so scholars and peace activists can better understand the abhorrent practice of mutual animosity.

THE IMPORTANCE OF THE RIVALRY STORY

The final story of how rivalries begin should combine aspects of all social and biological theory, plus historical processes and advanced statistical modeling techniques. Many past scholars have focused only on the efficacy of force and threats to achieve political gains; this path has not been fruitful in contributing to international peace. To explain how two states can come to hate each other requires more than just material explanations of the use of force. The size of a military or technological achievement in weapons development mean little unless there is a target these advancements are directed towards. To fully understand why rivalries begin and matter one must uncover the social, behavioral, interactive, biological, and structural reasons for the event.

The problem is that the complete story of rivalry development is often never told or investigated. The process has begun to be accepted as a logical fact. Maybe this is an extension of the Hobbesian view of man in the state of nature (Waltz 1959). If man is evil, selfish, and fearful, then we should not be surprised that rivalry between international states will develop. This school of thought believes that rivalry is a natural outgrowth of human relations. Most states active in the international system engage in some sort of rivalry, so why must we understand a fundamental concept in interstate life? To ignore the search for an explanation to such a critical event as rivalry is to accept that humankind is essentially doomed to perpetual conflict and war. This pessimistic and conservative view of international relations should no longer be propagated. Progress can be made. In international relations scholarship our first target of elimination should be long-standing rivals.

The story and process of rivalry development are important since rivalry as a situation is a direct contributing factor for most conflict in the system. To root out the disease (war), to destroy its influence on the course of human events, one must first understand how the process can be prevented from occurring in the first place. To do this we must tell the story of rivalry onset. This near uniformly tragic event in international life tends to occur because of power politics folklore and legend. When threatened by an opposing state, the next logical action is to threaten that state right back. The typical advice is to escalate, to fight back, and make the enemy back down. After all, it takes two to tango, as the saying goes (Hensel and Diehl 1994). Yet, this process is an ancient response that no longer fits with modern realities. Escalating and developing a rivalry is an immature response to international problems. The characteristics of a rivalry relationship are more suited for the playground than the forums of international diplomacy. Rivalries might be important in building state capacity (Thies 2005) early in the life of a state. Unfortunately as states become advanced developmentally the situation of rivalry only deters investment in social services, education, and research by diverting national attention away from internal issues. When the cumulative national project is focused on an external enemy and not internal improvement, the state can wither and degrade. States engaged in rivalries are more likely to end up on the ash heap of history (Morgenthau 1948) than those states who fail to play the power politics game.

There are many international examples of states that could focus their energies on more important aspects of international life than rivalry. Much of the Middle East, Pakistan, and Post-Soviet space have all failed to solidify and advance because of distractions, often devastating, posed by rival states. Even the United States of America spent treasure and resources confronting the Soviet Union in a vast positional rivalry (Thompson 2001) when the state should have been focused on consolidating its domestic achievements and society. While Israel has advanced economically and culturally since its founding, no one would claim that it would not be better off if the Israelis could put their fears of regional conflict aside and focus on internal improvement. Pakistan is beset by many political and economic problems, including a domestic insurgency that threatens other states in the region. Yet it fails to deal with these problems effectively as long as the state is focused on the long-standing existential threat posed by India. Perhaps Japan is the greatest example of the impact of rivalry distractions. Faced with the ability and unity to become a great power after World War I, Japan failed in its mission to achieve great power status. Japan instead focused on dealing with its rivalry with the United States and China. By launching a surprise attack against the United States at Pearl Harbor in 1941, in order to have a free hand in Asia, the Japanese government doomed the state to a long war and decades of recovery. Ultimately, rivalry is dangerous, devastating, and counterproductive for state interests.

There is perhaps no larger international concern than dealing with historic rivalries and preventing their development in the first place. By eliminating a central factor that can explain much of international conflict, the system can move towards a greater understanding of peace, progress, and harmony. These are not utopian ideals; they simply represent options that a state can try to focus on once an external enemy is no longer an obstacle.

Rivalry is very much like a story told over and over again. We all know how it ends, yet we read or listen to the story again and again. This tendency has to stop. Rivalry, repeated disputes, and intractable conflicts are all forms of relationships that should be made extinct and outmoded. Rivalry, as a form of relationship, can be replaced by better methods of peaceful negotiation and adjudication. We must then examine how one can avoid the process of rivalry in the future. Is there a way to stop the development of rivalry?

INTERSTATE RIVALRY AND THE STEPS-TO-RIVALRY THEORY

International relations scholarship holds the position that rival dyads (pairs of states) are more war prone and disputatious than any other type of dyad (Diehl and Goertz 2000; Thompson 2001). Thompson (2001) finds that 75 percent of all strategic rivals have engaged in war. Diehl and Goertz (2000) discover that over 50 percent of the enduring rivals (only sixty-three pairs of states) have fought a war at one time or another and account for the great majority of conflict experienced in the system. If interstate rivals are responsible for most of the war in the international system, a prudent course of action to decrease conflict is to focus conflict management techniques on states that are either already rivals or might become ones in the future.

An important advancement of the study of rivalry involves the assumption that disputes, crises, and wars are not independent events, but are connected across *time and space*. The rivalry research program brings the history of interactions between a pair of nations back into focus. This point is important and was so often missed by early conflict scholars. Crises and disputes were taken as unique or isolated events in statistical analysis. Of course, this is not the way leaders view conflicts, nor is it the way conflict should be studied. Wars and serious crises usually develop only with a long pattern of interaction that leads to escalation and conflict after hostility and animosity build up over time. Leaving time out of the equation is obviously faulty logic. One must consider the impact of time, history, and repeated events if scholars are going to make any headway in their investigation of the causes of international violence.

Rivalry is defined as constant competition and struggle between two or more actors over some stake or issue with a high degree of salience, but the issues at stake may vary over time. The relationship is characterized by the high probability of violence and the fact that relative positions matter more than absolute gains. In international politics, interstate rivalry involves the conflictual relations between two international enemies that are nation-states. A fundamental characteristic of a rivalry involves the willingness of the states involved to harm their own prosperity and progress in order to deny a gain to a rival state. There is no such thing as a "public good" in a rivalry. The only "good" during a rivalry is to hinder the progress of the enemy despite the negative consequences of such efforts on domestic progress.

As Most and Starr (1989) posited, states need both the opportunity and willingness to engage in international violence. States engaged in rivalry typically are willing to harm their own security to provide some net loss to their enemy. What of the opportunity to engage in conflict? States engage in rivalry because of issue disagreements (Mansbach and Vasquez 1981), which are central concerns for most international events. A state would only be willing to engage in a rivalry if faced with a threat to a vital issue that might hinder its existence or ability to operate. The willingness to engage in a rivalry is typically set off by a dispute over symbolic or transcendent issues. Types of issues that are symbolic include territorial disputes (Vasquez and Valeriano 2009), positional arguments (Colaresi, Rasler, and Thompson 2008), and ethnic considerations (Saideman and Ayres 2008). Territorial disagreements (Vasquez and Leskiw 2001) often are at the heart of interstate rivalries, yet rivals will fight about anything and everything once the rivalry situation starts.

The theory presented here builds on and refines prior models of conflict onset. The steps-to-war model (Vasquez 1993) holds that there are certain actions or foreign policy choices states make that increase the probability of war occurring within a dyad. Territorial disputes, power politics (alliance building, hard-liners in power, and arms races), and recurring disputes each move a state closer to war. "Power politics behavior, rather than preventing war, actually increases the probability that it will break out" (Vasquez 1993, 7). In combination, the issues at stake and how those issues are handled can provoke war if said issues are handled in a power politics manner. This constructivist view of interstate relations takes perceptions, intentions, and ideas into account when examining the process of rivalry development. I argue in this book that there are certain foreign policy practices that will increase the probability that a pair of states will become involved in an international rivalry, and that these steps occur prior to the outbreak of war, a major respecification of the steps-to-war hypothesis.

The model and theory of rivalry development proposed here suggests the initiation and escalation of rivalry is a stepwise process. Rivalry is the outcome to be explained before one can look to explaining how individual wars develop. States that utilize power politics strategies in response to a potential enemy will increase the probability that the potential enemy will become a full-fledged rival. When confronted with a symbolic or transcendent issue, states that utilize typical coercive strategies such as internal (military buildups) and external balancing (alliances) will become locked into conflict. Once locked in, the situation will escalate into a condition of dangerous rivalry. It is only through the interruption and termination of power politics practices that rivalry can ever be fully avoided and eliminated. It is the perpetuation of typical power politics strategies—such as alliances, arms races, constant use of force in other disputes, and the escalation of bargaining demands—that leads to the development of rivalry. This is the process that I will explain in this work. Hopefully careful attention to the causes of rivalry will lead to its avoidance in the future.

HOW TO EXPLAIN RIVALRY SCIENTIFICALLY AND ISLANDS OF THEORY

Long ago, Harold Guetzkow (1950) suggested that international relations research proceed with an "islands of theory" research model. The accumulation of knowledge on issues critical to war and peace will only come through the construction of basic explanations regarding different events or variables that might eventually join together to provide a macroexplanation of why conflict erupts. The goal is an all-inclusive model of conflict onset, yet we cannot hope to explain all wars and conflicts without recognizing that some wars are different than others and the conflicts that erupt have different preconditions (Vasquez and Valeriano 2010). Therefore, a careful construction of models that explain events in international politics is in order. The accumulation of knowledge is the goal, and this can be achieved through the patient construction of explanations for international events.

This research flows from the islands of theory proposal. The goal here is not to explain why wars are fought, when men kill, or why a crisis might erupt in the first place. Our task here is to explain why pairs of states lock into long-term rivalries. What accounts for the fact of international persistent enemies? This question is much different from the question of "why do states fight wars?" or "how do disputes begin?" This question should not be confused with the other levels of events because the goal is only to explain rivalry or repeated events. Instead of being divided by the relevant levels of analysis (Singer 1961), international relations research on the causes of conflict should be divided into three distinct domains that focus on war, rivalry, and disputes.[5]

The first domain is: Why do states engage in interstate warfare? What are the causes of interstate violence? These questions have been driving the field since its inception. The problem with this branch of study is that it has moved forward without explaining the more mundane task of who fights whom and why. There is some general agreement as to why states may fight (Geller and Singer 1998; Vasquez 2004; Vasquez and Valeriano 2010) yet very little understanding of where these factors come from in the first place.

This leads to the second domain and the one that is the most important. As a field, we need to have a better grasp of who fights whom repeatedly. Why do conflicts repeat, fester, and fail to be resolved? The task of this book is to explain how this undertaking can be managed through the patient construction of a theory that details how and when states engage in rivalry. Without explaining this level of events, it would be nearly impossible to target and manage ongoing conflicts (which account for most conflict in the system).

The last domain is tasked with explaining why disputes or crises arise in the first place. Why and when do the first signs of conflict come about? Explaining this island of knowledge will require more than simple explanations that focus on material power or the national interest. Explaining why states even begin to envy, fear, or hate another state will require a behavioral (Bennett and Stam 2004), genetic, cognitive, and psychological theory of why states choose to play the conflict game in the first place. This area of scholarship will become important in the future as scholars get a better handle on the individual motivations for conflict onset.

Each domain will require a different theory that will detail how and when conflict at this level will come about. This investigation will be mainly concerned with the second island outlined. What factors lead to rivalry? Little work has been done on this emerging research program, and it is hoped that this book will go a long way towards explaining the persistence of international enmity.

Reliance on the islands of theory concept also requires a reliance on the scientific study of international relations. The view of scientific enterprises is that only through the verification and testing of theories can one seek the accumulation of knowledge. Research builds upon other research efforts to eventually come to some sort of answer regarding pressing questions. In this case a theory is proposed and tested explicitly. This theory is generated from many other inductive studies of political events and also the deductive nature of historical learning. If the theory fails to be falsified, then we can have some confidence that the results accurately reflect the state of knowledge on the subject at the time. Reformulation might also take place if modifications of the theory are necessary, as are explanatory case studies that apply theoretical processes to current historical incidents.

Once a theory has demonstrated its empirical accuracy, logical consistency, and ability to explain the past, present, and future, it can then be said to scientifically account for a form of social and historical interaction. It must be remembered that when dealing with social realities our theories can never be 100 percent accurate. There is some randomness inherent in social forces; social science does not take place in a vacuum as some hard sciences do. In this book I have taken every measure to be both scientifically and historically accurate as well as honest about the limits of my theory in the application of real-world processes. It is only through the patient process of scientific study that humans can tackle the pressing problems in the international system.

PLAN OF THE BOOK

The argument of this book is that interstate rivalries develop under conditions where power politics foreign policy practices are utilized by international actors. When threatened with a persistent enemy, states respond in a fashion outlined by a power politics viewpoint (Morgenthau 1948). They "solve" the dilemma of a conflictual situation by building an alliance, participating in a military buildup, and participating in outward uses of force to show commitment and resolve. I find evidence that this is the case for the most dangerous forms of international enemies—rivals.

Chapter 2 of this book will outline the state of knowledge about rivals to this point. Very little work has been done overall about why rivalries develop, but there are quite a few relevant findings that might enlighten the path towards rivalry. Others suggest a punctuated equilibrium model of rivalry development (Diehl and Goertz 2000). Herein I posit that a process model (Bremer and Cusack 1995) is in operation. Events only add to and interact with preexisting conditions to produce an outcome. Rivalries develop; they do not manifest out of thin air. They neither truly evolve nor begin through calamitous events. Rivalries slowly build up, lock in through events and actions such as early wars, and then either escalate towards termination or settle into a period of managed conflict. There is no pattern to the life span of a rivalry, but there are patterns that can explain the development and onset of rivalry in the first place.

Chapter 2 will outline my steps-to-rivalry theory. The theory posits rivalry as a process whereby states take certain actions that increase the probability that they will become long-standing rivals. Rivalry is the most contentious form of conflictual relations, and states typically end up in this situation when they use power politics foreign policy tactics.

Chapter 3 is the first of the empirical chapters, and the goal is to undertake an exploration of the relationship between alliances, arms races, and rivalry as an outcome. I will first examine whether there is a relationship between alliances, arms races, and rivalry. I develop the logic for and test the proposition that these foreign policy practices represent probabilistic conditions for rivalry.

Chapter 4 takes my argument a bit further and looks at the relationship between timing and the occurrence of rivalry. I ask if the power politics factors investigated are present during different time periods prior to the start of the rivalry relationship. Will the results change if the analysis is shifted to a sequencing model that can account for the stages of rivalry throughout time? I will seek to understand when power politics strategies are used during the life of a rivalry. For my theory to be empirically accurate, it must show correct temporal ordering. It is also important to add the correct temporal ordering of events to models. Sequencing plays a very small role in theories pertaining to the onset of rivalry or war. The timing of events is critical. To that end, I provide an examination of time plots that display the life trend of a rivalry with critical variables specified in terms of when they occur during the life of a rivalry.

Chapter 5 summarizes and presents a complete rivalry model. This represents the combined and complete statistical test of my theory. Here, I seek to combine all the previous empirical findings of Chapters 3 and 4, plus other ideas, to show their relationship in the process of rivalry development. This model will add in findings on alliances, arms races, territoriality, and state power status to underscore each variable's relationship to the presence of rivalry. This chapter will also explore the pathways to rivalry, suggesting the most dangerous road to rivalry.

Chapter 6 seeks to place the theory and findings regarding rivalry dynamics in the post-9/11 world. Can my theory explain the onset of rivalry and war in a situation where it is not expected to? Can a theory of rivalry explain both the onset of intractable conflict and also why the Iraq War of 2003 erupted when there were more pressing security concerns for the United States to consider at the time? This chapter will focus on explaining how the theory is operational in the real world. It is an example of an explanatory case study that seeks to use rivalry theory to explain events of the past, present, and future. If an explanation cannot be applied to both the past and present, it cannot hope to explain future relations.

This book explains how rivalry develops and seeks to suggest ways that rivalry may be avoided. The last chapter in this book summarizes the findings presented in this book and throughout the field, and also suggests policy advice that may help entities avoid a state of rivalry in the future. All strands of research and empirical findings will be connected to tell the story of how a pair of states becomes an international rivalry. What do we know about rivalry now that this mammoth task has been completed, and where do we go in the future? Hopefully at the end of this project you will be convinced that my story is both accurate and important. There is no greater pressing concern than the avoidance of the scourge of warfare, and this work goes some ways towards figuring out how this devastating event can be avoided in the future.

2 The Steps-to-Rivalry Model

INTRODUCTION

Rivalries are relevant in every aspect of social life. They are common and prevalent and yet very deadly and distracting. Rivalries play an important role that either hinders progress or encourages determination in the face of adversity. Rivalries can be useful, but often they are damaging and dangerous. There are sports rivalries, interpersonal rivalries, and business rivalries that have either pushed individuals or groups to excellence or to ruin. Perhaps the most important form of rivalry, but also the least studied, is international rivalry. This type of rivalry plays a critical role on the path to war and peace in the international community. The absence of rivalry generally denotes a relationship of peace and cooperation. The presence of a rivalry denotes a high likelihood of war and constant conflict.

Interstate rivalries include a pair of recognized states who have formed a long-standing, conflictual relationship with each other. Rivals should be eliminated from international history because their negative consequences far outweigh any potential benefits. The steps-to-rivalry model presented here is rooted in an examination of the additive behavioral processes that bring about the situation of interstate rivalry. Rivalry is a process; it is a situation that develops through time due to reactions in response to context and stimuli. This action–reaction process is critical in explaining why and when rivalries begin.

Rivalries begin due to both events and responses to events. First some contentious issue must prove pressing and engaging enough to warrant the attention of at least two nation-states. The issue does not have to rise to the level of fully fledged crises, but it does have to be important enough to gain the attention of relevant decision-makers. Next, there must be a coordinated response by each side to escalate the conflict based on the issue situation that has developed. Once these steps are taken, rivalry will typically result if neither state disengages or stops escalating tensions as various disputes occur. Eventually the rivalry will either continue to fester until war and death, or it will settle into a period of managed hostility similar to the Cold War between the United States and the Soviet Union.[1]

It is the reaction to threatening situations and pressing issues that matters most for the process of rivalry and for the theory presented here. What happens after the first moves towards escalation are taken by the initiating side? We already know that certain issues can prove important in explaining who becomes rivals or who fights whom; yet we still need a theory to explain why each side took steps to lock a rivalry situation into existence. In short, why do states become rivals in the first place? Why do some states ignore the conflagration or settle the issue quickly, avoiding a long-term contentious relationship, while others press forward with conflict?

The answer to these questions lies in how states handle situations in which their interests are threatened. By making equal and escalatory threatening actions to resolve the situation that has brewed, states are doomed to perpetual conflict and rivalry. Deterrence or resolve almost never works in preventing recurring conflict; these types of actions tend to result in a security dilemma whereby actions taken to ensure state security end up threatening the other side and press that side to respond. Actions taken to protect the state almost always result in an equal or escalatory response by the other side, locking each state into rivalry. When faced with a salient international issue, it is almost never advisable that states settle these issues with power and force rather than negotiation and adjudication because power and force are factors that bring about rivalry.

What types of reactions produce rivalry and the security dilemma? Power politics foreign policy practices are the main culprit in uncovering the answer to the question of why certain states that press issue concerns become rivals. Territorial issues are dangerous, but alone they do not produce rivalry, although they make them more probable. The real problem is how states respond to pressing salient issues. When states take the typical power politics path of building alliances and escalating the military weapon acquisition process, rivalry typically results. Rivalry is a situation of protracted conflict whereby relative positions matter and there is a constant threat of conflict. The existence of a rivalry produces an existential threat to a state. Rivalry is a leading cause of war; therefore, it is a process that must be stopped and terminated before it leads to the escalation of violence and further international ruin.

This chapter will outline my theory of rivalry development, which is called the steps-to-rivalry theory. Power politics reactions to threatening situations will produce the outcome of rivalry. The way to stop the rivalry process is to eliminate the typical power politics response to threatening situations. First I will outline the prior state of knowledge about rivalry in the field, and then I will explain the path to rivalry through the model presented.

WHAT IS RIVALRY?

Rivalry as a Concept

The utilization of international rivalry as a concept has allowed the field of international politics to reconceptualize how the discipline studies conflict. In the past, the field concentrated on international war as the factor in need of explanation. If the rivalry situation accounts for over three-fourths of wars in the first place (Thompson 2001), the study of conflict and international politics should be orientated toward preventing and managing the most severe forms of rivalry before escalation to war takes place. If the purpose of international politics and peace studies is to prevent the outbreak of war, we must concentrate on what is observable, manageable, and preventable; in other words, we must concentrate on interstate rivalry.

Vasquez (1993, 75–76) defines a rivalry as "a relationship characterized by extreme competition, and usually psychological hostility, in which issue positions of contenders are governed primarily by their attitude toward each other." A rivalry essentially involves a hostile relationship with a recognized historical adversary. Rivalries are typically identified as some form of repeated, long-standing crisis or protracted conflict. They involve competition and struggle between two or more actors over some stake or issue that may change and vary from incident to incident.[2]

Some states are actually "addicted" to conflict with other states (Maoz 2004). The image of another state as an enemy endures in the relations between the states and in the minds of the elites and the mass public. Despite any information that may cause a reevaluation of the relationship, rivals typically are stuck in the situation because of the traits exhibited by addicts. Rivals tend to be impulsive, to be socially disconnected from each other, and to exhibit compulsive conflictual behavior. These are all traits one would expect to find in drug addicts, not responsible international actors. Rivalry as a situation is the height of irresponsible international behavior.

Denying gains to a rival is a central theme in rivalry. Rivalry assumes a zero-sum game where one side seeks to ensure their own security through the destruction or immobilization of another state. Zizzo and Oswald (2001) perform an experiment in which their subjects can reduce other players' monetary payoffs, but only if they give up some of their money first. They find that despite the assumption of self-interest, people put in this situation are willing to burn themselves rather than provide a gain for a rival. Two-thirds of the test subjects burned their opposing side even though it would be costly in terms of personal gains to do so. A similar dynamic works in rivalry situations. Rather than being focused on a narrow self-interest, states engaged in a rivalry are much more willing to go out of their way to deny a benefit to an enemy even if that means they harm their own security or personal well-being. Some rivals seek to wipe the other off the face of the earth; most simply wish to deny any gains to that rival. Either way, rivalry produces a destructive relationship that only detracts the state from more pressing problems internally. Rivalry focuses the collective state on the hatred of the "other" rather than self-improvement and advancement.

Rivalry simply means distrust with some expectation of future violence. As Colaresi, Rasler, and Thompson (2008, 12) note, during a rivalry each side exaggerates hostile actions and downplays the sincerity of cooperative actions. As a concept, rivalry is simply meant to denote a perpetual hostile relationship. It captures relationships characterized by selfishness, relative positions, mistrust, hostility, and animosity. Failure to include any of these sorts of characteristics would mean that rivalry as a concept is too underspecified to measure anything significant. Now that an explanation of rivalry as a concept has been elaborated on, we must seek to operationalize it as a factor or variable.

Operational Definitions of Rivalry

Many scholars in the past have investigated rivalry in an ad hoc manner by using case studies to test ideas. These scholars would describe the history of a case and generalize from that point forward. Modern research into the causes of conflict is much more precise about concepts and definitions. If we do not define concretely what a rivalry is, how would one know it when it is in existence? Careful definitions of what a rivalry is exactly are important so that others can have confidence that the concept we are studying is both valid and reliable. Validity suggests that the concept of rivalry as measured in empirical analysis actually reflects what one means by the term *rivalry*. Concept reliability suggests that others in the future can use the same operational definitions and investigate the same processes achieving similar results. Perhaps the exemplar of rivalry scholarship was produced by Gary Goertz and Paul Diehl beginning in the 1990s. While they were not the founders of the study of rivalry, they were the ones who defined the term as it is used today, operationalized it, released a data set, and encouraged others (like me) to study the process on their own.

Empirically, Goertz and Diehl (1992, 1993) define and operationalize rivalries as repeated conflicts with a certain degree of competitiveness and connection of issues. Competitiveness suggests that there is a consistent and conflictual relationship between the two parties with some expectation of future conflict. For rivalries to be observed, there must be some degree of serious competition. A connection of issues is also important for Diehl and Goertz (2000), since rivalry for them is not an isolated incident of conflict but should have linkages between disputes throughout the relationship.

In coding rivalries, a militarized interstate dispute (MID) is used to operationalize the competitiveness requirement.[3] Goertz and Diehl (1992, 1993; Diehl and Goertz 2000, 44–46) operationalize an enduring rivalry as those pairs of states with six MIDs within a period of twenty years. Proto-rivalries are those dyads that have up to five MIDs but fail to reach the enduring rivalry requirement in a twenty-year period. Isolated conflicts, on the other hand, are those conflicts between dyads that involve one or two disputes and do not escalate to the proto or enduring rivalry stage. Goertz and Diehl consider isolated conflicts undeveloped rivals; yet they are truly isolated confrontations that either lack salience in relation to the issue at stake or are clashes between states otherwise distracted by more pressing problems. Isolated conflicts also seem to be confrontations between states, likely democracies, which are able to deal with their issues either diplomatically or legally.

Before the introduction of the Diehl and Goertz (2000) data set, scholars had a limited ability to test propositions about repeated disputes in a manner that truly accounted for the rivalry situation.[4] New rivalry data sets allow investigators to analyze the history of interactions for all international enemies, not just a select few. There clearly is a pattern in that only 25 percent of the MIDs witnessed occurred between disputants that only fought once or twice (Diehl and Goertz 2000, 60–63). Disputes and crises are usually not independent events, but part of an ongoing hostile relationship.

There are some flaws with the earlier Diehl and Goertz (2000) data set that necessitated an update. The new data set (Klein, Goertz, and Diehl 2006) covers the 1816 to 2001 period and does not consider isolated conflicts as rivals since these are not dyadic rivalries but short confrontations. Other changes include a more specific selection of who the rivals are. While the competitiveness rules have not changed much, now the Klein, Goertz, and Diehl (2006) data set eliminates those dyads in which there was no clear contact between the disputing parties and those dyads that were coded as fighting but actually left or entered the dispute before the other party did. They also eliminated disputes if the conflict had nothing to do with the overall rivalry context.[5] For reference, Table 2.1 lists all the Klein, Goertz, and Diehl (2006) rivals by the number of disputes the dyad is engaged in.

The data set also now considers only one category of rivalry, eliminating the distinction between proto and enduring rivals.[6] This change means that there are now shorter rivals in the data set since there is no minimum time requirement, but it allows for longer rivalries in that the time between disputes has been increased up to fifteen years if the rivals are still fighting over the same issues.[7] The final data set includes 915 cases of isolated contact and 290 rivals.[8] "Of the 290 cases of rivalry, 115 are enduring and 175 are proto-rivalries under the previous coding criteria" (Klein, Goertz, and Diehl 2006, 340). Because there is a focus on a high probability of future conflict and reliance of militarized disputes for coding of rivalries, the Klein, Goertz, and Diehl (2006) data set will be relied on for most of the analysis in this book.

16 *Becoming Rivals*

Table 2.1 List of Rivalries

Rival A	Rival B	Begin Date	End Date	number disp
United States	Russia	19460415	20001231	59
Russia	China	18620601	19940630	54
Russia	Japan	18610313	20010411	53
Syria	Israel	19480514	20010701	51
India	Pakistan	19470922	20011231	46
United States	China	19491001	20010817	36
Egypt	Israel	19480514	19890603	36
Greece	Turkey	19580101	20011231	34
China	Japan	18730601	19580507	34
North Korea	South Korea	19490505	20011127	32
Iran	Iraq	19341201	19990610	31
United States	North Korea	19500627	20000323	28
China	Taiwan	19491001	20010831	27
Iraq	Kuwait	19610625	20010331	25
Honduras	Nicaragua	19570419	20010331	22
United Kingdom	Russia	19390325	19990611	22
China	India	19501116	19870604	22
Ecuador	Peru	18910801	19550927	21
Turkey	Iraq	19580715	20010826	21
France	Germany	18300828	19400622	20
Bolivia	Paraguay	18860810	19380721	19
United Kingdom	Iraq	19580715	20011003	19
South Korea	Japan	19530203	19990219	19
Russia	Iran	19080416	19871102	18
Thailand	Cambodia	19531101	19980502	18
United States	Iraq	19870517	20011010	18
United States	Cuba	19590114	19960224	17
United States	Mexico	18360404	18930931	17
Chile	Argentina	19520701	19841019	17
United Kingdom	Russia	18760501	19230611	17
Greece	Turkey	18661001	19250430	17
Russia	Norway	19560130	20010219	17
China	Vietnam	19751123	19980930	17

(continued)

Table 2.1 (continued)

Rival A	Rival B	Begin Date	End Date	number disp
Somalia	Ethiopia	19600814	19851022	16
United States	Libya	19730321	19960402	15
Cyprus	Turkey	19650316	20010720	15
United Kingdom	Turkey	18270816	19340716	14
Italy	Turkey	18800914	19241131	14
Russia	Afghanistan	19800301	20011115	14
Turkey	Syria	19550326	19981119	14
Armenia	Azerbaijan	19920126	20011212	14
United States	Spain	18500601	18980812	13
France	Turkey	18800701	19380628	13
Uganda	Sudan	19680514	20011030	13
Jordan	Israel	19480514	19731024	13
Afghanistan	Pakistan	19490301	20011031	13
Thailand	Laos	19600825	19880219	13
Ecuador	Peru	19770621	19980813	12
Russia	Turkey	18760513	19210531	12
Uganda	Kenya	19650515	19970228	12
Ethiopia	Sudan	19670702	19970113	12
China	Philippines	19500930	20010531	12
India	Bangladesh	19760419	20010430	12
United States	Yugoslavia	19920716	20001128	12
Colombia	Venezuela	19820713	20001123	12
Iran	Turkey	19810921	20010825	12
North Korea	Japan	19940326	20011222	12
Ghana	Togo	19611101	19941210	11
Congo	Democratic Republic of the Congo	19630815	19971008	11
China	South Korea	19500930	19941031	11
United States	Iran	19791104	19971003	11
United Kingdom	China	19500817	19681117	11
Hungary	Yugoslavia	19910822	20001128	11
Albania	Yugoslavia	19921209	20010208	11
Cameroon	Nigeria	19810520	19980911	11

(continued)

Table 2.1 (continued)

Rival A	Rival B	Begin Date	End Date	number disp
Zambia	South Africa	19680406	19870425	11
Chile	Argentina	18730315	19090707	10
Greece	Bulgaria	19130428	19520813	10
Iraq	Israel	19480514	19981220	10
Belize	Guatemala	19931015	20010513	10
Nicaragua	Costa Rica	19771013	19980831	10
United Kingdom	Yugoslavia	19920716	20001128	10
France	Iraq	19900808	19991022	10
Croatia	Yugoslavia	19920120	20000930	10
Yugoslavia	Turkey	19920716	20001128	10
Russia	Turkey	19930907	20000913	10
Libya	Egypt	19750804	19851202	10
Iran	Afghanistan	19790318	19990516	10
Afghanistan	Uzbekistan	19930303	20011031	10
Sudan	Egypt	19910201	19960331	9
Cambodia	Republic of Vietnam	19560201	19670224	9
United States	Haiti	18691101	19150909	8
United States	Ecuador	19520801	19810120	8
United States	United Kingdom	18371229	18611226	8
Venezuela	Guyana	19661014	19991009	8
Peru	Chile	18520602	19211213	8
Belgium	Germany	19140802	19400528	8
France	China	18700725	19270328	8
Spain	Morocco	19571123	19800617	8
Yugoslavia	Bulgaria	19130418	19521026	8
Democratic Republic of the Congo	Zambia	19710429	19940930	8
Syria	Jordan	19490426	19820224	8
Lebanon	Israel	19480514	20011231	8
Thailand	Vietnam	19610420	19950531	8
United States	Spain	18160727	18250331	8
Canada	Yugoslavia	19980611	20001128	8

(continued)

Table 2.1 (continued)

Rival A	Rival B	Begin Date	End Date	number disp
Netherlands	Yugoslavia	19920716	20001128	8
Belgium	Yugoslavia	19920716	20001128	8
France	Yugoslavia	19920716	20001128	8
Spain	Yugoslavia	19920716	20001128	8
Germany	Yugoslavia	19920716	20001128	8
Italy	Yugoslavia	19920716	20001128	8
Yugoslavia	Greece	19920716	20001128	8
Russia	Georgia	19920613	20011018	8
Zambia	Zimbabwe	19651111	19791221	8
Afghanistan	Tajikistan	19930303	20011010	8
China	Republic of Vietnam	19560830	19740204	8
United States	Canada	19740914	19970528	7
Colombia	Peru	18990401	19340519	7
United Kingdom	Germany	18870601	19211105	7
Germany	Italy	19141020	19431018	7
Italy	Yugoslavia	19230824	19560411	7
Iraq	Saudi Arabia	19610701	20010824	7
China	Japan	19780413	19990715	7
United States	Mexico	19110125	19200225	7
United States	Egypt	19560419	19680213	7
United Kingdom	Italy	19271028	19430909	7
Netherlands	Indonesia	19510816	19620817	7
France	Italy	19251201	19400610	7
Greece	Iraq	19820809	19991022	7
Chad	Libya	19760909	19940531	7
Uganda	Rwanda	19910127	20011030	7
Zimbabwe	Botswana	19690301	19790810	7
Iran	Saudi Arabia	19840426	19880424	7
United States	Peru	19550129	19920424	6
Honduras	El Salvador	19690624	19930220	6
Honduras	Nicaragua	19070105	19290709	6
Guyana	Suriname	19760401	20000930	6

(continued)

Table 2.1 (continued)

Rival A	Rival B	Begin Date	End Date	number disp
Brazil	United Kingdom	18380801	18630105	6
Democratic Republic of the Congo	Uganda	19770428	20010630	6
Morocco	Algeria	19620702	19840615	6
Israel	Saudi Arabia	19570112	19811109	6
Trinidad and Tobago	Venezuela	19961030	19990831	6
United Kingdom	Taiwan	19491018	19550119	6
United Kingdom	Japan	19320131	19450814	6
France	Libya	19780415	19870911	6
Portugal	Yugoslavia	19980611	20001128	6
Poland	Yugoslavia	19990309	20001128	6
Czech Republic	Yugoslavia	19990309	20001128	6
Italy	Ethiopia	19230101	19430614	6
Croatia	Bosnia and Herzegovina	19921020	19961018	6
Yugoslavia	Norway	19980611	20001128	6
Yugoslavia	Denmark	19980611	20001128	6
Yugoslavia	Iceland	19980611	20001128	6
Russia	Turkey	18170404	18290914	6
Russia	Israel	19561105	19740828	6
Tanzania	Burundi	19950615	20000531	6
Eritrea	Yemen	19951113	19990821	6
Libya	Sudan	19720920	19840331	6
Egypt	Jordan	19480601	19621222	6
Egypt	Saudi Arabia	19621001	19670514	6
China	North Korea	19930100	19971025	6
United States	Syria	19700916	19960630	5
Brazil	Paraguay	18500901	18700301	5
Bolivia	Chile	18570820	18840404	5
United Kingdom	France	18880201	18981104	5
United Kingdom	Egypt	19420204	19581024	5
United Kingdom	Yemen Arab Republic	19490701	19670422	5

(continued)

Table 2.1 (continued)

Rival A	Rival B	Begin Date	End Date	number disp
France	Tunisia	19570531	19610905	5
Portugal	Senegal	19611201	19730525	5
Germany	Russia	19361112	19450507	5
German Federal Republic	Russia	19610813	19800319	5
Austria-Hungary	Italy	18480115	18771131	5
Italy	Albania	19140913	19390408	5
Macedonia	Yugoslavia	19940500	19990610	5
Bulgaria	Turkey	19350823	19520501	5
Russia	Ukraine	19920714	19960324	5
Russia	Sweden	19811022	19920921	5
Russia	Turkey	19400201	19620817	5
Russia	Taiwan	19490721	19580908	5
Russia	South Korea	19591228	19830901	5
Liberia	Sierra Leone	19910331	20010618	5
Uganda	Tanzania	19710127	19790603	5
South Africa	Botswana	19840826	19880721	5
Iraq	United Arab Emirates	19900716	19991022	5
Saudi Arabia	Yemen Arab Republic	19621005	19800215	5
China	Thailand	19510120	19711231	5
Malaysia	Philippines	19680404	19880818	5
United States	Dominican Republic	19000101	19170529	4
United States	Germany	19150210	19181111	4
United States	Germany	19391024	19450507	4
United States	Afghanistan	19980820	20011115	4
United States	Japan	19320131	19450814	4
United States	Vietnam	19610101	19730127	4
Canada	Russia	19990408	20001231	4
Haiti	Dominican Republic	19860131	19940929	4
Haiti	Germany	18720611	19110803	4
Guatemala	El Salvador	18760201	19060720	4

(continued)

22 Becoming Rivals

Table 2.1 (continued)

Rival A	Rival B	Begin Date	End Date	number disp
Nicaragua	Costa Rica	19480419	19570623	4
Nicaragua	Colombia	19940400	20011130	4
Venezuela	United Kingdom	18810101	19030219	4
Venezuela	Netherlands	18490501	18690231	4
Peru	Spain	18590401	18660509	4
Argentina	United Kingdom	19760204	19830809	4
Argentina	Yugoslavia	20000327	20001128	4
United Kingdom	Iceland	19580827	19760601	4
France	Italy	18600910	18660709	4
France	Russia	18330622	18560330	4
France	Russia	19180628	19201001	4
France	Russia	19480321	19611028	4
France	Thailand	19401123	19520307	4
Spain	Italy	19271028	19401001	4
Portugal	Guinea	19620311	19730120	4
German Federal Republic	German Democratic Republic	19610813	19710129	4
Poland	Russia	19930620	19970321	4
Poland	Lithuania	19190404	19380320	4
Austria-Hungary	Italy	19040901	19181103	4
Austria-Hungary	Yugoslavia	19081006	19181103	4
Austria-Hungary	Turkey	18760513	19051206	4
Hungary	Yugoslavia	19380924	19521026	4
Albania	Macedonia	19930626	19970313	4
Albania	Greece	19940410	19970917	4
Yugoslavia	Bosnia and Herzegovina	19920406	19940131	4
Yugoslavia	Romania	19930130	20001128	4
Yugoslavia	Russia	19980817	20001128	4
Yugoslavia	Lithuania	19980817	20001128	4
Bulgaria	Turkey	19081005	19150922	4
Russia	Latvia	19940110	19990205	4
Russia	Azerbaijan	19930200	19990330	4
Armenia	Iran	19930900	19940317	4

(continued)

Table 2.1 (continued)

Rival A	Rival B	Begin Date	End Date	number disp
Armenia	Turkey	19930400	20000911	4
Guinea	Liberia	19990813	20010525	4
Guinea	Sierra Leone	19970527	20010604	4
Congo	Angola	19950513	19971015	4
Democratic Republic of the Congo	Rwanda	19960922	20010630	4
Democratic Republic of the Congo	Angola	19941023	19970531	4
Kenya	Somalia	19631229	19890920	4
Djibouti	Eritrea	19951200	19981231	4
Eritrea	Sudan	19941100	19990131	4
South Africa	Lesotho	19940907	19941216	4
Tunisia	Libya	19770520	19850822	4
Iraq	Syria	19760606	19910303	4
Iraq	Bahrain	19860826	19941020	4
Saudi Arabia	Yemen	19941023	19980719	4
Yemen People's Republic	Oman	19720506	19821207	4
Afghanistan	Kyrgyzstan	19930303	19970531	4
Mongolia	Japan	19350108	19450814	4
Taiwan	Japan	19950108	19960906	4
Taiwan	Vietnam	19940416	19950325	4
India	Sri Lanka	19841217	19920317	4
India	Nepal	19620401	19690931	4
Cambodia	Vietnam	19690328	19790107	4
Laos	Vietnam	19581205	19730215	4
Vietnam	Philippines	19980800	19991030	4
Indonesia	Papua New Guinea	19820526	19901029	4
Papua New Guinea	Solomon Islands	19930305	19961129	4
United States	Cuba	19120815	19340131	3
United States	Nicaragua	19820317	19880331	3
United States	Nicaragua	19090103	19260923	3

(continued)

24 Becoming Rivals

Table 2.1 (continued)

Rival A	Rival B	Begin Date	End Date	number disp
United States	United Kingdom	19020701	19031020	3
United States	Czechoslovakia	19530310	19611028	3
United States	Romania	19401213	19511124	3
United States	Russia	19180112	19201001	3
Haiti	United Kingdom	18830701	18870430	3
Guatemala	United Kingdom	19720127	19770719	3
El Salvador	Nicaragua	19070312	19090525	3
Colombia	Ecuador	18571101	18631206	3
Colombia	United Kingdom	18360120	18570131	3
Colombia	Italy	18850701	18980814	3
Peru	Chile	19760911	19770831	3
Brazil	Argentina	18720322	18751230	3
Chile	Spain	18620810	18660509	3
Argentina	United Kingdom	18420101	18460326	3
Argentina	France	18420101	18460326	3
United Kingdom	Germany	19380826	19450507	3
United Kingdom	Greece	18860426	18970815	3
United Kingdom	Russia	18491006	18610921	3
United Kingdom	Japan	18630406	18651124	3
United Kingdom	Indonesia	19510903	19660425	3
Netherlands	Iraq	19900821	19991022	3
Belgium	Democratic Republic of the Congo	19911027	19930131	3
France	Austria-Hungary	18400801	18590712	3
France	Greece	19160111	19220729	3
France	Morocco	19040601	19110630	3
France	Iran	19851018	19880120	3
France	Turkey	18270816	18330710	3
France	China	19491214	19530727	3
France	Japan	18630720	18651124	3
Spain	Morocco	19070808	19111230	3
Portugal	Zambia	19660518	19730614	3
Portugal	India	19540807	19611219	3

(continued)

Table 2.1 (continued)

Rival A	Rival B	Begin Date	End Date	number disp
Germany	Saxony	18640212	18660726	3
Germany	Czechoslovakia	19340725	19390316	3
Germany	Greece	18860426	18970815	3
Germany	Russia	19140725	19200201	3
Germany	Norway	19110718	19180111	3
Germany	Turkey	18760513	18970815	3
Germany	Iraq	19910106	19991022	3
Germany	China	18971114	19010907	3
German Federal Republic	Czechoslovakia	19840420	19860922	3
Poland	Russia	19190101	19201118	3
Poland	Russia	19380923	19390929	3
Austria-Hungary	Papal States	18470717	18490701	3
Austria-Hungary	Greece	18860426	18970815	3
Austria	Yugoslavia	19910627	20001128	3
Hungary	Romania	19190410	19230131	3
Italy	Albania	19520608	19570608	3
Italy	Greece	18860426	18970815	3
Italy	Russia	19180628	19201001	3
Italy	Iraq	19900821	19991022	3
Albania	Yugoslavia	19150612	19211018	3
Albania	Greece	19460301	19490813	3
Greece	Russia	18860426	18970815	3
Bulgaria	Romania	19130628	19260723	3
Bulgaria	Russia	19121102	19171215	3
Bulgaria	Turkey	18860720	18871003	3
Moldova	Russia	19920331	19930215	3
Russia	Sweden	19520616	19640924	3
Russia	Turkey	18491101	18560330	3
Mali	Burkina Faso	19741101	19860731	3
Mauritania	Morocco	19800229	19870418	3
Guinea	Ghana	19660310	19661104	3
Liberia	Nigeria	19980200	19990409	3
Chad	Rwanda	19980929	19990430	3

(continued)

Table 2.1 (continued)

Rival A	Rival B	Begin Date	End Date	number disp
Democratic Republic of the Congo	Angola	19751224	19780320	3
Burundi	Rwanda	19640122	19730629	3
Mozambique	South Africa	19830412	19871227	3
Iraq	Egypt	19590310	19620228	3
Iraq	Egypt	19900811	19991022	3
Iraq	Oman	19910224	19941020	3
Syria	Lebanon	19630205	19691113	3
Saudi Arabia	Yemen Arab Republic	19310101	19340623	3
Saudi Arabia	Qatar	19920930	19950628	3
China	Myanmar	19560730	19691107	3
China	Nepal	19560214	19600801	3
China	Laos	19610402	19790315	3
China	Australia	19500930	19711231	3
China	New Zealand	19500930	19710631	3
Taiwan	Republic of Vietnam	19650425	19740204	3
Malaysia	Indonesia	19630211	19651114	3
Vietnam	Republic of Vietnam	19601108	19750430	2

Source: Klein, Goertz, and Diehl (2006).

Diehl and Goertz (2000) have come under their fair share of public and private criticism because coding of rivalry is dependent on the observation of actual conflict in the form of militarized disputes. For some, conflict should be a dependent variable, not something that is contained within a model. In addition, using the dispute density approach might oversample the major powers in the data; so, it would be prudent to discuss and utilize alternative methods of coding rivals when possible. Defining rivalry by the number of MIDs within a dyad may limit the ability of the operational definition to capture the true meaning of rivalry and to account for all cases. Thompson and coauthors believe that for a rivalry to be active, each side must regard the other as competitors, be the source of actual or latent threats, and recognize each other as enemies (Colaresi, Rasler, and Thompson 2008, 25). Using historical research, Thompson (2001) identifies a population of dyads (173 rivals from 1816 to 1999) that are strategic rivalries.

Hewitt (2005) creates a new rivalry data set based on the Interstate Crises Behavior (ICB) data set (Brecher and Wilkenfeld 1997; Brecher, Wilkenfeld, and Moser 1988a, 1988b). While following the Diehl and Goertz (2000) rivalry data set closely, the ICB-based data set has the potential to be important in that it examines only those instances of crises behavior and not just dispute behavior. The data set also has much more information on actions of leaders as crises brew. Unfortunately the crises-based data contain many of the same flaws that other ICB-based articles have to deal with, such as a limited temporal domain, reliance on high-level crises that might miss important low-level disputes, and a skewed population sampling since the methodology behind the MID project is much more comprehensive. The final data set concludes that since 1918 there have been thirty-one enduring rivalries that lasted for longer than twenty years and experienced at least three crises as counted by the ICB data set.

The Thompson (2001) and Hewitt (2005) data sets provide interesting alternative conceptualizations of rivalry. What rivalry data set researchers use really depends on personal preference and familiarity with the options. Since most scholars in the conflict studies field are familiar with the MID data set, the Klein, Goertz, and Diehl (2006) and Diehl and Goertz (2000) tend to be used most often. As Colaresi, Rasler, and Thompson (2008, 72) note, "analysts who prefer the high conflict emphasis are likely to be more comfortable with dispute-density approaches." Since the goal here is to root out serious conflict in the system the Klein, Goertz, and Diehl (2006) data will be the foundation of most empirical analysis in this book. The Thompson (2001) data will be used to provide an alternative test of the propositions presented here.

WHAT DO WE KNOW ABOUT RIVALRY DEVELOPMENT?

The literature on interstate rivalry has only begun to identify factors leading a pair of states to initiate or develop into a rivalry. We therefore know little about how rivalries actually come about. Most factors that are said to account for the onset of rivalry either fall in the category of events to induce the situation right away or factors that accumulate to ultimately produce the outcome of rivalry. My own theory of rivalry development focuses more on factors that collectively help bring about the situation rather than shocks that bring about the event right away.

Diehl and Goertz (2000) theorize that a political shock is a "virtual necessary" condition for the initiation and termination of a rivalry. A political shock is a traumatic event in either the international system (e.g., world wars, changes in power distribution, and periods of territory shifts) or internal-domestic politics (e.g., regime change and civil war). In an empirical analysis, Diehl and Goertz (2000) find a political shock to be associated with rivalry initiation 95 percent of the time (sixty to sixty-three cases) for enduring rivalries. They theorize that a political shock allows a "window of opportunity" for rivalry initiation.

Colaresi (2001) looks at global war as a political shock that might bring about rivalry using a population of Thompson's strategic rivals. He finds that a war shock only leads to the termination of rivalry, not the initiation. It does seem clear that most rivalries begin at state birth (Colaresi, Rasler, and Thompson 2008, 84), which is a form of a political shock (Goertz and Diehl 1995) discussed in the literature.

Rivalries typically evolve or experience a trend of increasing conflict throughout their life. Hensel's (1999) escalating evolutionary approach to rivalries holds that rivalries are likely to advance and become "enduring" if the outcome of the first dispute is not resolved to both states' mutual satisfaction. Leng (1983, 1993, 2000) makes a similar point through many case study examinations. The evolutionary approach also holds that high levels of severe conflict (war) early in the life of a rivalry make confrontations in the future less likely yet still push the states to lock into rivalry early. In essence, choosing not to respond to a militarized dispute with the use of force diminishes the probability of future disputes (Hensel and Diehl 1994) and rivalry.

Dissatisfaction is likely to play a large role in rivalry relationships. Maoz and Mor (2002) find that dissatisfaction with the status quo and equality of capabilities are factors that influence the continuation of a rivalry. Rivalries will endure as long as neither side has the ability to demonstrably change the relationship and both sides are dissatisfied with the outcome of past disputes. Hensel's (1996, 1998a, 1998b) notion of evolutionary learning during a rivalry likely explains much of why dissatisfaction tends to fester. Suspicion, hostility, and grievances only grow through time, making it more likely that a rivalry will lock in and endure. Dissatisfaction also plays a part in the analysis conducted by Goertz Jones, and Diehl (2005), which finds that stalemate outcomes early during a rivalry push the dyads to endure as enemies (see also Hensel 1996). These facts might lead us to conclude that how disputes are handled early in the life of a rivalry matter the most. If behaviors are exhibited that exacerbate hostility and mistrust early, the rivalry is then likely to endure because of mutual dissatisfaction and animosity that build up during the prerivalry condition.

One cannot forget the importance of domestic politics in the analysis of rivalry situations. Domestic factors such as leadership tenure (Colaresi 2001) and domestic instability (Mitchell and Prins 2004) can produce the outcome of rivalry. Leaders sometimes need external enemies to galvanize the population in support of their policies and will only choose to deescalate a rivalry if they are in a secure power position internally (Colaresi 2005). The unfortunate consequence of this tactic is that it likely makes rivalries endure and lock in. In fact, rivalries are almost impossible to terminate if both the public and leadership do not agree to end the hostile relationship. Leaders must play the ratification game on many levels (Putnam 1988) in order to achieve victory on policy initiatives. Domestic opinion can either force the continuation of a rivalry (Hensel 1998a) or induce peace (Mor 1997).

Internal regime dynamics are also important factors in determining who might become rivals. Democracy reduces the likelihood of states entering into a rivalry in the first place (Hensel, Goertz, and Diehl 2000). There have only been two serious cases of rivalries beginning between two democracies and only one of those cases (the United Kingdom versus the United States) contained two stable democracies for the entire duration of the conflict. By breaking down the different types of IGOs contained in institutional data sets, Valeriano and Leskiw (2010) conclude that shared membership in regional rather than universal IGOs makes it less likely that two states will engage in rivalry. Other scholars have found evidence that IGOs reduce the duration of rivalries (Cornwell and Colaresi 2002; Prins and Daxecker 2007), but none of these studies have looked at the origins of rivalry and the impact on external institutions.

Stinnett and Diehl (2001, 735) argue that rather than having one cause, "[rivalries] emerge from the conjunction of a large number of small, individually weak factors." Stinnett and Diehl (2001) find that behavioral factors (linkages between disputes and dispute outcomes) and structural factors (political shocks and great power involvement) each have a small impact on rivalry initiation. Colaresi and Thompson (2002) take a similar line and suggest two rivalry paths, one for positional rivalries—those concerned with global/strategic issues—and one for spatial rivalries—those concerned with territorial questions. Contiguous rivals are likely to begin over spatial/territorial questions (Colaresi, Rasler, and Thompson 2008, 169, 180). Nondemocracy, militarization, and major power status increase the likelihood of positional rivals (Colaresi, Rasler, and Thompson 2008, 203) whose main source of disagreement seems to be based on geopolitical positioning rather than specific locations and territories.

Colaresi, Rasler, and Thompson (2008, chap. 7) take a step back and ask if the factors that lead to war as uncovered by Bremer (1992) lead to rivalry instead. Their analysis concludes by finding that dyads that are contiguous (being neighbors), are militarized, and contain a state that is either a regional or major power all contribute to the onset of rivalry in general. While these factors are important, they are also likely only factors that we should control for in our analysis and not evidence of processes that actually cause rivalry.

To summarize, there is a direct relationship between rivalry and war. This relationship may be a function of the number of disputes that rivalries engage in, yet this cannot be a tautological fact. Most wars only occur because of rivalry; rivalry leads to war. In fact, most wars occur near the beginning of the rivalry (Klein, Goertz, and Diehl 2006, 342). This suggests that the road to war and the outcomes of said wars may play a pivotal role in rivalry development.

Democratic dyads are unlikely to become rivals, and those states committed to international institutions tend to avoid rivalry also. Shocks can be important factors in explaining onset, yet many of these factors seem too large and systemic to have a direct impact on the development of a rivalry. The shotgun approach is what the shock theory of rivalry onset seems to suggest. Large disruptions can cause a noticeable impact on interstate relations. While large disruptions to systemic processes can play a role in the onset of rivalry, these factors also fail to directly explain why each shock produces rivalry. Newly independent states tend to engage in rivalry, but this is because of the characteristics of the territorial disputes that newly independent states engage in. Territoriality as a factor and the salience of issues seem like better avenues to pursue regarding the onset of rivalries and issues rather than contiguity and independence.[9]

Overall, we know relatively little about the development of rivalries. Knowledge of the behavior processes that predate the onset of rivalry is particularly lacking. There has been a tipping point in that investigations that look at the structural factors of rivalry have turned up many ideas but no concrete explanations of the process of rivalry onset. Little has been done in the way of explaining processes that actually affect the decision-making calculus of states as they choose whether or not to engage in conflict. Why and when do states make the choices they do that lead them down the rivalry path? States that are newly independent, lack the characteristics of democracies, or fail to engage in relevant international organizations are likely to become rivals, but these factors are largely processes that are outside the domain of foreign policy action and behavior. Becoming a newly independent state is not a foreign policy choice. Neither is becoming a democracy. Signing and participating in regional institutions can be a choice, but this factor is largely exogenous to the decision to start a rivalry. So how do rivals become rivals? How do we explain the behavioral development of the process? To explain the process of rivalry onset, we must develop a constructivist theory of power politics behavior on the road to conflict.

CONSTRUCTIVIST THEORY, POWER POLITICS, AND THE SECURITY DILEMMA

The theoretical perspective behind the work I am presenting here is a version of a constructivist theory of international political relations (Ruggie 1993, 1998; Wendt 1999). Context matters when discussing the causes of international violence. Rivalry is a situation that begins through stimuli and events that are specific to the process. Rivalries do not develop in a vacuum; the situation requires that attention be paid to the nuances particular to the history and culture of the states engaged in the situation. Past studies of rivalry routinely fail to engage history and culture in explaining why states commit to long-term animosity. The theory presented here largely attempts to bring these factors back into the analysis. History, culture, and tradition do matter for rivalry onset. Power politics foreign policy practices central to the theory presented here are examples of how history, culture, and tradition can influence the onset of rivalry. As Thies (2008) notes, constructivism is not antithetical to empirical rivalry research. We can understand culture, identity, and tradition in a macroinvestigative context.

While material security variables might inform this analysis, reality often works in an opposite manner of how realist theorists tend to expect it to operate. The idea that the national interest is determined by power alone (Morgenthau 1960) is wrong. What is in the national interest typically relates to who the enemy is, where they are located, and what the issue at stake is. The national interest becomes relevant after a rivalry has begun, not before it starts. Absent a rivalry, threats to the national interest are likely inflated and used by state leadership to inflame the domestic population against an actor so the public is distracted from more pressing political problems (Levy 1989). Concern for the national interest is empty without a serious enemy to consider.

It is issues and how issues are handled that matter most in international relations (Hensel 2001). If one believes that issues and the allocation of values surrounding such issues (Mansbach and Vasquez 1981) are of utmost importance in international politics, then the type of theory is constructivist in that views on issues and how to handle these issues are socially constructed processes (Berger and Luckmann 1966). How to respond to events in the context of issues is a process born out of social reality rather than material interests or deterrence dynamics. A state will build up its military in response to a threat because that is what is advised; it is dictated by realist culture and folklore (Johnston 1995). This reaction is the typical response that most leaders would never be able to reject because it is what is expected of them. If setting and situation demand some sort of action, this action is constructed through social interactions rather than pure power calculations. The ultimate advice that can be gathered from this theory is that leaders and states should do the opposite of what is expected; otherwise they will become in engaged in a deadly rivalry that will sap materials, strength, and future avenues of progress. Reacting to threats with power politics tactics might seem like the optimal or easy path, but it is a path that has repeated often in history and the results tend to be the opposite of what one expects.

Before we proceed to my theory, I must elaborate on how power politics is utilized as a constructed concept in this book. Power politics responses are not advisable, nor are they useful in world politics. Unfortunately, they tend to be the dominant form of international diplomatic communication. All too rarely do states throw away the devices of power and threats in favor of reconciliation and adjudication.

Power politics is a condition in foreign policy practice where force and power are utilized to settle disputes and exert influence on other states or actors. Vasquez (1983, 216) defines power politics practices as "actions based on an image of the world as insecure and anarchic which leads to distrust, struggles for power, interest taking precedence over norms and rules, the use of Machiavellian stratagems, coercion, attempts to balance power, reliance on self-help, and the use of force and war as the ultima ratio."

Power allows a state to do what it wants, take what it wants, and to flaunt the conventions of international norms. Yet our notion of stable international affairs is shaped by conventional international norms such as respect for other countries, state sovereignty, and international institutions. Power and the use of force come in direct conflict with notions of peace and stability in the system. The problem is that, at least in the minds of state leaders, state survival depends on the realities of power rather than realties of international norms and positive action.

Concern for the state's survival is critical for all states. No state can operate in the interstate system if it does not mind its own security. While there are examples of states that have given up their offensive capabilities (Costa Rica) or became pacific to a large extent (Scandinavian states), these states are rare in the system. Realists such as Morgenthau believe that power is evident in all aspects of international politics. "Whatever the ultimate aims of international politics, power is always the immediate aim" (Morgenthau 1948, 13). Notions of security and survival cannot be divorced from power. Order through force is the dictum of power politics.

The problem is that concern for survival generally leads directly to the security dilemma (Herz 1950) and perceived insecurity. The security dilemma is a process whereby actions taken to ensure the survival of a state are seen as endangering the security of another state. States attempt to guard their survival by forming alliances, engaging in military buildups, fighting over territorial acquisitions, and participating in relentless conflict enterprises. These factors are meant to ensure state survival when in reality they only bring about an equal and escalating response from the other side. These actions increase tensions and eventually lead to rivalry. Therefore, the security dilemma as a process is central to the theory presented here. My work here is not suggesting that a power politics approach is advisable; it suggests that a power politics approach leads to the opposite outcome of what is intended when the choice of such outcomes is made.

When the interests of the state are threatened, tradition dictates that the state act in a certain way to preserve its stability. The norm should be mediation and diplomacy, yet the norm often in use is force and power politics practices. The theory presented here considers power to be a negative rather than a positive factor. As history tells us, power and force are not ways to state security, but paths to war. This idea will be a central characteristic of my theory.

THE STEPS-TO-RIVALRY MODEL

Foundations

The steps-to-war theory (Vasquez 1993) is the starting point for this project. Therefore it is important to discuss the steps-to-war model before I describe the steps-to-rivalry model, which provides the foundation for the analysis. Science does not progress forward in isolation; we learn from the advances of others, and this theory is heavily indebted to earlier pathbreaking work that modeled how states enter into war. Unfortunately war is not the end of the story; we first must understand why states engage in rivalry before wars begin.

The steps-to-war model (Vasquez 1993, 2009) holds that there are certain actions or foreign policy choices states make that increase the probability of war occurring between two states. Territorial issues, power politics practices, and recurring disputes are all factors that push states to war when states choose to utilize these options (Senese and Vasquez 2008).

Power politics foreign policy practices lead a state down a path to war. Each step taken increases the probability that the outcome will be observed. Since only the probabilities of war increase, the outcome is not evitable but only probable. States can end the movement towards war by settling an issue or simply taking a step back during the escalation process. They can also opt out of the power politics path by utilizing institutional structures such as legal bodies to solve pressing policy concerns.

The model and theory in operation reconceptualize the onset of war into a new decision tree. First a state must escalate an issue to a dispute in the first place. Then they must escalate a dispute to a rivalry. Finally, war will result generally only during the rivalry situation. Therefore, it is critical that we rethink how our models of warfare account for the factor of rivalry in the first place. War is an outcome predicated on rivalry in most occasions. Discovering why disputes emerge in the first place is of less importance than answering why disputes repeat and fester in the form of rivalries.

Any model of an event should explain the process by which the event emerges. The steps-to-rivalry model predicts that the development of rivalry will occur through a series of steps that combine to make a rivalry outcome probable. The steps-to-rivalry model is not a deterministic process but a process model whereby each action a state takes on the road to rivalry increases the probability of the event occurring. Events along the road to rivalry only make a rivalry outcome more probable, not automatic. The factors most likely to result in rivalry are power politics strategies such as the construction of alliances, participation in military buildups, and escalating bargaining demands. When the application of these strategies is examined, it is found that each factor actually leads to the development of rivalry rather than deterrence and peace. Threatening actions rather than preventing further conflict actually make it more likely.

This theory is counterintuitive to conventional wisdom in many ways since the practices I suggest bring about rivalry are typically seen as symptoms of rivalry, not causes. The empirical evidence here will demonstrate that these processes are more than symptoms and help tell the story of how rivalry comes about in the first place. Aggressive power displays only result in a prolonged rivalry situation that can be dangerous to a state's long-term security interests. Factors that might be considered symptoms are actually causes. They are observed before and after the onset of the event (rivalry).

Preconditions

A few assumptions must be outlined from the onset. This investigation is only looking at states that already have experienced at least one conflict or dispute prior to the engagement in rivalry. As stated in Chapter 1, there are three different islands of investigation in interstate conflict research. Rivalry is but one aspect, and our goal here is to explain the beginnings of protracted conflict. Rivalry cannot develop without some form of conflictual contact first. Hatred is not brewed out of thin air. The Thompson (2001) data set does not depend on disputes to discover rivals, but nearly every strategic rival has had a number of disputes throughout their history. The first pre-step to rivalry is a militarized relationship as measured by an MID (Ghosn, Palmer, and Bremer 2004).

Without an established militarized relationship, how would scholars be able to distinguish between general animosity and hostility leading towards war? This project is not interested in diplomatic rivalries or economic rivalries since these conflicts are serious but not necessarily deadly and dangerous. The goal here is to eventually root out war in the system, and militarized rivalry is a symptom of just about every war since the age of Napoleon. The concern here is with violence that will produce fatalities, not frivolous disputes that will rename what Americans call fried potatoes.[10]

Another assumption is that the states engaged in rivalry are interstate system members. While it would be interesting to look at the onset of internal or nonstate actor rivalries, this is beyond the scope of this project. The states that matter the most for this analysis are those members of the recognized interstate system as determined by the correlates of war project (Small and Singer 1982). The coming of globalization pushed forth the idea that states no longer matter; they are withering away (Strange 1996). The main conclusion of the modern era can only be that states matter more than ever despite the protestations of globalization scholars. States continue to retain a monopoly on violence, social services, and protection (Tilly 1985).

States are the residential organizing unit in the international system and thus are the focus on this research.

The final assumption has to do with the narrow nature of the research question in that we can only explore the onset of rivalry between two interstate system members. While looking at complex or multiparty rivals is an interesting project, it is beyond the scope of our intent since complex or multiple rivals would be rivals of a different sort (Valeriano and Powers 2010; Valeriano and Vasquez 2010). Here I only seek to explain the onset of dyadic rivalry.

The Model

This model considers the development of rivalry as a stepwise process. States that use realpolitik strategies in response to a potential enemy will increase the probability that the pair of states will eventually form an intense rivalry. Using these power politics strategies will make states lock into conflict that will escalate to the condition of dangerous rivalry and, quite likely, war.

By reorienting our theories away from explaining war towards explaining the process of variable accumulation towards protracted conflict, we must also modify our theories to take into account a shift in priorities. The steps-to-war model needs reformulation and reconsideration. The variable of interest is now rivalry, and some factors thought to lead to war likely lead to rivalry first.

The movement between stages of rivalry takes the form of steps. There are certain actions that a pair of states takes that increase the probability of rivalry. Each step will take the form of an independent variable in future analysis. The causal mechanism in this model is either fear or hubris. Fear activates the process when one state fears for its existence when posed with a threat. The motivation to take each step forward towards rivalry comes from the mistaken assumption that ensuring state security can only come through material demonstrations of power. Fear motivates a mistaken reliance on deterrence, which then typically results in protracted conflict. On the other hand, the mechanism for initiating states can be hubris. Overreliance on power and threats creates an inflated sense of accomplishment that will lead to future conflict based on the assumption of superiority.

It should be noted that the relationship between the steps and war is not path dependent; rather, there are steps that can be taken (settling an issue, consulting an international organization, or a larger threat can emerge) to avert rivalry once the process has started. Rivalry occurrence has to do with increasing the probability of a certain outcome as actions are taken. There are always ways to end a rivalry, and rivalry is never an inevitable outcome. When a state buys into fear or hubris, there is a high likelihood that rivalry will result; the goal should be to eliminate fear and hubris in the process of foreign policy decision making.

Step One: The Issue

The first step in the model is the existence of a contentious issue in dispute between two states. The trigger of many disputes is not the underlying structural forces or personality considerations of specific actors, but an issue on which two states disagree. Issues are critical to world politics because they provide the justification for extreme action. There would be no disputes or wars without issues to divide states. Issues provide context and motivation at the same time. World politics is not about the distribution of influence in general, but about influence as it pertains to the decision-making calculus surrounding issues of important to external state relationships.

Early on, Diehl (1985) uncovered a connection between contiguity and major power rivalry. We now know that territorial issues are more critical than simple location dynamics (Senese 2005), yet early work on contiguity was important in highlighting the importance of territorial issues as steps towards rivalry (Colaresi, Rasler, and Thompson 2008; Huth 1996b; Tir and Diehl 2002).

Territorial issues produce greater commitment by states in that the nature of the conflict becomes symbolic rather than divisible (Vasquez and Valeriano 2009). Issues are more difficult to resolve when they contain transcendent properties because solutions must deal with the abstract qualities of the issue under consideration. Territorial issues tend to generate realpolitik responses (Hensel 2000) due to the symbolic and abstract qualities of the territory under question. Rarely is a territorial dispute fought over a tract of land with a sure value; instead, territorial disputes tend to be fought over desolate or inaccessible locations. While territory is concrete and divisible, in practice the disputes over territorial questions are never very simple to solve because of their transcendent properties. Would India settle for the division of Kashmir right down the middle of the territory? Would Argentina be happy with half of the Maldives/Falkland Islands?

Realpolitik actions aim to increase the security of one state but usually end up creating a decrease in security of its potential rival. Perceiving a decrease in its own security, the opposing state employs its own realpolitik tactics in the context of pressing issues. The state seeks to "burn" or harm the enemy by denying them any sort of gain on pertinent issues. The situation develops into a conflict spiral and security dilemma, making the use of power politics tactics over salient issues the initial step on the road to rivalry.[11]

Various issues may prompt a state to respond to a threat in a power politics fashion. Territorial disputes alone do not bring about rivalry. It is how territorial disputes are handled that contributes to the factor's increased probability of war. Ethnic disputes handled in a similar fashion will also produce rivalry. The mechanism in operation is the choice of power politics strategies. Why a state may choose to pursue the power politics path is a question that will be tackled later, but it does seem clear that these choices produce an outcome of rivalry. When posed with a threat by an enemy, it is likely that power politics responses seem the most logically suitable option. Unfortunately these responses are directly related to the onset of rivalry and also tend to be associated with territorial disputes and then war (Vasquez and Leskiw 2001). The process of interest for this project is the path to rivalry as started by issue disagreements.

Step Two: Alliances

Throughout history many have argued for the utility of alliances as instruments of security and against alliances as impediments to stability. George Washington's quote during his farewell address warning of the dangers of alliances comes to mind. "'Tis our policy to steer clear of permanent alliances with any portion of the foreign world." Yet even to this day alliances are touted as a path to peace and prosperity. NATO is an untouchable institution in the United States. Why? What benefit do alliances provide for the state? The model in operation here considers alliances steps towards rivalry.

Alliances are written formal agreements between at least a pair of states that commit a state to intervene in a conflict, agree to remain neutral in a conflict, or to consult the other state if a conflict erupts (Gibler and Sarkees 2004). Traditionally alliances have been seen as factors that either add to power or as ways to deter aggression by opposing states. These two views have been challenged by history, which suggests alliances actually detract from power by being restraining factors (Schroeder 1994) or extending deterrence commitments to third parties, rendering direct deterrence irrelevant and illogical.

Alliances are the key trigger to the rivalry process. It seems that alliances are factors that lead to the onset of rivalry and also contribute to the onset of complex wars (Valeriano and Vasquez 2010). They are not directly tied to the onset of dyadic interstate war when one considers that rivalry likely comes before war and alliances are observed before rivalries.[12] Alliances are meant to increase the security of one state but tend to decrease the security of both sides (Vasquez 1993). Instead of adding to the power of state, demonstrating resolve, or deterring an aggressor state, alliances seem to lock states into a rivalry relationship by encouraging the development of similar strategies in the opposing side––either to catch up and achieve a balance of power or due to the psychological need of the leadership to demonstrate activity in the face of threats.

There has been a plethora of research that demonstrates that alliances are factors than can increase the probability of war. Starting with Singer and Small (1968), scholars have demonstrated that alliances are necessary conditions for war (Levy 1981, 1983). Certain types of alliances increase the probability of war (Gibler 1996, 1997, 2000; Gibler and Vasquez 1998). Left unexplored is the relationship between alliances and rivalry. Might it be that alliances conceived of during the initial hints of animosity contribute to the onset of rivalry?

To explore the logic of this proposition, we must uncover the purpose of alliances in world politics. Some alliances are used to prepare for war, but most are intended to never be used as tools during war. Looking at the commitments in existence, it is generally hoped by the signatories that alliances will never have to be used in actual combat. The language contained within the text of alliances speaks of future agreements to hash out specific military commitments (Gibler 2009). If alliances are not tools of war and are not factors used in direct deterrence, then why do states still use alliances?

The true purpose of alliances leaves only one conclusion. Alliances are either meant to settle past conflicts and confer bonds of friendship (Gibler 1997), or they are used to target specific enemies on the road to rivalry (Walker 2001). It is those alliances that target specific enemies that are of interest here since these alliances activate the security dilemma (Snyder 1997). Alliances signal intent to another potential rival. Alliances increase insecurity and provoke military buildups and counteralliances rather than submission.

The response to alliances formed by threats tends to be one of threat, reaction, and then protection. There is a threat to a pressing issue at stake, and the other side responds. It chooses to escalate and not back down. When this happens there are few options left to decision-makers short of war, and one option is the formation and utilization of alliances to deter future escalation. Unfortunately alliances tend to engender continued power politics responses and further escalation. Alliances do not deter future conflict but only encourage it. Alliances are early steps towards rivalry and thus should be avoided as tools of conflict management.

Step Three: Military Buildups/Arms Races

An arms race, or mutual military buildup, signifies the rapid buildup and acieration of two opposing state's military capabilities. A military buildup is a process by which two states compete to develop their capabilities to prevent attacks by another state. Two main elements comprise the arms race relationship: interaction and acceleration (Richardson 1960; Sample 1998). An arms race signifies a competition between one state and another. A single state can have a military buildup, but this process is not mutual unless another state also competes and races. The other element fundamental to the arms race process is acceleration. The buildup of military capabilities must be significantly higher than in previous years to constitute a real threat to the other side. Without a significant buildup, how would the other side know that there was a strategic danger posed by their enemy?

Since World War I, theorists, historians, and practitioners have asserted that arms races are a direct cause of war. The system of linking arms races in Europe compelled each state to increase its own arms to counter a potential rival (Stevenson 1988, 1996). The arms race process is relatively simple in that one state builds up its arms for either internal (domestic industry, internal threats, leadership turnover) or external (threats, force modernization, weapons advancements) reasons (Valeriano, Sample, and Kang 2011). This buildup then compels a developing enemy to do the same, locking each side into rivalry. Uncovering why military buildups begin is an important task, but at this point I am focused on discovering the consequences of such actions. In this work I will demonstrate that mutual military buildups are positively associated with the onset of rivalry.

Counterintuitive to conventional wisdom, mutual military buildups actually decrease the security of both sides instead of providing for protection like most policy makers seem to believe. Building up an arsenal only increases the probability that the opposing side will build up its own arsenal in a similar manner. In this case, the security dilemma results whereby alliances and mutual military buildups create a context and provide the opportunity for the development of rivalry. A strategy of peace through strength sets in motion the security dilemma common in international politics (Herz 1950; Jervis 1978). Jervis (1978, 169) writes, "the security dilemma exists when many of the means by which states try to increase its security decrease the security of others." Making an alliance or building up one's military may not always lead to war, but it will certainly be associated with rivalry relationships and development of the rivalry conflict spiral because of the psychological and strategic impact of such processes.

A military buildup prepares a state for the eventual use of force, creating the means by which a state may conduct conflict operations. Interacting with other conditions such as alliance ties and territorial disputes, mutual military buildups become a step to rivalry. Using a multivariate model, Sample (1997, 1998, 2002) is able to demonstrate that even when controlling for issues, military defense burdens, and nuclear weapons, mutual military buildups are positively associated with the onset of war. Our question is if these processes lead to rivalry in the first place. Early evidence (Vasquez and Valeriano 2010) suggests that in combination, the factors of alliances, arms races, and rivalry provide a path to war. Do some of these factors provide a path to rivalry? A study by Gibler, Rider, and Hutchinson (2005) finds further evidence arms races lead to militarized disputes, but unfortunately they used Thompson's (2001) strategic rivals to code arms races so we have no clue about the independent effect of arming on rivalry onset.

Early studies in the field suggested that militarization (Bremer 1992) or mobilizations (Van Evera 1999) are causes of war and disputes. Just having weapons or preparing to use them is not a cause of rivalry or war. We have to be more careful about causal processes than simply linking the means to war with the onset of conflict. Instead factors like mobilization and militarization are symptoms to the eventual event, not causes. Our concern for this study is the mutual and accelerated process of arming and the responses these moves lead to in the other side. When conducted in a climate of fear, threats, and aggressive posturing, arms races will lead to the development of rivalries.[13] The question is: when do arms races occur and do they occur early enough in the timeline to cause rivalry and not just wars?

The famous Roman dictum of peace through strength is not accurate. Increasing one's security through power politics activates an action–reaction pattern of conflictual relations. This pattern, once activated, decreases the security of the opposing side and increases the probability of escalating hostilities. Such underlying factors encourage military disputes to recur, which by definition produces rivalry. We know that arms races are associated with war (Gibler, Rider, and Hutchinson 2005; Sample 1998); the remaining question is if they are associated with rivalry development.

Step Four: Escalating Bargaining Demands

One constant truth in international interactions is that threats more likely beget threats when demands are made in the context of repeated demands. Threatening other international actors with violence and extreme demands only brings about the onset of international rivalry, not the resolution of the issue concerns. Under certain contexts, threats and provocations can be ignored as frivolous. What cannot be ignored is when the threats take on an escalating nature of increasing impact and demands as time goes on. As threats escalate in terms of consequences, the probability of rivalry then increases.

Leng's (1983, 1993) early studies are important to uncover this behavioral process critical to the onset of rivalry. The power politics style of international diplomacy focuses on utilizing power and resolve to spur concessions and achieve results. Unfortunately demands escalate as successes are achieved in other arenas (Leng 1983). Actors who participate in escalating threats are rejecting the prudential version of realism (Morgenthau 1948) in favor of a more offensive version of realist political theory (Mearsheimer 2001). The offensive version of realism fails to conform to reality and thus can lead a state to make bad decisions (Valeriano 2009). One such bad decision is the use of coercive bargaining tactics (Leng 1983) because they are assumed to be required responses when in fact they only set up the situation of rivalry. Pushing and poking only bring about equal and escalatory responses from the other side.

Studies (Leng 1993, 2000) confirm that coercive bargaining demands lead to more disputes and war since the opposing side is unlikely to back down in the face of such extreme provocations. The outcomes of previous disputes are important; if left resolved or if both sides fail to be appeased, then conflict is likely to continue. If successful in prior conflicts, states may choose to continue to use threats to achieve diplomatic ends. Success promotes learning, and states can learn that force works. The problem is that force may work in isolated situations, but, more often than not, force begets more force. As demands become more escalatory as time goes on, the overall conflict becomes intractable and develops into rivalry because of the nature and context of the threats that are made. One threat alone is not sufficient to bring about rivalry. Threats must be of an increasing nature and also seek to humiliate the enemy into a submissive posture.

Unfortunately escalation is an unsuitable way to tackle a threat from an enemy. When an animal is threatened, cornered, and beaten, it tends to lash out rather than submit. Even in the face of overwhelming defeat an opposing actor will lash out rather than be humiliated without responding. In many cases leaders make the choice that defeat is better than capitulation and demonstrated weakness. When a state is threatened, cornered, and beaten into submission, it likewise lashes out.

Vasquez and Valeriano (2010) demonstrate that escalating bargaining demands early in a rivalry are important correlates of some types of war. The remaining question is how escalating bargaining demands impact the process of rivalry development. We must not only look at the issue and responses to issue conflicts, but we also must study the types of responses used by international actors. Are the threats increasing in nature? Do they seek to make the other side submit or simply convey a point about preferred bargaining outcomes? The prediction here is that when demands escalate early in a rivalry the states will likely lock in as permanent rivals.

Step Five: Rivalry Linkages

Very few scholars have investigated the impact of linkages between disputes. By *linkages*, I do not mean how issues within a rivalry are linked, but how two different dyadic rivalries are linked to another set of rivals or enemies. In short, how are rivalries connected and how does this impact the development of a rivalry? Of course, rivalry does not occur in isolation. When India fights Pakistan, every other state in the region is a witness. What is unclear is what impact the observation of these behaviors will have on relationships between developing enemies.

The view presented in this work follows the overarching power politics theme outlined in my steps-to-rivalry theory. When states utilize power and threats to spur favorable action in the opposing side, they are more likely to provoke an equal and escalatory reaction from the other side. This is the power politics path within a rivalry, but what about the path outside of a rivalry? What happens when states threaten and participate in disputes with other states while they already have an ongoing conflict with an emerging enemy? The theory presented here suggests that movements to protect state security outside of a rivalry will escalate the rivalry of interest at the same time. Threats to another enemy will only provoke that enemy into responding and might also provoke other regional actors to join the developing fray. Acting like a negative regional actor who threatens others will only provoke enemies and rivalries, not produce stability.

The actions within one dyadic pairing will link up and impact the relationship of another pair of states. This type of interactive relationship is what I term a *rivalry linkage*.[14] Rivalries do not exist independently of other disputes between states. A dispute is linked to a rivalry if a party outside the dyad has a dispute with one member involved in a rivalry during the lifetime of that rivalry. The linkages between other disputes connect a rivalry to its ongoing threat environment in the region or international community.

Rival linkages help lock states into rivalry relationships by pushing a dyad into a tighter bond of rivalry. Even through the offending threat is made outside of the relationship in question, the threat still has an impact on local rivalry. Think of the relationship between Iraq, the United States, and Iran during 2003. Later we will discuss in depth if the states in question do indeed have a rivalry. What is not really up for debate is the fact that threats made against Iraq also hardened the views of those within Iran pushing the U.S. and Iran to become greater enemies. Threats and the eventual invasion of Iraq only suggested to Iranian decision-makers that they were next and communicated that the United States was serious about launching military action if nuclear weapons were being developed. The response by Iran was to harden internal options and accelerate or restart the production of nuclear weapons, thus exacerbating a potential rivalry between the U.S. and Iran.

The theory of war weariness has resulted in very little empirical support. War does not wear down a state unless said state is vanquished almost completely. Instead we tend to find that the probability of conflict increases as states are engaged in more disputes in general. We also know that the more actors involved in a dispute, the less likely it is that said dispute is to be settled short of war (Cusack and Eberwein 1982; James 1988). Huth (1996B) early on finds that when states are engaged in other ongoing disputes the level of threat for territorial disputes in question tends to minimize. The idea is that new disputes tend to decrease the severity of an ongoing dispute. For this study I am interested in the impact of new threats and rivalry. What happens when new rivals emerge?

One would think preoccupation might constrain a state from taking on new threats, but this would only be true outside of developing rivalries. When faced with a pressing issue and other power politics moves (alliances and arms races), a state engaged in multiple simultaneous disputes will likely end the others and focus on the new rival. The use of power politics tactics in other disputes only increases the probability the same steps will result in rivalry if other conditions are met. This type of rivalry linkage is what I term *rivalry commitment dynamics*. States likely to engage in rivalry are committed to the use of power politics tactics when threatened by opposing states. Since power politics tactics are thought to lead directly to rivalry, we also observe states engaged in what might be called rivalry clusters. One dispute in one area of the region might set off multiple other disputes over the same issues and tactics used by the offending state. This is the type of dynamic we see in the Middle East and also in Southeast Asia. One rival begets another.

Major Powers

Major power status should also be included as a factor that can help predict who will become rivals. Major power states are those states that have expansive foreign policy portfolios and power projection capabilities. Post the development of the United Nations, major powers tend to be actors with permanent Security Council status. Bremer (1992) discovered so long ago that major power status increases the probability of war. The same process should be even more in operation during the development of rivalry. Only a certain amount of states have the ability to constantly fight and threaten an enemy. While minor powers engage in many rivalries (Colaresi, Rasler, and Thompson 2008), this is because there are many more minor powers in the system than major powers. Major power state status is fairly rare; it therefore should be reasonable to expect that where major powers are engaged in issue-based conflict, their foreign policy choices will likely utilize the typical power politics tactics that induce rivalry.

Major power states fit the profile of the type of state likely to engage in rivalry. They have expansive issue concerns, making it more likely they will conflict with any state in the system over a foreign policy concern. Major power states have the economic ability to fund weapons purchases and increases, making military buildups more likely. Finally, major powers are typically sought–after alliance partners because of their power projection capabilities. Considering these three facts leads one to theorize that major powers will be more likely to engage in rivalry than minor powers.

CONNECTING THE DOTS

Now that the theory under consideration has been presented, we must further dissect the assumptions and processes the theory implies. Few scholars interested in outcomes actually investigate the sequence of events as they take place to produce the outcome of interest. What assumptions are made about the model, and how does it play out in the real world in terms of temporal ordering? Two important issues that require coverage are the timing of events and if events combine or add to outcomes as they occur to produce new outcomes. The theory presented here has much to say about timing and the temporal ordering of events.

Timing clearly matters. It is troubling that the field of international relations has failed to explain how the timing of events is a critical step to explaining how events come to fruition. Statistical scholars control for time in that they look at lagged effects in models or model the duration between events, yet few fully explain how timing and sequencing are critical aspects of their theories. It seems hard to fathom how timing is left out of so many studies. The dependent variable should come before the event of interest, but when before and in what order?

This theory of rivalry onset depends on the timing of events to explain an outcome. By tossing all the factors thought to cause rivalry into a large statistical soup and running regressions, we fail to fully explain the process of the outcome. Correlation does not explain causation unless the factors come before the event. They must come before an event but also directly contribute to the ordering of outcomes as the process continues along. How can we know when and why each factor contributes to rivalry without exploring how the sequencing of events plays a large role on why states become rivals? This theory would be empty and bankrupt if I fail to explain how timing matters in historical data.

The steps-to-war theory largely has failed to account for sequencing of events on the road to war (Vasquez 2009; Colaresi 2008, 260). In discussing the ordering of the steps-to-war, Colaresi, Rasler, and Thompson (2008, 223) seem to just lump the steps-to-war variables of interest into an interactive circle with no account for the sequencing of events. In later analysis, Colaresi, Rasler, and Thompson (2008, 251) investigate the pattern of contested territory to rivalry, finding that in four cases rivalry led to contested territory and in four cases contested territory led to rivalry. The dominant outcome was contested territory leading to militarized disputes but not rivalry. They conclude by finding that contested territory is most dangerous in combination with rivalry, but they fail to present a full account of the timing of events on the road to rivalry besides looking at territorial issues.

In specifying how and when rivalry will occur, this theory makes a pressing theoretical statement about the importance of timing in the explanation of conflict onset. For rivalry, the ordering of events matters. Alliances, arms races, escalating bargaining tactics, and linkages to other disputes are all factors that must be observed before the onset of rivalry for these factors to contribute to the development of the event. They may also occur later in the life of a rivalry, but the critical issue is whether or not they occur early in the life of a rivalry first. Once used, these factors are likely to be used again in a rivalry, but what matters is that they contribute to the story of how states become rivals in the first place.

It is also hypothesized that the independent variables outlined in this study are additive. It makes little sense for binary events to multiply on themselves. This theory does not investigate the magnitude of each variable, only its presence. Empirically, it matters little how many alliances are in operation or who the alliance partners are. What matters is that the alliance is in existence in the first place and the other power politics variables are in operation as threats to the other side. The number of allies or types of weapons are questions more relevant to the onset of war than the onset of rivalry.

If the magnitude of the variables is irrelevant, the important question that remains is how and when events add on to each other to produce events. In combination, a certain amount of factors is likely to produce rivalry. If an event is observed once, it becomes likely that the opposing decision-maker gets the message and makes concurrent plans. It therefore stands to reason that events that build up to produce a rivalry build up through additive process rather than interactive factors. Different chapters of this book will explore the additive hypotheses and also the different causal paths available to explain rivalry onset. Herein a full account of the life cycle of rivalries will be examined so as to fully outline the beginnings of rivalry.

RESEARCH QUESTIONS GUIDING THE REST OF THE BOOK

Gartzke and Simon (1999) argue that empirical research on the concept of rivalry suffers from what can be called a "hot hand" error, where rivals are seen as no more than a pattern of unrelated events. They note (1999, 779), "for the enduring rivalry research to progress . . . it must justify why researchers should only examine certain cases. Further, the approach can only be rationalized if it is shown that subsequent disputes are caused by factors unique to the presence of rivalry." This research will test the specific hypothesis that the foreign policy practices of rivals are different for dyads that do not escalate to situations of serious rivalry. We know little about the process of rivalry formation but hope to show that rivals are unique dyads in that they exhibit different foreign policy patterns when compared to other types of dyadic pairings. The rivalry research program is not equivalent to a "hot hand" but represents a real exploration of a setting of mutual animosity between states.

This research is positivist and scientific to a large extent. Theory confirmation and evaluation should first come with the demonstration that the hypotheses generated by models and theories are empirically accurate. If my theory does not confirm to real-world historical data, then what is the point in purporting to explain how rivalries begin? My theory should be able to explain and account for the development of past, present, and future rivalries. Once a theory is judged to be empirically accurate, one can then focus on other aspects of theory confirmation that include parsimony, policy relevance, and research fertility. After testing the theory presented herein extensively, I will then reevaluate its accuracy and reformulate the ideas presented based on evidence and facts. The future is a tricky topic, and this study will conclude with predictions about the course of rivalry dynamics in the immediate future.

My general query in this work is to determine what factors make pairs of states that have already experienced some conflict and contact become fully fledged rivals. The hypotheses and predictions tested here treat rivalry as the dependent variable and seek to explain the process of rivalry development. The central theme is that handling crisis with responses associated with power politics practices will increase the probability that an issue conflict will develop into a rivalry situation. The use of power politics strategies leads a state on the path to a rivalry conflict spiral rather than a situation of peace through deterrence. Each state identifies the other as an enemy and attempts to deny benefits to that enemy. During the life of a rivalry, states send signals to each other. The formation of alliances and arms races are negative signals that may increase hostility between a dyad. From this logic, hypotheses 1 and 2 would be expected to be true.

> H1: *Pairs of states that form politically relevant alliances against each other are more likely to become involved in dangerous rivalries.*
> H2: *Pairs of states that participate in mutual military buildups are more likely to become involved in dangerous rivalries.*

If alliances and arms buildups are observed more often in rivalries this discovery does not document a causal process. The findings might be a typical example of a spurious relationship unconnected to how events occur in reality. However, the question remains: are alliance formations and arms races responses to being in an advanced stage of rivalry or processes that push a pair of states towards rivalry? What effect does alliance formation or participation in arms races have on recurring conflict?

A possible spurious finding should prompt the investigator to look at the historical process that resulted in the pattern. We must first look at the variables suggested here to see if they show a temporal ordering consistent with the theory to account for causation. Otherwise this work would have a clear endogeneity problem. Although it is difficult to address causes in any analysis, this project will look at the timing of alliance formation (and arms races) to determine if these factors are possible causes of rivalry escalation. Chronologically, which comes first: power politics strategies or recurring crises? This study predicts that politically relevant alliances and military buildups will lock in early during the life of the rivalry and contribute to the escalation (or steps) towards the manifestation of rivalries.

> H3.1: *When a relevant alliance is exhibited in a rivalry, it should be formed early in the life of the rivalry.*
> H3.2: *When a mutual military buildup is exhibited in a rivalry, it should be formed early in the life of the rivalry.*

The next hypothesis deals with linkages between rivalries. As stated earlier, the theory is counterintuitive to the war weariness hypothesis. States likely to engage in rivalries are likely to fight with anyone in the surrounding system using the same foreign policy tactics. The initiation of one rivalry will increase the probability that both states will engage in other rivalries. The only reason some disputants become rivals and others do not depends on the type of issue causing friction and the power status of the opposing side.[15] When one state commits to multiple ongoing rivalries and continues to escalate disputes with other states, the likelihood that the pair of states contesting over a new issue concern will become rivals is high. Due to the addiction to the use of power politics tactics, any state that frequently uses these tactics in other disputes will also be likely to continue the use of these tactics when a new threat emerges.

The cliché that it is hard to teach old dogs new tricks applies here. The same process occurs for foreign policy actors. What has been used before in the past, even if unsuccessful, will likely be used again the future because it is what is suggested by folklore and represents the typical response available to political actors. Contagion in rivalry seems to be an important predictor of who will be future rivals. When confronted with a critical issue, a state that has followed the rivalry path before will follow that path once more. It might be that a rivalry will only end when a new principal threat (Thompson 1995) emerges, but this does not preclude the existence of multiple rivals if new rivals that emerge are not principal threats.

> H4: *States that participate in multiple rivalries at one time will be likely to escalate new disputes to the rivalry stage.*

This book will conduct various tests of the hypotheses and predictions laid out in this chapter. Hypothesis 5 presents the additive probability hypothesis. This prediction is the accumulation of other theoretical bets tested throughout this book. Here we add in the factors of issues at stake and major power status to better predict which states will become rivals in the future. In combination, the factors of politically relevant alliances, mutual military buildups, major power status, and territorial disputes are likely to lead to rivalry.

> H5: *Pairs of states that form politically relevant alliances against each other, participate in mutual military buildups, are major powers, and have a significant amount of territorial disputes are more likely to become involved in a rivalry than pairs of states that do not engage in these types of behaviors.*

Future chapters and analysis will more fully specify how these predictions will be tested and what types of resources will be used to model the predictions. Some hypotheses will be tested with empirical data and statistical analysis. Others will be tested with qualitative techniques that are better able to account for causal processes. Finally, these predictions will be explained and evaluated using the U.S.–Iraq case to examine the relevancy of this work in the context of a recent conflict and also to provide some contemporary policy advice regarding current conflicts.

POTENTIAL FLAWS TO THE MODEL

Scholars should be open about the potential flaws to their models. Only through a frank discussion of limitations to an analysis can we be honest about the progress we are making towards answering the big questions in political science research. This analysis represents an accumulation of two decades of research on rivalry processes, yet it is not without its faults.

Important questions are: When are rivalries born? How do we measure inception? These are not questions that are critical for the Thompson (2001) or Klein, Goertz, and Diehl (2006) coding of rivalry, but they are critical for this study. For this analysis the inception of a rivalry will be counted as the third militarized dispute observed during the rivalry history. This choice reflects early coding choices of other scholars (Goertz and Diehl 1992) and also prior research by Leng (1983) that looked at the number of crises relevant for war.

Selecting the third dispute is not a perfect way to count rivalry inception, but it seems to be the best of many other flawed options. First, we have to admit that rivalry is meaningless if there is no observed conflict in the form of militarized threats. Therefore, the observation of a certain amount of militarized challenges is critical to determine when rivals begin. Since all Klein, Goertz, and Diehl (2006) rivals reach the three dispute threshold, this data set will be the focal point for much of this research. But we can also use the Thompson (2001) data as long as there are a certain number of disputes counted. Beginning a rivalry at first militarized contact does not seem accurate since we would want to count repeated conflict outcomes, not singular attempts to threaten another actor. Locating the initiation of a rivalry at dispute one would be an invalid way to measure onset.

Endogeneity is another potential criticism of this research. One point would be that the variables examined here are endogenous. One variable, such as alliances, is assumed with the outcome of rivalry, so how can alliances be a causal predictive factor? To alleviate this potential concern, all effort has been made to examine and illuminate the causal process at it occurs throughout history. A component statistical examination that examines the timing of events will be conducted, and this will be supported through case study research, time plots, and pathway analysis. It should be fairly clear that this study outlined all possible avenues of rivalry onset controlling for timing and event ordering.

The issue of selection effects has been important in the study of conflict in recent years (Reed 2000; Signorino 1999). *Selection effects* refer to one stage of a process that can impact the next stage of model. Choices made early in a relationship may determine the future choices and outcomes of a relationship. Early critics (Reed 2002) of the rivalry approach point out that the program cannot explain why states initiate the first instances of conflict. Why do enemies even begin to interact? As stated in the first chapter, this question is beyond the scope of this analysis. No attempt is made here to explain why certain states engage in conflict; the only goal is to explain repeated conflict.

I expect the question of selection effects to have no impact on the overall value of the findings in this study. Other studies (Bennett, Baker, and Stam 2002; Senese and Vasquez 2003, 2008) have found a similar absence of impact. However, it may still be important to investigate if there is a selection process at work. There may well be selection effects evident when pairs of states engaging in MIDs are likely to act differently than those who do not. That fact is not surprising, and it is suggested in the theory. When analyzing rivalry, it is important to focus on how disputes are handled once they occur, not why they occur in the first place. This task is contained within an entirely different research enterprise since addressing the origins of disputes constitutes a research program of a different sort when compared to the goals of the rivalry research program.

The final potential problem is advice to ignore the power politics path. Responding to threats with power politics tactics is the norm in the international system. Due to the implications of the use of power politics strategies, I am hesitant to ever recommend their usage, but there are benefits to the path. One is that a show of force is what is expected, and if a leader fails to do this, there might be electoral or internal punishment for one who chooses the more cooperative path. Avoiding the power politics path is advisable, but tangible actions need to be taken when threatened. Sometimes the power politics path might be the only path available. I just want to be clear that this path only begets more threats, rivalry, and war.

It is also advisable to use the power politics path to deter, corner, and minimize a pressing threat early, before it gets out of hand. Squashing a bug might be the best way to deal with the situation. This advice suggests that these options be used early and to maximum effect. One such example might have been the optimal strategy of France and the United Kingdom when threatened by Adolf Hitler as he rearmed Germany in the early 1930s. The caveat is to do this early, before the opposing side can gain enough power to hold off external threats and before the other side learns the lesson that militarized diplomacy works. Militarized diplomacy should never be the optimal strategy in the international system, and it is up to the states in the region to reject this course of action when mad men advocate the path.

ASSESSMENT AND CONCLUDING REMARKS

The central expectation derived from the theory presented here is that issues matter, and how issues are handled will determine if a pair of states will become rivals. When states utilize power politics responses to threats posed by other states, they are likely to become rivals. Rivals are likely to fight wars and engage in frequent conflict, and they tend to avoid dealing with internal problems and reform. Solving the dilemma of rivalry will remove many obstacles that impede international progress and domestic harmony. Ending the scourge of rivalry will be an important step towards international peace.

This theory is largely behavioral. The resulting implication is that behavior matters more than intentions, ideas, and material capabilities. In the absence of other forms of information, states can only judge other states on their ability to conduct themselves in a decent manner in the international system. Decency is counterintuitive to a rivalry. The existence of rivalry means that all conflict options are on the table; all forms of behavior are condoned to deal with the existential threat posed by an international enemy. All sorts of crazy behavior can result from interpersonal rivalries, and we can only observe more of the same at the international level.

How do we know the story presented here is accurate? Theories need to be tested empirically first. We can have no confidence in the ideas posed here unless they actually apply to reality as we know it. Without the empirical application of theory, theory remains isolated as a normative idea of how the world should work. When we have information that details how the international interactions have worked, then why would one avoid investigating if theory applies to reality as measured? Very little is gained by ignoring the application of theory to data. This book could be a typical effort in ransacking history if empirical evidence was not evaluated in a consistent manner. We can never be sure the case studies chosen are value-free. What I term *theoretical incest* is a real problem in international relations. So often scholars develop theories by examining one case and then test their theory with the same case. Many scholars have used the Cold War example to develop and test theories at the same time. The only way we can be sure theory testing is value-free is by utilizing a variety of methods to explore the question. This book will not be an effort in selected case studies, caveats, or counterexplanations.

Once we have investigated how the world has worked in the past, we must then turn to more nuanced examinations of theory. Mechanisms, pathways, and processes cannot be left out of the story. They typically require the application of qualitative theory investigations quantitative scholars so often ignore. Correlation is not causation, but correlation can lead to the examination of causation if done accurately.

The final task would be one of explanatory power and relevance (Vasquez 1998). Theory must explain how the world has worked, but it must also explain how the world is working now to be relevant. What use is a theory that only applies to past action? Relevancy also requires the application of suitable policy advice. International relations scholarship is bankrupt if one fails to explore the policy implications of findings. It is only through the investigations of empirical application, casual pathways, and policy relevance that one can say his or her theory is interesting, important, and meaningful. The rest of this book will be an effort to empirically test this theory and also to apply policy lessons based on past historical experience to current situations.

3 The Empirical Dynamics of the Steps-to-Rivalry Model

MODELING RIVALRY DEVELOPMENT

A theory accounting for the development of rivalry should be able to correctly determine which types of states will enter into a rivalry relationship. Rivalry is a long-standing situation of mutual animosity where the stakes between the actors are high and competition over issues varies due to the existential threat the competitor poses to a state. The goal is prediction, but we should also be able to target certain states and situations for intervention before the process gets out of hand, becoming detrimental to the global good, the public within each state, and any bystander caught in the middle of the conflict. These considerations signal how important predicting rivalry is as an enterprise. The stakes are life or death in the international system. Few areas of inquiry in the field of international relations are of more import.

This chapter builds on the prior chapters, which outline the process of rivalry development, and suggests a theory that accounts for the rivalry situation as it arises in the international system. The theory is based on power politics considerations being negative factors in international relations. The typical approach when one encounters a competitor is to either overwhelm them with one's own internal development (military buildups) or external support (allies). In fact, either policy virtually ensures that a competitor will become a threat now and an enemy later. How one handles a potential threat generally becomes a self-fulfilling prophesy that leads to rivalry if power politics tactics are utilized.

This chapter will outline the goals of the scientific enterprise concerning rivalry, present a research design that guides the statistical investigations, and analyze the data available to test hypotheses on the development of rivalry in relation to power politics inputs. By the end of this chapter, the reader should have some sense of what factors push states towards rivalry.

MAKING PREDICTIONS

Every social scientist has to place bets. Without predictors, inclinations, and testable hypotheses, science would be empty and would avoid taking sides on

The Empirical Dynamics of the Steps-to-Rivalry Model 53

the perspective being offered. While this is not an effort at true science in the vein of chemistry or physics, one can try to approximate political and social reality as best as possible to get at the dynamics of international events. There is no true control group for intervention studies, but there is a comprehensive sample, variation in the data, reliable indicators of concepts, and statistical techniques we can use to analyze the impact of various factors on the outcome of interest, rivalry.

All theories need a way to judge if the predictions inherent in the statement are either right or wrong. The central question, a question that is sometimes overlooked, is how one knows if one is wrong. When is a theory falsified? This is the role of testable series of hypotheses. All these issues were covered in Chapter 2, but it is useful to go over some of the basic questions here.

The hypotheses presented here treat rivalry as the dependent variable and seek to explain the process of rivalry development. This study will be concerned with factors that distinguish isolated conflicts from more serious forms of rivalry. Vasquez (2000, 349) poses the question, "are there certain foreign policy practices that distinguish dyads that are rivals from those that are not?" This pressing question is the jumping-off point for much of the work presented here on rivalry. We know rivalry is important; it is a form of relationship different from other sorts of international relationships, and it is deadly. However, we do not really know the factors that distinguish the rivalry process from nonrivalry situations.

Handling international challenges with responses associated with power politics behavior will increase the probability that an isolated conflict between two states will become a rivalry situation. The use of power politics leads a state to the path of a rivalry conflict spiral. Each state identifies the other as an enemy and attempts to deny benefits to that enemy. During the life of a rivalry, states send signals to each other. The formation of alliances and arms races are examples of negative signals that increase the hostility within a rival dyad.

The concept of a security dilemma is critical for this analysis and is an outgrowth of the policies that precede rivalry. In fact, it is a strategy of peace through strength that sets in motion the security dilemma common in international politics (Herz 1950). Jervis (1978, 169) states, "the security dilemma exists when many of the means by which states try to increase their security decrease the security of others." The process of building up one's strength either externally or internally directly leads to a security dilemma. A security dilemma is part of a rivalry relationship.

Making an alliance or building up one's military may not always lead to war, but it will certainly be associated with rivalry relationships and development of the rivalry conflict spiral. Increasing one's security through power politics activates an action–reaction pattern of conflictual relations that decreases security and increases threat perceptions, hostility, and conflict. Such underlying factors encourage military disputes to recur, which is the essence of rivalry if it is observed in the system. From this logic, one would expect hypotheses 1 and 2 to be supported by historical evidence.

> H 1: *Pairs of states that form politically relevant alliances against each other are more likely to become involved in dangerous rivalries.*
>
> H 2: *Pairs of states that participate in mutual military buildups are more likely to become involved in dangerous rivalries.*

To take a step back, the hypotheses presented here are very specific to the available data scholars have to investigate power politics questions. The more general hypothesis is clearly the prediction that power politics strategies exacerbate competitor relations and push states towards rivalry. It takes two to tango, and when two states do more than dance but also begin to bluster, poster, and pose in a manner akin to a pre–boxing match press conference, the situation escalates into low-level conflict and then, later, outright rivalry.

> *Pairs of states that utilize power politics strategies meant to display power and deter a competitor from challenging the status quo will end up in a rivalry.*

Now that our bets are placed, the question is how do we know when there is enough evidence to accept a hypothesis or, at the very least, not reject an idea? The heart of this study is about making a connection between power politics behavior and the increasing chances of a pair of states entering into a rivalry relationship. To that end, many different forms of evidence will be presented to support the main contentions I am making throughout this book. This chapter will proceed with a basic examination of the data. This means that summary statistics will be used to provide context and background for the relationship between power politics and rivalry behavior. The chapter will then move on to utilize more advanced statistical procedures to predict rivalry onset and control for a number of intervening factors.

DESIGN OF THE STUDY

In testing the additive models of rivalry development, this study relies on both bivariate statistics and various forms of binary logit modeling to determine the impact of each independent variable on the outcome. A key independent variable in this chapter is politically relevant alliances, which are taken from the work of Senese and Vasquez (2005, 2008). In their data, alliances are relevant only if they include a major power or a minor power state from the same region as the dyad. The alliance must be formed at least three months prior to the dispute in question. Further, only outside alliances are counted here (either both sides or one side had an alliance), and alliances where the states are allied to each other are excluded. No distinction was made between types of alliances or the purpose of the alliance. In the future it might be useful to further investigate the types of alliances that lead to rivalry, but first we must uncover the basic dynamics at work. Alliance information is taken from Correlates of War alliance version 3.0 (Gibler and Sarkees 2004) and Gibler's (2009) reference volume on alliances.

The data for the key independent variable, mutual military buildups, are taken from the updated military expenditures data used in the capability data (Singer, Bremer, and Stuckey 1972) that include both major and minor power mutual military buildups (Sample 2002). Sample's (1996, 1997) data code a mutual military buildup as occurring if both states exhibit an overall increase in military spending in the ten years prior to a militarized dispute, an operationalization based on a measure developed by Horn (1987). Over a ten-year window, there must be a marked increase in expenditures compared to the prior ten-year period. The first dependent variable will then be a Horn (1987) mutual military buildup.

The Horn measure is too restrictive to capture simultaneous racing behavior in the system. Instead I also follow Gibler, Rider, and Hutchinson (2005) and use a measure that codes a mutual military buildup if there is an 8 percent spending increase over three years. The 8 percent figure is standard in the field (Horn 1987) and used to distinguish from natural fluctuations in capital or exchanges that might influence how spending numbers are calculated. This new measure of a mutual military buildup was developed by Valeriano, Sample, and Kang (2011), and it differs from the Gibler, Rider, and Hutchinson (2005) measure in that it does not rely on Thompson (2001) rivalries to indentify competing partners. This would obviously bias the results, and thus it is appropriate to use a measure that just looks if the buildup is interactive over a certain period of time for all dyads. The second measure will be called Valeriano, Sample, and Kang (2011), but there are plans to release a public version of this data, and it will likely become the Sample, Valeriano, and Kang measure in the future.

The main dependent variable in this analysis is taken from Diehl and Goertz's (2000) coding of rivalry as updated by Klein, Goertz, and Diehl (2006). Diehl and Goertz distinguish which pairs of states are enduring rivals, i.e., those states that have had at least six disputes over a twenty-year period and states that only engage in sporadic conflict. The basic conception of rivalry requires at least three disputes over a short time span. A 2011 update of the data was used for this analysis that corrected a few problems with the prior version. The years covered are 1815 to 2001.

Two control variables are used in this study. The first is contiguity. States that are contiguous are most likely to get into disputes (Bremer 1992). It is important to control for contiguity to ensure that findings on alliances are not spurious or driven by proximity rather than other factors. We also include status as a predictive variable. Major states are more likely than any other type of state to become involved in conflict (Bremer 1992).

THE IRRATIONALITY OF RIVALRY

It should be noted that rivalry is an irrational project in most cases. While the process might be natural and evolutionary, it does not mean that it makes much rational sense. In fact, the bargaining theory has little to say about rivalry. During a situation of rivalry, the stakes, preferences, and goals of various actors make little difference. It is true that these factors are important for specific disputes—usually early in the life of enmity between two countries—but it is not the case in the relationship between rivals. Often, states engaged in rivalry have no real idea how the whole process started. Like the infamous Hatfields versus the McCoys, both sides have been fighting for so long they no longer have any memory of how the dispute started in the first place. Preferences and goals can matter little when an entire society is focused on persecuting an "other" as an enemy.

In most cases a rivalry will start out as a strategic process, and there is generally some gain to be made, through territorial concessions, resource allocation, or support of general policies. Unfortunately, once this process starts—however rational the initial motives may have been—irrationality soon takes hold. The entire course of the dispute becomes an "us versus them" stake that cannot be solved through simple concessions or strategic statements. Long-standing rivalries like the U.S. versus the Soviet Union or India versus Pakistan illustrate the totality of enmity in some rivalry relationships.

The U.S.–Soviet rivalry is an interesting example to use here. One would have thought the rivalry terminated with the end of the Cold War, but this was not the case. In fact, the decline of both the Soviets during their Afghanistan war and the United States during Vietnam should have demonstrated to both sides that the strategic goals they were trying to implement were doomed to failure. Yet, the dispute persisted until the Soviet Union was relegated to the ash heap of history, and enmity with the Russians continues to this day (Valeriano and Maness 2012b).

The animosity between the Russians and the United States continues mainly through a clash of policy goals in areas such as Kosovo, Syria, the War on Terror, and energy politics. But the general relationship continues to be one of strategic competition that is not rooted in any real source of hatred. The source of discord now seems to be functional rather than rational. The United States and the Russians clash based on perceptions of intentions and goals rather than coming to blows over the actual stated goals of each state. The reaction to the ballistic missile defense shield promoted by the United States is a perfect illustration of this problem. The U.S. is now willing to share plans, move installations, and do just about anything to allay Russian fears, but the reaction remains negative with the stated suspicion that the shield program is really just targeting Russia. The only way to move beyond this conception of hostility in the relationship is to rebuild a system of trust between the two sides.

The question must be asked, what does it mean that rivalry is an irrational process? Like most disputes over serious issues, the irrationality of the demands is a central reason there is no resolution of the disagreement. One cannot be satisfied with objective measures of assurance or concrete goods unless one has a reasonable grasp over what assurances or goods one wants out of the relationship. Because rivalry as a process is irrational, we should expect to find that symbols, actions, and events take on a greater meaning than intended on most occasions. This is why power politics behavior is so important on the path to rivalry. Behavior matters during the development of a rivalry, and behavior consisting of blustering, posturing, and displays of force only exacerbates the situation, pushing the outcome towards its natural conclusion. The irrationality of the rivalry process ensures that simple calculations of who should and should not be involved in a rivalry matter little. What matters in this relationship is action and how actions are perceived by each opposing side.

SUMMARIZING RIVALRY DEVELOPMENT

This section will examine the basic dynamics of a rivalry relationship in relation to the factors promoted as causes of rivalry development. Most scholars tend to utilize advanced statistical techniques to examine questions in the conflict studies field. While these methods are important in a complete analysis of international events, sometimes the utilization of basic bivariate techniques can be an illuminating way to examine relationships. Here, simple tables are presented to marshal evidence pinpointing what factors are important in the development of rivalry.

Alliance Basics

To test hypotheses 1 and 2, I first construct basic bivariate tables that show whether or not power politics strategies are present in each rivalry phase. Some may find the basic results unnecessary when later forms of analysis will utilize a more advanced model of rivalry development. I prefer to build towards this more advanced model by first examining bivariate relationships. The first step should be an examination of the basic outline of the data in relation to the dependent variable of rivalry occurrence.

Table 3.1 outlines the basic bivariate relationship between rivalry and relevant alliance formation. The first thing that can be understood from this table is that relevant alliances are not sufficient conditions for rivalry. In other words, not all alliances lead to rivalry. In fact, there are 687 alliances observed during the isolated conflict stage. Furthermore, relevant alliances are not *necessary* conditions for rivalry. Stated differently, rivalries sometimes form even without the presence of alliances.

In terms of expected counts, it is interesting that there should have been 265.8 alliances observed during rivalry, but instead we observe 284 cases. The same goes for the lack of alliances; based on basic proportions, we should observe 65.2 cases without alliances during the rivalry stage, but instead we observe 47. What is important to discover, however, is if the probability of rivalry increases when relevant alliances are observed. This will be the next task.

Table 3.1 Rivalry and Relevant Alliances 2x2

	No Alliance	Alliance	Total
Isolated Conflict	191	687	878
	(172.8)	(705.2)	
	21.75%	78.25%	
	80.25%	70.75%	
Rivalry	47	284	331
	(65.2)	(265.8)	
	14.20%	85.80%	
	19.75%	29.25%	
Total	238	971	1,209

Notes: Pearson Chi^2 = 8.6771 Pr = .003.
Percentages are calculated for row and column values.
Expected count in parentheses.
*Allied to each other not counted as a relevant alliance.

As Table 3.1 demonstrates, 29.25 percent of the total number of relevant alliances observed occur during a rivalry. However, the table also shows that for almost every dyad in a rivalry (284 of the possible 331 cases, or 85.8 percent), either one or both sides have an outside alliance. It is also telling that the percentage of cases that exhibit alliance behavior increases according to the number of disputes a dyad experiences. In particular, of the eighty-six dyads engaging in enduring rivalry behavior (more than six disputes over more than twenty years), seventy-seven (89.5 percent) cases exhibit alliance behavior. Those pairs of states allied to each other were not counted as positive observations.

Alliance Multivariate

Table 3.2 presents results for a basic logit model that tests hypothesis 1. In particular, the model examines if pairs of states that form politically relevant alliances are more likely to become involved in rivalries than states without these types of alliances. This portion of the study utilizes a rivalry history research design and provides us with a total of 1,209 cases to analyze. This model tries to determine if the hypothesized factors of rivalry development are actually present in the cases that form the unit of analysis. A dyad enters this data set if it ever engaged in at least one militarized dispute. Here we examine if alliances increase the likelihood that a dyad engages in a rivalry while also controlling for the factors of contiguity and major power status. These two factors are controlled for since they may help account for the dynamics of rivalries for those states that use alliances. We would have no confidence in the overall theory if it could not pass this basic test. The results support the proposition that states forming

Table 3.2 Relevant Alliances and Rivalry Coefficient Estimates, Logit Model for Rivalry Type

	Outcome Rivalry			
Independent Variables	Coefficient	S.E.	ZScore	P>|z|
R. Alliance	0.782	.190	4.11	0.000
Contiguity	1.362	.142	9.56	0.000
Major Powers	1.044	.281	3.72	0.000
Constant	-2.171	.193	-11.23	0.000

Notes: N = 1209.
Prob > chi2 = 0.000.
Log likelihood = -652.097.
Isolated Conflict is the reference category.

relevant alliances against each other are more likely to become involved in a rivalry, as coded by Klein, Goertz, and Diehl (2006), but are less likely to be observed in isolated conflicts.

For the rivalry category, relevant alliances generate a coefficient of 0.782 and are statistically significant at the 0.001 level. Major power dyads generate a coefficient of 1.04 and are statistically significant at 0.001 level. Contiguous states are also likely to engage in rivalry behavior, as the coefficient for this variable is 1.362 with a p value less than 0.001.

The analysis performs as expected; alliances make it more likely that a state will engage in rivalry. Pairs of states that include contiguous states or a state that is a major power also are more likely to become involved in rivalry, but these factors do not diminish the import of the alliance variable. They likely add to the process rather than account for it fully. This idea will be explored more fully in Chapter 5.

Predicted probabilities (Table 3.3) illustrate the statistics in a different way and allow one to determine if, in addition to achieving statistical significance, the variables are important in a substantive sense.[1] If the values on all variables are set at zero, the base probability for rivalry is 0.102. However, for rivalry, if an alliance occurs, the probability jumps from .102 to .199.

If the values for relevant alliances and contiguity are set at one, the probability that a dyad will engage in rivalry increases to 0.493. Lastly, when there is an alliance present, the states are contiguous, and there is a major power involved, the probably of rivalry is .734, a significant increase from the base probability. These results demonstrate a consistent pattern; alliances increase the probability of rivalry occurrence and each additional factor increases the probability even more.

60 Becoming Rivals

Table 3.3 Predicted Probabilities for Alliance and Rivalry

	Isolated Conflict	Rivalry
All Variables = 0	0.897	0.102
Alliance = 1	0.800	0.199
Difference	-0.097	+0.097
Alliance = 1 + Cont = 1	0.506	0.493
Difference	-.391	+.391
Ally = 1 + Cont = 1 +Major = 1	0.265	0.734
Difference	-.632	.632

Mutual Military Buildups Basics

Tables 3.4 and 3.5 outline the basic bivariate relationship between rivalry and mutual military buildup occurrence. As stated earlier, two different measures of mutual military buildups are used. The first is the standard Horn (1987) measure used by Sample (1997, 1998) to examine the question of arms races and war. The second is called *mutual military buildup* (Valeriano, Sample, and Kang 2011) and has a less restrictive coding and makes more theoretical sense since such a long time period under observation (i.e., ten years) is not always relevant to the rivalry situation.

These tables are the first test of hypothesis 2, which states that mutual military buildups should make the presence of rivalry more likely. The first thing we notice is that not all mutual military buildups lead to rivalries. For instance, there are sixty-one buildups during the isolated stage (i.e., 61 of the total 879 isolated conflicts have buildups, or 6.94 percent) for the Horn measure and thirty-nine for the military buildup measure (i.e., 39 of the total 879 isolated conflicts have buildups, or 4.44 percent). While this shows that buildups are not sufficient conditions for rivalry, it also demonstrates that very few isolated conflicts take place in the context of mutual military buildups (i.e., only 6.94 percent when using the Horn measure and 4.44 percent when using the Valeriano, Sample, and Kang measure).

The expected count of mutual buildups during a rivalry is 29.5 based on proportions, but the actual observed count is 47. This demonstrates unexpected observation of factors when compared to what is expected from the data. We also see less observed buildups during the isolated state than would be expected by the proportions. What is critical is if the probability of rivalry increases with the presence of these events.

For rivalry dyads, the relationship between mutual military buildups is evident. For the Horn measure, 47 of the 331 cases of rivalry have buildups. Although this only encompasses 14.2 percent of the total number of rivalry dyads, fully 43 percent of all the mutual military buildups that occur take

Table 3.4 Rivalry and Horn Mutual Military Buildups 2x2

	No Buildup	MMB	Total
Isolated Conflict	818 (800.5) 93.06% 74.23%	61 (78.5) 6.94% 56.48%	879
Rivalry	284 (301.5) 85.80% 25.77%	47 (29.5) 14.20% 43.52%	331
Total	1102	108	1,210

Notes: Pearson Chi² = 15.589 Pr = 0.000.
Percentages are calculated for row and column values.
Expected count in parentheses.

place during a rivalry. For the Valeriano, Sample, and Kang (2011) measure, 57 of the 331 cases of rivalry have buildups present (Table 3.5). Again, while this indicates that only 17.2 percent of the total number of rival dyads have buildups, it is telling to note that 59 percent of the total number of mutual military buildups occur during a rivalry. The Valeriano, Sample, and Kang (2001) measure also demonstrates the unexpected observation of the factor during the rivalry stage with only 26.3 expected mutual military buildups, but here we observe 57. Furthermore, while a relatively low percentage of rivals have buildups (i.e., 14.2 percent and 17.2 percent, respectfully) isolated conflict dyads—as indicated earlier—have even fewer (i.e., 6.94 percent and 4.44 percent). The multivariate test will provide a fuller picture of this relationship.

Table 3.5 Rivalry and Valeriano et al. Mutual Military Buildups 2x2

	No Buildup	MMB	Total
Isolated Conflict	840 (809.3) 95.56% 75.40%	39 (69.7) 4.44% 40.63%	879
Rivalry	274 (304.7) 82.78% 24.60%	57 (26.3) 17.22% 59.38%	331
Total	1,114	96	1,210

Notes: Pearson Chi² = 53.797 Pr = 0.000.
Percentages are calculated for row and column values.
Expected count in parentheses.
*In the tables to follow, *military build* refers to mutual military buildups.

Mutual Military Buildups Multivariate

Tables 3.6 and 3.7 present results of logit models testing hypothesis 2 and examine whether or not mutual military buildups promote the development of rivalry. The results support the proposition that states participating in mutual military buildups against each other are more likely to become involved in rivalries.

Using the more restrictive Horn measure or the Valeriano, Sample, and Kang measure does not produce drastically different results. The difference in the measures will become clear for other forms of analysis later in this book. Here I just want to present the basic relationship. For the Horn buildups (Table 3.6), mutual military buildups generate a coefficient of 0.593, and this factor is statistically significant at the 0.05 level. Major power states generate a coefficient of 1.139 that is statistically significant at the 0.001 level. Contiguity also has a positive coefficient and is significant at traditional levels.

When using the Valeriano, Sample, and Kang (2011) measure (Table 3.7), mutual military buildups generate a coefficient of 1.18, and this factor is statistically significant at the 0.001 level. Major power status dyads generate a coefficient of 0.945 that is statistically significant at 0.001. Contiguity remains significant and positive.

Table 3.8 displays the predicted probabilities for the Horn buildup measure. The probabilities show that if the values for all variables are set to zero, the probability of rivalry is 0.176. If there is a positive observation of a buildup, the probably of rivalry then increases to 0.279. What is interesting is that the probability of rivalry increases when there is a Horn buildup, just as there is a similar increase for the alliance variable.

Table 3.6 Horn Mutual Military Buildups and Rivalry Coefficient Estimates, Logit Model for Rivalry Type

Independent Variables	Coefficient	S.E.	ZScore	P>|z|
Military Build	0.593	.217	2.72	0.006
Contiguity	1.208	.138	8.74	0.000
Major Powers	1.139	.280	4.07	0.000
Constant	-1.540	.093	-16.56	0.000

Outcome: Rivalry

Notes: N = 1210.
Prob > chi2 = 0.000.
Log likelihood = -657.916.
Isolated Conflict is the Reference Category.

Table 3.7 Valeriano et al. Mutual Military Buildups and Rivalry Coefficient Estimates, Logit Model for Rivalry Type

Independent Variables	Outcome Rivalry Coefficient	S.E.	ZScore	P>|z|
Military Build	1.180	.231	5.10	0.000
Contiguity	1.156	.140	8.27	0.000
Major Powers	0.945	.288	3.28	0.001
Constant	-1.561	.093	-16.80	0.000

Notes: N = 1210.
Prob > chi2 = 0.000.
Log likelihood = -648.430.
Isolated Conflict is the Reference Category.

If Horn military buildup and contiguity are set at one, the probability that a dyad is engaged in a rivalry is 0.565, representing an increase by over a factor of three from the baseline model. The relationship is even stronger when the values are set to one for a military buildup, contiguity, and a major power dyad. When a dyad has all three of these factors present, the probability that it will become engaged in a rivalry is 0.802. This is an increase of nearly five times from the baseline model.

Table 3.9 displays the probabilities for rivalry occurrence in relation to the factor of a mutual military buildup following the example of Valeriano, Sample, and Kang (2011). The results here are stronger, suggesting that when the variable for mutual military buildup is coded using a three-year observation period, it has a more substantial relationship with rivalry than the prior Horn (1987) measure that required a ten-year observation period.

Table 3.8 Predicted Probabilities for Horn Buildup and Rivalry

	Isolated Conflict	Rivalry
All Variables = 0	0.823	0.176
Horn MB = 1	0.720	0.279
Difference	-0.103	+0.103
Horn MB = 1 + Cont = 1	0.434	0.565
Difference	-.389	+.389
MB = 1 + Cont = 1 + Major = 1	.197	.802
Difference	-.626	.626

64 Becoming Rivals

Table 3.9 Predicted Probabilities for Valeriano et al. Military Buildup and Rivalry

	Isolated Conflict	Rivalry
All Variables = 0	0.826	0.173
MB = 1	0.594	0.405
Difference	-0.232	+0.232
MB = 1 + Cont = 1	0.315	0.684
Difference	-.511	+.511
MB = 1 + Cont = 1 +Major = 1	0.151	0.848
Difference	-.675	.675

The direction of the findings is the same and only increases in power. For example, if a military buildup occurs at all, holding other variables constant at zero, the probability of rivalry is .405, while the basic probability of rivalry when using the Horn measure is only .279. Adding the positive values for a mutual military buildup and continuity increases the probability of rivalry to .684. Finally, if the values are set to one for a mutual military buildup, contiguity, and major power, the probability of rivalry is .848.

ASSESSMENT OF FINDINGS

Relevant alliances are the first and most important factor investigated. Those pairs of states that participate in relevant alliances (at least one outside alliance) are more likely to become involved in rivalry. Very few "enduring" rivalries do not have alliances present. The basic probability of a rivalry is .199 when an alliance is present and only .102 when there are no alliances.

This analysis also shows that rivalry is more likely if states are involved in mutual military buildups. The probability of the occurrence of rivalry increases when mutual military buildups are present. Accordingly, the probability of isolated conflict decreases when mutual military buildups are present. While the effects of mutual military buildups are consistent with the hypotheses presented here as probabilistic sufficient conditions of rivalry, they are not necessary conditions. Not all rivals have experienced mutual military buildups, and some buildups occur outside of a rivalry. This issue will be explored more fully in Chapter 4.

The basic dynamics are clear, mutual military buildups and alliances increase the probability of alliances. This chapter has sought to illustrate this relationship in many ways. From two-by-two tables, to logistic regression results, to probability tables, there is a clear pattern of power politics factors being related to the development of rivalry. The next question relates to the timing of events. When exactly do these events occur on the timeline of rivalry? Chapter 4 will investigate this question.

4 Timing and the Steps-to-Rivalry Model

TIME AND RIVALRY RELATIONSHIPS

The relationship between social units and time should be at the heart of all forms of analytical examinations. Surprisingly, scholars often fail to explore the timing of events in the processes they are trying to predict, explain, or examine. Often it is deemed sufficient to simply lag a variable by a year or two in order to examine how the variables are accounted for through time in a model. This is an inadequate way of investigating such a critical question or factor. The timing of events is likely one of the most critical elements to be examined in a causal process, yet a major flaw is the lack of methods that can account for timing in binary data investigations.

The basic axiom of quantitative research is that a factor can be said to be a cause of an event if it comes before the event, correlates, and is not spurious. Often scholars can deal with two of the three requirements, but the third factor of timing tends to be problematic. Correlations are relatively straightforward relationships to pinpoint, either statistically or through qualitative analysis. The goal of the prior chapter was to establish that there is a correlational relationship between power politics strategies and rivalry development. The potentially spurious nature of social relationships can be outlined with a solid theory that predicts and accounts for how factors will impact outcomes and by specifying the causal mechanisms inherent in a process. The remaining factor left to explore is time.

Time matters because a factor cannot be said to have an impact on an event unless it comes before the outcome temporally; this is the most basic function of time in an empirical relationship. The analysis of variables through time can account for the shifting relationship of time in relation to events, or concurrent causality. It is even possible that just the expectation of a factor's occurrence can start the chain of events that leads to an outcome with the causal factor remaining unobserved. An example of this is the mobilization processes prior to World War I, where the mere assumption of full Russian mobilization triggered full German mobilization. Expectations of an event's occurrence can change the outcome in question.

More critically, a factor must have enough time to be observed so that it can set off the causal mechanisms inherent in a social process. An event can come before an outcome, but that does not mean that the event had enough lead time to result in a change in behavior. Sometimes inputs are not realized in social reality for various reasons, the actors may be distracted, some other event can take precedence, or there is a variable that is omitted that might be more important for the event's occurrence than an investigator thought in the first place. It could also be that an event that fails to occur before an outcome in a statistical examination did not really fail to occur during the correct temporal ordering, but rather the analysis failed to pick up evidence of the event or there is something inherent about the event that the analyst overlooks that truly is the trigger in a causal process. All these contingencies matter and are critical to the examination of social realities through time.

Here, the goal is to demonstrate that power politics practices come before rivalry events. We will examine why certain events should occur during different time periods, when they should occur, and what evidence is sufficient to accept that a factor contributes to the onset of a process. The timing at which events occur is important, as is the ordering and sequencing of events. Here I will present data that deconstruct the timing of power politics events. I will also present time plots that display the life history of a rivalry so the timing of events is clear to see for any observer.

ORDERING AND SEQUENCING ON THE ROAD TO RIVALRY

Related to the issue of time is the consideration of ordering and sequencing. The move towards quantitative approaches to political science has seemingly discarded simple methods that can account for sequences important in examining behavior. Most forms of conflict analysis and security studies leave the process out of any scholarship suggesting the causes of conflict. This is a tragic development that I hope to not repeat. The ordering of events is an important part of the explanation for how events come about in the first place.

Waltz (1979) was rightly faulted by many in the field for failing to take into account how change comes about in the system and when. The sequences critical for examinations of a balance of power relationship are missing in his analysis of the system. Instead, the substitute was to simply wait for the prediction to come true no matter how long that took. Proper theory and analysis should be able to predict when an event will occur and how its occurrence sets off a causal chain of events. Devoid of this logic, theory can be empty and useless.

Leaving out the factor of ordering and sequences is also the main weakness of the steps-to-war theory proposed by Vasquez (1993). In the original (Vasquez 1993) work and subsequent extensions (Senese and Vasquez

2008; Vasquez and Valeriano 2010; Vasquez 2009) the theory accounts for a large proportion of wars fought since the end of the Napoleonic era. The work remains a masterpiece of international relations theory and empirical scholarship, yet it still fails to take into account the processes inherent on the steps towards war. In short, the sequences and order of events are ignored due to methodological limitations and conventional norms in the field at the time.

It is hoped that this research can represent a step forward and consider how events occur during the process of rivalry development. This is a major restatement of the course of war as suggested by the steps-to-war theory. The proper sequencing between events and outcomes should be observed. Power politics strategies, when correctly observed in social reality, will occur early in the life of a rivalry and push a pair of states towards becoming long-standing enemies.

PREDICTING THE TIMING OF RIVALRY EVENTS

The basic path to rivalry is through the use of power politics strategies. Tactics such as the use of alliances, building up the military to deter a potential enemy, and the use of escalated bargaining techniques and demands will push a pair of states away from the path of cooperation and towards the situation of rivalry. While this path is neither automatic nor assured, nor can it account for all instances of rivalry, if correct, it will account for a great proportion of cases that end up as rivals. It addition, the theory should be supported quantitatively through the use of statistical controls to account for a wide swath of history and qualitatively to demonstrate a causal mechanism.

The expectation is that these power politics moves or strategies will be evident before the onset of the rivalry situation. For our purposes, a state is engaged in a rivalry after the onset of the third militarized dispute. This is clearly not the optimal way to code the onset of rivalry, yet it is the best option available at the time that helps account for the timing of events on the path to rivalry. The Thompson (2001) coding of rivalry defines the start of rivalry when perceptions of animosity are high on both sides, but this coding does not account for the preconditions of a rivalry through time. A more accurate, but unfeasible, consideration of rivalry onset might be a qualitative historical account (for all cases) of the enmity between the two sides and why that enmity escalated. Using the Klein, Goertz, and Diehl (2006) data to approximate this situation is a suitable way to judge rivalry development for our purposes, but I will also endeavor to use other methods like the time plots presented later in this chapter.

Chapter 2 spelled out the theory inherent in this analysis; generally power politics strategies will provoke an equal and opposing reaction in the target. This reaction will produce a conflict spiral that will trigger the onset of rivalry and enmity that endures. While we know that alliances and mutual arms buildups are observed more often in rivalries, this finding alone does not document a causal process. The question remains: are alliance formations and arms races responses to being in an advanced stage of rivalry or processes that push a pair of states towards rivalry?

The possibility of a spurious causal relationship should prompt the investigator to look at the historical process that resulted in the pattern; this will be one of the tasks of this chapter. The data used in this work are based on historical cases and should be seen as historical quantitative reasoning. Unpacking the data and their origins is the next step on the road to documenting a process towards rivalry. We must first look at the variables suggested here (alliances and arms races) to see if they show a temporal ordering consistent with the theory to allow for causation. While it is difficult to address causes in statistical analysis, this project will look at the timing of alliance formation and arms races to determine if these factors are a possible cause of rivalry development.

Chronologically, which comes first, power politics strategies or recurring crises? This study predicts that politically relevant alliances and military buildups will lock in early during the life of the rivalry and contribute to the escalation (or steps) towards the manifestation of rivalry. This study also predicts that military buildups and alliances will occur early in the life of rivalry and contribute to the movement towards the more severe forms of rivalry.

> H 3.1: *When a relevant alliance is exhibited in a rivalry, it should be formed early in the life of the rivalry.*
> H 3.2: *When a military buildup is exhibited in a rivalry, it should be formed early in the life of the rivalry.*

The hypotheses presented here are general expressions of the power politics path to rivalry. Specific factors and when these events will occur depend in some sense on the data used to answer the question. This chapter will proceed with two tests of the general propositions here. The first will be a comprehensive account of the timing of power politics events during different rivalry stages. The second sort of evidence presented will be grand historical accounts generated through time plots that sketch out the events that occur on the path to rivalry and when these events occur.

RIVALRY AND POWER POLITICS EVENT OCCURRENCE

Alliances

To test the timing of events outlined in hypothesis 3.1, I code alliance formation timing according to stages. Disaggregating the disputes within each rivalry to look at the timing of alliance formation allows for a more complete view of how the stages of rivalry matter. It must now be determined when, in the life of a rivalry, a state forms politically relevant alliances and participates in arms races. This is an important empirical issue that deals with the endogeneity problem that could surface as a result of the empirical findings presented in the prior chapter.

To investigate this question, I code when states make power politics foreign policy choices through time. Using the COW alliance (Gibler and Sarkees 2004) data set, it was first noted when the relevant alliance that was in the data set occurred and then this observation was counted with the appropriate code given the timing of the rivalry situation. The Diehl and Goertz (2000) data were used to facilitate the examination since they clearly break the rivals down by periods for each dispute. The periods are the isolated conflict stage for disputes one through two; the proto-rivalry phase for disputes three to five; and, then, the enduring rivalry stage for disputes that occur after the sixth instance and over a period of twenty years.

Table 4.1 Alliance Timing Distribution

During Early Conflict Stage

Alliance Timing	Early Stage
No Alliance	181 (20.5%)
With Alliance	699 (79.4)
Total	880

During Intermediate Rivalry Stage

Alliance Timing	Intermediate Stage
No Alliance	32 (14.3%)
Alliance at Early Stage	188 (84.3)
Alliance at Intermediate Stage	3 (1.3)
Total	223

During Advanced Rivalry Stage

Alliance Timing	Advanced Stage
No Alliance	3 (4.7%)
Alliance at Early Stage	55 (87.3)
Alliance at Intermediate Stage	4 (6.4)
Alliance at Advanced Stage	1 (1.5)
Total	63

70 *Becoming Rivals*

Table 4.1 presents the results regarding the timing of alliance formation according to rivalry stages. This examination covers only those conflicts that were militarized in some sense. First, each rivalry unit was separated out according to its classification of isolated conflict, proto-rivalry, or enduring rivalry. Then it was determined when during the unit's history of conflict the factors of interest occurred.

During the early stage, over 79 percent of cases had relevant alliances that occurred during the profoundly early stage of the conflict, during the prerivalry phase. Only about 20 percent of the cases out of a total of 880 displayed no alliance behavior at all during the early stage.

It should be clear that alliances alone are not sufficient conditions of rivalry. Alliances increase the probability of rivalry occurrence but do not completely account for their formation. We must consider that rivalry development is a multicausal phenomenon. Early investigations give us confidence that alliances are step towards rivalry, but other factors have to be accounted for also.

During the intermediate rivalry stage (or proto-rivalry stage), 188 alliances occurred when the first two militarized disputes where observed (87.3 percent). A great majority of proto-rivals utilized alliance tactics early in the life of a rivalry. Only three alliances were formed late in the life of the rivalry. Fourteen percent had no alliance behavior at all. This shows that for intermediate rivalry, alliances do occur early in the lifetime of the rivalry and can contribute to the existence of recurring disputes.

During the advanced rivalry stage, fifty-five enduring rivalries formed alliances during the early stage. Four enduring rivalry dyads formed alliances during the intermediate stage, and one alliance was formed during the advanced stage, after dispute six. This shows once again that alliances contribute to the existence of serious rivalries and occur early in the life a rivalry. Hypothesis 4 fails to be falsified to this point. Alliances, when they occur during a rivalry, occur early in the life span of a rivalry. In combination with evidence from the prior chapter, alliances increase the probability of rivalry, are quasi-necessary conditions for rivalry, and occur early during the life of rivalries.

Mutual Military Buildups

To test hypotheses 3.2 on the timing of military buildups and rivalries, I coded mutual military buildups according to stages. Here I disaggregate the disputes within each rivalry to look at the timing of the mutual military buildup. Using Sample's (2002) data on mutual military buildups, one can look for when the buildup counted in the data set occurred during the life of the rivalry.

It should be made clear that data limitations allowed only the investigation of mutual military buildups and not singular military buildups. Alliances were counted if only one side had an outside alliance early in the rivalry, but for military buildups, the buildup has to be mutual because the data available are trying to account for the concept of an arms race. Table 4.2 presents the results regarding the timing of mutual military buildups, according to rivalry stages.

Table 4.2 Mutual Military Buildup Timing Distribution

During Early Stage	
Military Buildup Timing	Early Stage
No Military Buildup	835 (94.9%)
With Military Buildup	45 (5.1)
Total	880

During Intermediate Rivalry Stage	
Military Buildup Timing	Intermediate Stage
No Military Buildup	196 (87.9%)
Military Buildup at Early Stage	17 (7.6)
Military Buildup at Intermediate Stage	10 (4.4)
Total	223

During Enduring Rivalry Stage	
Military Buildup Timing	Advanced Stage
No Military Buildup	38 (60.3%)
Military Buildup at Early Stage	3 (4.7)
Military Buildup at Intermediate Stage	7 (11.1)
Military Buildup at Advanced Stage	15 (23.8)
Total	63

During the early stage, there were forty-five observations of mutual military buildups. This number was much higher than one would expect to observe by chance alone. Ninety-four percent of the isolated conflicts observed no mutual military buildups at all.

During the intermediate or proto-rivalry stage, seventeen buildups are observed during the early stage. There are ten observations during the intermediate stage, and 87.9 percent of the cases observe no mutual military buildups. When a military buildup occurs in a proto-rivalry, it is likely to occur early, but evidence for this statement is weak since there are so few cases of buildups during proto-rivalry.

During the advanced rivalry stage, there are three military buildups during the early stage. There are seven observations during the intermediate stage and fifteen during the advanced rivalry stage. This finding demonstrates that when mutual military buildups occur during enduring rivalries, they tend to occur later in the life span of a rivalry. At this point we cannot reject hypothesis 5, but the hypothesis is on shaky ground. For the proto-rivalry stage, mutual military buildups occur early in the life a rivalry and during the enduring stage; they are more likely to occur during the later

Table 4.3 War and Mutual Military Buildups at the Early Conflict Stage

War	No Military Buildup	Military Buildup	Total
No	716 (85.7%)	21 (46.7%)	737
Yes	119 (14.3)	24 (53.39)	143
Total	835	45	880

stages of rivalry rather than the early stages. More investigation needs to be done on the factor of military buildups and rivalry.

Taking a step back to the early rivalry phase, it might be interesting to explore the cases of isolated conflict that have mutual military buildups present and understand why these cases exist since they defy predictions by others. Breaking down the early stage according to war occurrence, it is found that twenty-four of the forty-five military buildups resulted in war; Table 4.3 displays these dynamics. Over half of the buildups led to war, likely ending the rivalry early and settling the issues under contention. Those pairs of states with military buildups during an early stage are primed for rivalry but sometimes do not engage in enough disputes for rivalry to occur.

Military buildups can directly lead to war, and this is likely why some military buildups are observed in isolated conflicts. It could also be that these cases expose the flaws of the mutual military buildup measure in that it depends on concurrent racing around a militarized dispute. Could be that these cases are not racing but only captured as they are dragged to war by other parties.

The discussion of war as a dependent variable is critical here so that we may explain the finding of mutual military buildups not resulting in rivalry on many occasions. Clearly the answer might be that some military buildups result in war and thus terminate the rivalry when the issue at stake is settled with militarized means in the form of warfare.

Assessment

One factor I investigate is politically relevant alliances. Those pairs of states participating in politically relevant alliances at an early phase of conflict lead to an increased likelihood of rivalry involvement. It is clear that alliances are important for the development of rivalry, no matter which research design is employed to investigate the question.

Politically relevant alliances occur early in the life of rivalry. Prior to or during the first two disputes, it is likely that in a proto-rivalry or enduring rivalry, at least one state has used alliances to bolster their security.

This usually results in the formation and development of a rivalry itself rather than a decrease in tensions as policy makers typically hope. Deterrence through alliances does not prevent future conflict if the outcome in question is a rivalry. Any attempt to increase a state's security early in the process usually results in a perceived decrease in security for the opposing side. The power politics processes these events trigger become the causal mechanism for the development of rivalry.

We also observed that the timing of mutual military buildups varies. No consistent pattern has been determined. For some rivals the mutual buildup occurs early; for others, the mutual buildup occurs late in the life of a rivalry. The existence of a mutual military buildup signals that a pair of states is involved in an enduring rivalry. If a military buildup occurs at the isolated conflict stage, the dyad is likely to engage in war and end any potential rivalry. Mutual military buildups are strong factors that push the relationship between disputes and escalation to war (Sample 1996, 2002).

This research shows that mutual military buildups clearly do not occur only in the context of rivalry as some suggest (Diehl and Crescenzi 1998). There are forty-five cases of mutual military buildups during the early rivalry stage, and twenty-four of these led directly to war, thus ending the rivalry. Twenty-one of these cases did not lead to war, and these cases need further investigation. One cannot assume that arms races will occur only during a rivalry relationship; rather, a significant number of mutual military buildups occur outside of rivalries. The remaining question is: what of monadic military buildups? Might we be missing part of the explanation by only focusing on those pairs of states who engage in military expenditure racing behavior at the same time?

Gibler (2007) performs another potentially relevant test of the steps-to-rivalry theory. He finds that states that settle their disputed boundaries early tend not to use power politics tactics and establish themselves as democracies. The expectation would be that avoiding territorial disputes in the first place eschews the triggers found in the steps-to-war theory (Vasquez 1993), including rivalry development.

Throughout the life (mainly early) of an enduring rivalry, both states will form politically relevant alliances and participate in mutual military buildups to counter the original threat. It seems that the temporal pattern typically is a territorial dispute, relevant alliance, early forms of rivalry, and then a mutual military buildup. This pattern, however, is not always consistent, with mutual military buildups coming early in the life of a rivalry in quite a few cases and later in the life of a rivalry for some other cases.

These findings do not support a realist theory of international politics since the findings are counterintuitive to the theory. While elites and leaders may think about the future and prepare for rivalry, the theoretical foundation critically depends on the expectation of deterrence through threats of force. Of course, the opposite tends to happen, and rivalry results when these behaviors are exhibited. The fact that states form alliances prior to and during the life of a rivalry does not represent a condition of peace but is a factor that leads to both war and rivalry.

PLOTTING RIVALRY RELATIONSHIPS THROUGH TIME

In an effort to better understand the dynamics of rivalries over their lifetime, it would be useful to present time plots of rivalry events. Each plot here details the events during the life of the major power versus major power enduring rivalries. Disputes are marked with lines that indicated their level of hostility (between five and zero). Alliances are indicated, along with the date and participants. Arms races (mutual military buildups) are also indicated along with the date of their inception.

A potential issue for the data used in this project is the timing of individual alliances during a rivalry. The alliance data set can contain alliances formed previous to the rivalry, but also those alliances still in effect when the rivalry forms. It can also contain alliances that are renewed during the rivalry; all this information is lost in quantitative examinations. The alliance variable is much more nuanced than is evident from the binary variable used in the investigations here.

In an examination of alliance information in relation to rivalry, the majority of the cases experience alliance formation after or prior to the first dispute. In an effort to alleviate any potential concerns about the timing of alliances, rivalry plots will be used to illustrate the events during the life of a rivalry. This is a more fine-tuned display of alliance dynamics during the lifetime of a rivalry.

Each rivalry plot takes an individual major power enduring rivalry and plots out the duration of the rivalry. Within each rivalry, it is noted when on the timeline the rivalry become a proto-rivalry (dispute number three) or enduring rivalry (dispute number six). Each militarized dispute during the life of a rivalry is plotted, along with the level of intensity for each side during the disputes. Taking the alliance data set, each politically relevant alliance is plotted according to its initiation. Arms races are also plotted according to their initiation. These plots will help show the course of rivalry events in an easy to digest format.

United States and USSR (1947–1989)

This rivalry is interesting because of the multiple alliances formed during its duration. Both states were actively engaging in power politics strategies. Early in the rivalry, the USSR formed alliances with China, Yugoslavia, Poland, Rumania, Hungary, Bulgaria, and Finland. The United States also formed the NATO alliance prior and during the commencement of the proto-rivalry (dispute three).

Each state continuously formed and reformed alliances during the rivalry. There is a marked increased in alliances between the proto and enduring stage, suggesting that these alliances may have been important factors in pushing this rivalry to the forefront of each state's foreign policy

Timing and the Steps-to-Rivalry Model 75

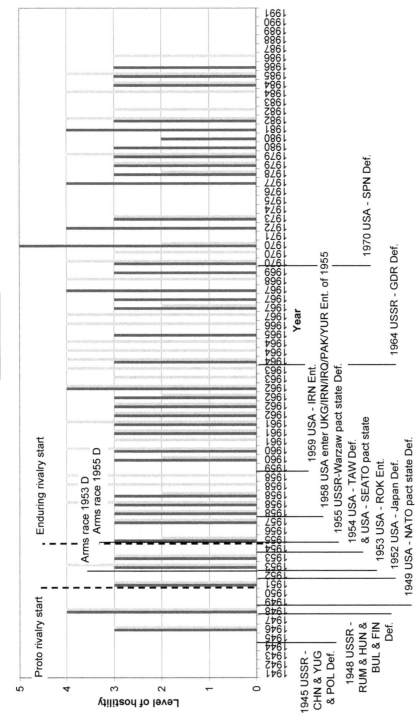

Figure 4.1 United States and USSR (1947–1989).

focus. By the initiation of the enduring rivalry (1955), each state had alliances arrayed against each other to prepare for possible conflict. Issues such as the post–World War II management of Europe and Berlin may have been the most important events for the rivalry, but the continuous use of alliances is also a clear factor when time plots are viewed.

As far as arms races go, this rivalry follows the typical pattern. The arms races do not come early, but, then again, they do not exactly come late in the life of the rivalry. Here, there are two arms races in 1953 and 1955, before and during the sixth dispute and the onset of the enduring rivalry. The arms races seem to be a significant factor driving these states to rivalry, not a symptom of an advanced rivalry.

United States and China (1949–1974)

Early in the rivalry, the United States signed significant alliance pacts that are relevant to the Asian region. The NATO alliance was formed during and around the first disputes with China, and it is relevant here because of its focus against Communism and inclusion of major powers. After a series of three disputes in a short period of time, the United States also formed alliances with the Philippines and Australia in 1951 and Japan in 1952, as well as South Korea in 1953. The United States also signed a defense pact with the Republic of China in 1954; Taiwan was China's main rival. China formed a few relevant alliances late in the rivalry, but the state does shy away from alliances in general, likely due to their position as a Communist state and the ebbs and flows of the relationship with the USSR at the time.

Between the onset of proto-rivalry and enduring rivalry, the United States and China engaged in two arms races in 1951 and 1953. In total, this rivalry fits the steps-to-rivalry theory quite closely. It must also be remembered that this rivalry is deeply coupled with the USSR and United States rivalry. Events in that rivalry are linked to the United States and China rivalry.

United Kingdom and Germany (Prussia) (1887–1922)

This rivalry began with a short burst of disputes around 1887. Three disputes quickly drove this rivalry to the proto-rivalry stage. Early, there are alliances evident in the rivalry. In 1887, the United Kingdom signed an entente with Italy and Austria-Hungary, removing potential allies of Germany from any conflict with Britain. Germany also signed a nonaggression pact with Russia in 1887.

Through the life of this rivalry, there are multitudes of important alliances that are formed and reformed. This dyad exhibits the shifting patterns of alliances during this time. Alliances change in composition, but intent remains the same.

There is an arms race around the onset of the enduring rivalry in 1919. An important naval rivalry began around the turn of the century, and this event is not captured through the data. The significance of the naval arms race cannot be understated, and some argue this was the cause of the rivalry in the first place because it orientated the threats facing the United Kingdom away from France towards its more immediate naval competitor.

Timing and the Steps-to-Rivalry Model 77

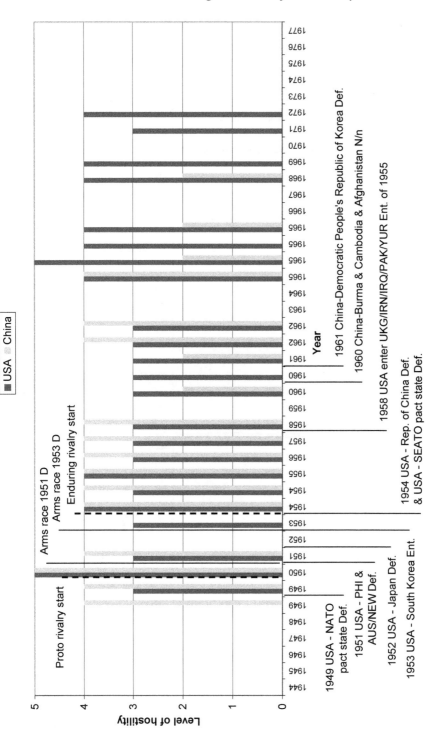

Figure 4.2 United States and China (1949–1974).

78 *Becoming Rivals*

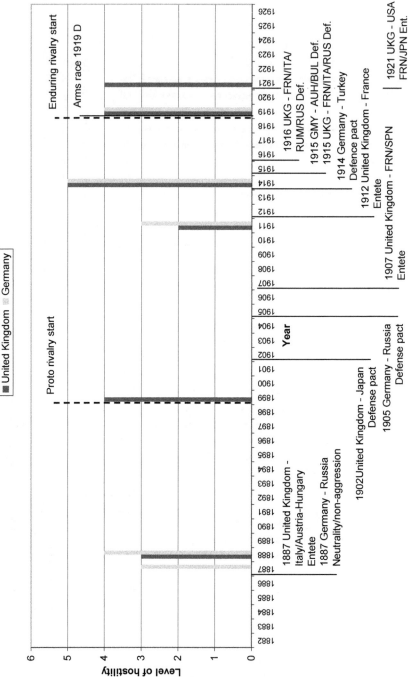

Figure 4.3 United Kingdom and Germany (Prussia) (1887–1922).

Timing and the Steps-to-Rivalry Model   79

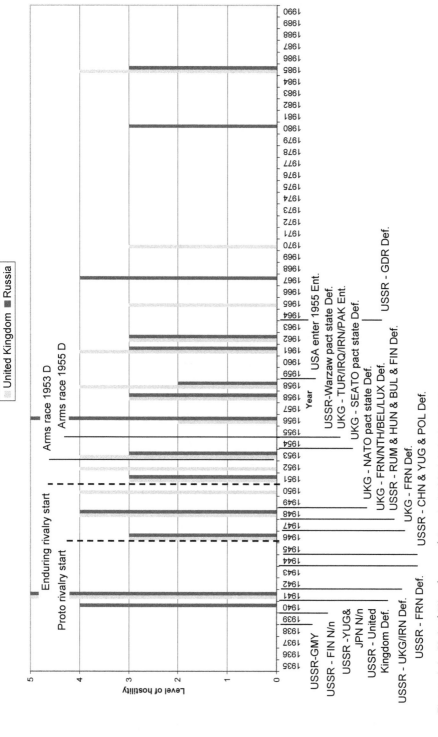

Figure 4.4   United Kingdom and Russia (USSR) (1940–1985).

United Kingdom and Russia (USSR) (1940–1985)

It is evident that the United Kingdom and Soviet rivalry began with the constant formation and reformation of relevant alliances in the context of various foreign policy disagreements. Immediately before and during the first few disputes in this rivalry, Russia allied with Germany, Finland, Yugoslavia, and the United Kingdom itself. The rivalry lay dormant for a few years while the two sides were allied with each other during World War II. Once the war was over, the rivalry began anew and once again was punctuated by alliance commitments. Most importantly, the United Kingdom joined the NATO (with the United States) alliance in 1949.

The USSR formed the Warsaw Pact in 1955, a little after the start of the enduring rivalry. Two arms races are also identified in 1953 and 1955, after the start of the enduring rivalry. Even though the arms races occurred after dispute number six, it is clear they did come early in the life of the rivalry, and the buildup on the United States side also drove the dyad towards rivalry.

While World War II clearly delayed the onset of an intense rivalry between these states, the relationship has always been characterized by power politics moves. Even after the termination of the Cold War rivalry, the two sides continued to play power politics games with various alliances and arms buildups occurring after 1995.

Russia (USSR) and Japan (1895–1984)

The longest rivalry in the data set is one of the most interesting. The Russian and Japanese rivalry is another conflict that is punctuated by early power politics moves. Both Russia and Japan formed relevant alliances around and after the first dispute. In 1894, Japan signed a defense pact with Korea, while Russia signed a defense pact with China in 1896. Up to and after the Russo-Japanese war, there are quite a few relevant alliances formed. The alliances all take place before the onset of the enduring rivalry stage.

As far as arms races go, there are quite a few late in the life of the rivalry. There are five arms races between 1935 and 1941. There are also three arms races between 1963 and 1969. While the arms races are not power politics events that came early in the life of this rivalry, they did help the rivalry become locked in and endure for such a long time.

Russia (USSR) and China (1862–1986)

The Russian and Chinese rivalry is another long-standing Asian rivalry that does not follow the typical power politics path. Although there are numerous relevant alliances observed during the life of the rivalry, none are observed before the proto-rivalry stage. There are quite a few alliances formed between the proto-rivalry and enduring rivalry stage, suggesting that these events could help drive the rivalry to its enduring stage.

It should be noted that China, like most Asian states, did not rely on alliance politics to dictate foreign policy decisions. It seems the culture of alliance politics is much different in Asia than it is in the rest of the world.

Timing and the Steps-to-Rivalry Model   81

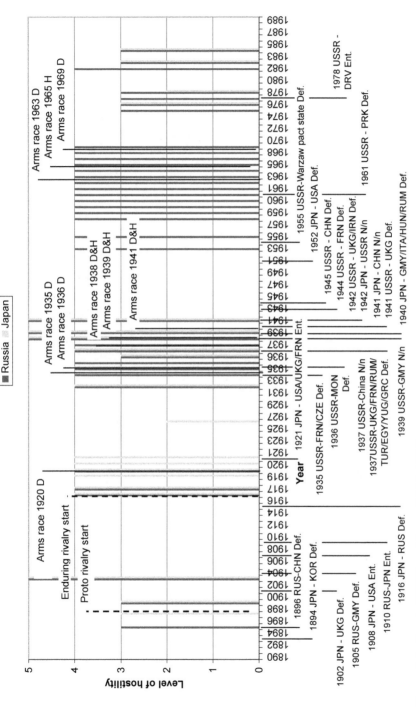

Figure 4.5   Russia (USSR) and Japan (1895–1984).

82 *Becoming Rivals*

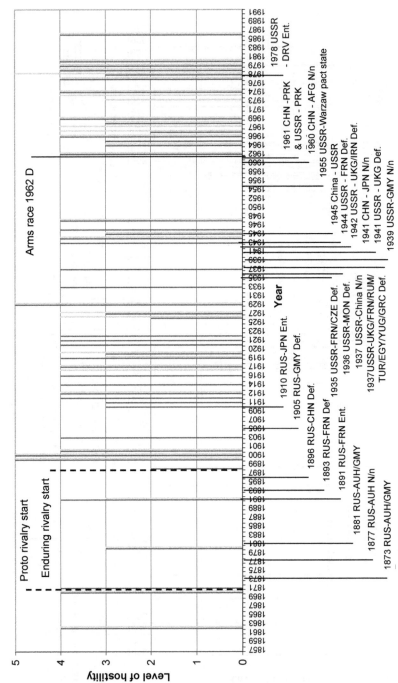

Figure 4.6 Russia (USSR) and China (1862–1986).

Timing and the Steps-to-Rivalry Model 83

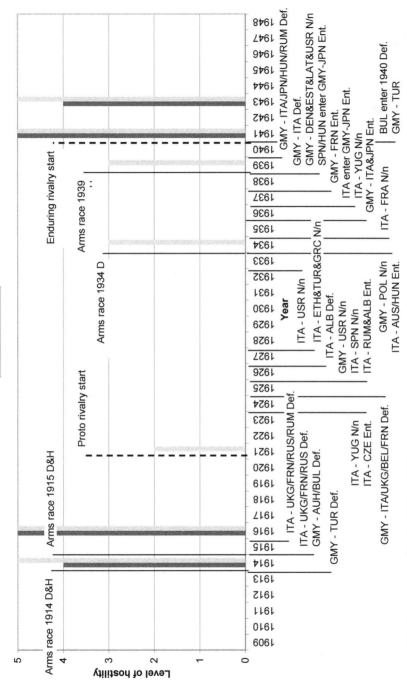

Figure 4.7 Germany and Italy (1914–1943).

China did not see a marked increase in alliance formation until the rise of Communist China after 1949.

In this dyad, there is one arms race in 1962, very late in the rivalry. It is likely this event did not drive the rivalry to become enduring and most likely represents the direct preparation for war between the two states.

Germany and Italy (1914–1943)

Germany and Italy, although frequently allied to each other, did have a long-standing rivalry. Very early in the conflict, there are numerous power politics events. Both states were active in the alliance politics before the outbreak of World War I. Germany allied to Austria-Hungary and other regional powers. Italy sided with the allied powers in World War I because it could not side with Austria during the war.

The two states also participated in two arms races in 1914 and 1915. Alliances and arms races in this dyad both seem to drive the ongoing rivalry and constrain the choices and strategic alignments each side could take against each other. While not exactly bitter enemies, they did have long-standing issues at stake and did not find themselves on the same side until World War II.

France and Germany (Prussia) (1830–1887)

Early in this rivalry, both sides formed relevant alliances to deal with the real security threat each posed to the other side. Germany allied with Austria and Russia in 1832. France allied with Spain, Portugal, and the United Kingdom in 1833. Both of these events can be seen as direct reactions to the first few disputes in this rivalry.

During the rivalry's lifetime, there are numerous relevant alliances observed. It is also important to note that during the start of the enduring rivalry stage (dispute six) there was an arms race. This observation would suggest the arms race came late in the life of the rivalry, but that point is debatable depending on what one considers late.

The rivalry between France and Germany (also known as Prussia during this time) is one of the best examples of a long-standing enduring rivalry. This rivalry experienced many wars during its duration, and the rivalry was not settled until the outstanding territorial issues between the two states were finally resolved after World War II. Looking at this rivalry plot, it is evident that each side was continuously seeking to revise and enhance its security posture the face of the threat of its rival. Neither side was content to keep existing alliance alignments and continuously swapped partners in response to the ongoing security environment of Europe during the time.

France and Germany (1911–1944)

This rivalry lay dormant for twenty-four years before starting up again prior to World War I. Like many rivals, these states were born fighting. Each side engaged in alliance formation moves early in the life of the rivalry. France allied with the United Kingdom, Italy, and Russia. Germany allied with Austria, Turkey, and Bulgaria before the onset of the proto-rivalry stage.

Timing and the Steps-to-Rivalry Model 85

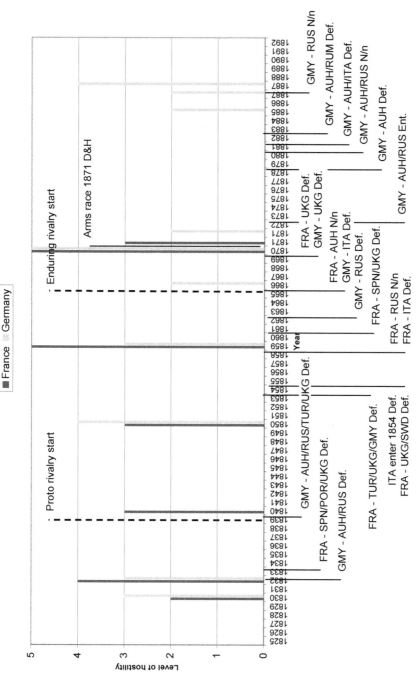

Figure 4.8 France and Germany (Prussia) (1830–1887).

86 *Becoming Rivals*

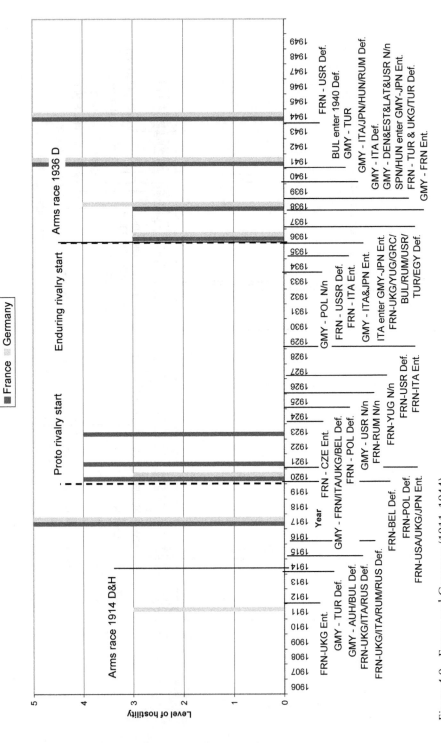

Figure 4.9 France and Germany (1911–1944).

Timing and the Steps-to-Rivalry Model 87

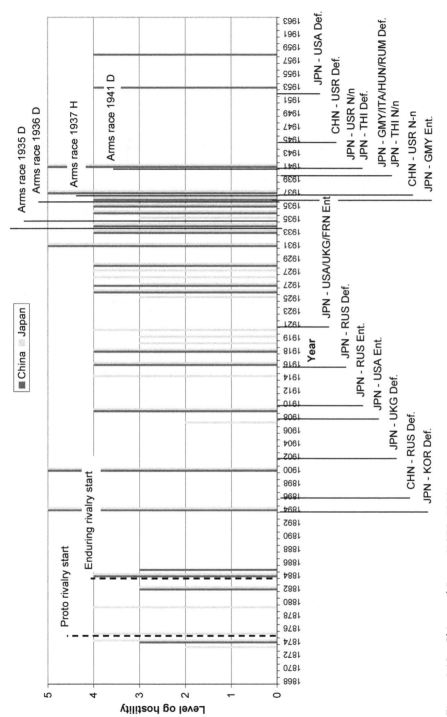

Figure 4.10 China and Japan (1873–1958).

88 *Becoming Rivals*

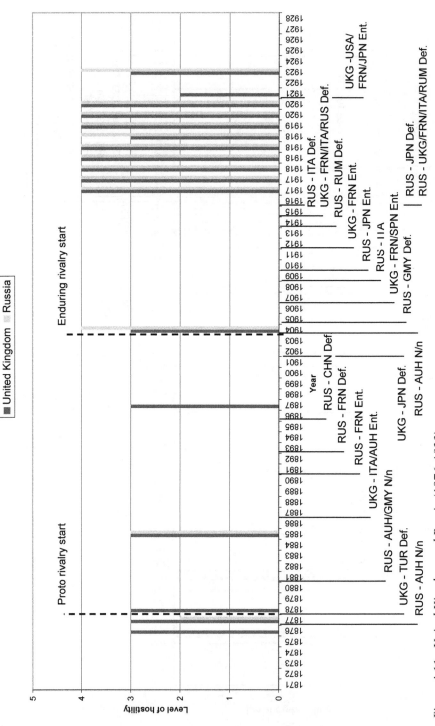

Figure 4.11 United Kingdom and Russia (1876–1923).

This rivalry experiences an early arms race (before the proto-rivalry stage) in 1914, primarily a result of the impending war in Europe. They also experienced an arms race in 1936. Perhaps most significantly, the two nations were participating in an ongoing land arms race during the rivalry's lifetime. Each military continuously revamped their plans and strategy in the face of their rival. This also meant the revision of force structure plans that had a direct influence on the course of the rivalry.

China and Japan (1873–1958)

This rivalry represents the outlier for the typical pattern of rivalry development, at least for major–major status enduring rivals. There are no alliances or arms race early in the life of the rivalry. What this rivalry does show is the typical power politics strategies of Asian regional nations. There is a marked nonuse of alliance commitments for all Asian nations until after World War II. Around that time, and the 1930s, this rivalry showed an increase in the use of power politics.

There are repeated arms races observed in 1934, 1935, 1936, 1937, and 1941. There are also repeated and shifting alliance commitments after this time. It is clear that this rivalry did not need to rely on power politics to push the rivalry to the proto or enduring stage.

United Kingdom and Russia (1876–1923)

During this rivalry, both sides formed relevant alliances before the onset of the proto-rivalry stage. The United Kingdom allied with Turkey in 1877. Russia also allied with Austria in 1877. There is also evidence of constant alliance reshaping and formation before the onset of the enduring rivalry stage.

There are no arms races observed at all in this dyad. Neither side was able to settle their issues until the end of World War I. Even then, the rivalry restarted again during the Cold War when it became a multiparty conflict.

ASSESSMENT OF RIVALRY PLOTS

The aim is that these rivalry time plots illustrate the relationship between rival states. The ebbs and flows of this type of relationship are difficult to pinpoint with statistical analysis. Here, we can see the timing of the onset of the rivalry along with when power politics moves are made. It is clear that most power politics moves are made early in the life of the rivalry. This finding mainly holds for alliance developments, which here show the nuanced and fluid relationship between alliances and the development of rivalry.

Arms races follow the typical pattern of late development as they tend to be observed later in the proto-rivalry stage or early in the enduring rivalry stage, if they are observed at all. These plots show that arms races happen during the advanced stages of a rivalry but not near the end. It is possible that these arms races, while not driving the onset of rivalry, are important factors that make rivalries endure and make them more fully developed antagonistic relationships.

Another important aspect of these plots is that they describe the evolutionary nature of rivalries. Here, partners shift and balance according to international events. The rivalries do not develop in isolation but are influenced by the events in their surrounding neighborhoods and the greater international system at large. While alliances may help a rivalry lock in early, the alliances themselves are not locked in and continuously shift during the rivalry according to the dictates of the political environment.

To keep information to a manageable and presentable size, only major–major status enduring rivalries are analyzed here. Plots were generated for all enduring rivalries, and these do not differ much from the major–major rivalry plots presented here. The major–major rivalries are only used as a baseline since there are more ongoing events during their lifetime, making it easier to see and describe the rivalry timeline.

CONCLUSION AND FUTURE TASKS

The question of when events occur during a causal process is an important query that many scholars seem to skip. This is especially true of quantitative scholars. Hopefully this chapter has gone a long way to demonstrate the path to rivalry and when important events occur during this path.

The path to rivalry is nuanced and fluid, as the time plots presented here demonstrate. Power politics tactics are used over and over, shifting according to the dictates of the contemporary international system. Alliances demonstrate this pattern best and clearly are important factors that occur early in the life of a rivalry, locking the relationship in during its early phases.

Arms races are much rarer and tend to occur late in the life of a rivalry, usually during the proto-rivalry stage or early in the enduring rivalry phase. It is likely that the relationship of rivalry is not enfranchised enough to motivate both sides to commit to massive military spending projects at the same time.

Recent work by Valeriano, Sample, and Kang (2011) explored the development of military buildups in the monadic sense and provides a clue as to when military buildups will help produce rivalries. The goal was to determine what factors would increase the probability of a military buildup. Scholars seemed to have skipped a step and suggested arms races contribute to conflict onset without examining the process by which arms races start in the first place. To uncover why arms races occur in the system, one must unpack the concept and examine why military buildups occur. The answer seems to be that military buildups are a result of territorial disputes, economic capacity, and internal instability as measured by coups, riots, and strikes (Valeriano, Sample, and Kang 2011). Rivalry does not increase the probability of a military buildup, confounding the expectations of some who expect that military buildups should be a function of a rivalry relationship.

Clearly, a problem with this analysis is the inconsistent relationship the mutual military buildup variable has with the timing of rivalry initiation. Some buildups occur early, some during the middle stages, and some late. Some states even have buildups outside of the rivalry situation. With this finding we could reject the hypothesis that arms races lead to the development of rivalry, or we could take a step back and reexamine the hypothesis. Since rivalry is not a cause of a military buildup, it is prudent to wonder if a rivalry itself is really the cause of a military buildup, especially in the interactive sense. Likely, rivalries do not lead to monadic buildups that threat has already accounted for and strategized against before the rivalry began. It is likely that military buildups come before rivalries, and then mutual military buildups come after the rivalry starts to develop.

As currently coded, an arms race is measured as concurrent mutual military buildups that occur during a militarized dispute (Sample 1997). This concept of an arms race is problematic for rivalry origins since there is not an observation of directed racing behavior, nor should the coding of an arms race have to occur during a militarized dispute. This issue demonstrates the importance of being specific in the construction of data and how data are used in the field. In the rush to quantify the concept of arms races, scholars forgot to examine when and why each side chooses to build up the military in the first place. It is likely these choices, which are important, should be investigated more closely in the future.

5 The Complete Steps-to-Rivalry Model

INTRODUCTION

The goal of this chapter is to provide a comprehensive analysis of the steps-to-rivalry model. Previously, Chapter 3 found a link between the factors of alliances and mutual military buildups and the development of rivalry. The question now moves to whether these factors promote the development of rivalry when considered in combination. Further, I also ask if there are other factors that can be added to the equation to help determine with greater certitude what variables contribute to the onset of rivalry.

Here, I reevaluate all the previous empirical findings in order to depict the process of rivalry development through the use of an additive probability model. I combine the effects of each independent variable (specifically politically relevant alliances and mutual military buildups) and add some tests for new independent variables (territorial disputes) to determine which pairs of states are more likely to become rivals.

The steps-to-rivalry theory presented throughout this book suggests that the path to rivalry can be found by examining the steps taken by a pair of states on the road to rivalry. These steps usually take the form of power politics foreign policy strategies. In particular, politically relevant alliances and mutual military buildups should increase the likelihood that a rivalry develops.

In testing the steps-to-rivalry theory, I seek to examine and explain the additive impact of each factor on the process of rivalry development; each step taken combines with the others to increase the probability of rivalry occurrence. Once a pair of states participates in a few of these steps, it becomes more likely to participate in a militarized rivalry. At the end of this chapter I present the most likely paths to rivalry.

The analysis presented here suggests that pairs of states that form politically relevant alliances, participate in military buildups, fight in territorial disputes, and are major powers are likely to become rivals. This finding represents the most likely road to rivalry in light of the theory presented here.

HYPOTHESIS AND RESEARCH DESIGN

The goal here is to present a process model of rivalry. In particular, this chapter attempts to determine which factors, when considered in combination, increase the probability of rivalry. In addition, this chapter presents the most likely path to rivalry, according to probabilities available. This is necessary since Chapter 3—despite delineating some possible paths to rivalry—was neither additive nor cumulative.

In this additive model, I add a new set of hypotheses relating to territorial disputes. As stated previously in Chapter 2, territorial disputes increase the probability of rivalry occurrence. In this chapter, I retest this proposition, adding a territorial dispute variable to my combined model. These findings add to the literature on rivalry in a number of ways. Past studies have found a relationship between rivalry and territorial disputes (Vasquez and Leskiw 2001), but here this relationship is reconfirmed with the updated rivalry data and also with an alternative rivalry data set.

Hypothesis 5—originally presented in Chapter 2—suggests the additive probability hypothesis. The hypothesis asserts that the factors of politically relevant alliances, mutual military buildups, and territorial disputes are more likely to lead to dangerous rivalries.

> H5: *Pairs of states that form politically relevant alliances against each other, participate in mutual military buildups, and fight over a significant amount of territorial disputes are more likely to become involved in rivalries than pairs of states that do not engage in these types of behaviors.*

Once again, the main dependent variable is taken from the Klein, Goertz, and Diehl (2006) data set that extends from 1815 to 2001. It is also important to test the major components of this analysis against an alternative rivalry data set. The Thompson (2001) data are used here to examine if my theory of rivalry development is consistent across different conceptualizations of rivalry. This analysis is different in that a rivalry history dyad is not used since the Thompson data are not compatible with that measure as it is presently constructed. Here, I use a data set of all MIDs and code whether or not the MID occurred during a Thompson rivalry. The standard independent variables used throughout this book are added into the analysis to produce a result consistent with the other statistically significant results presented throughout this work.

Chapter 3 discussed the research design choices for this chapter. In testing the additive conditions of rivalry, I rely on bivariate statistics, standard logistic regression, and multinomial logistic models to determine the impact of each independent variable on the outcome. The first main independent variable in this chapter is politically relevant alliances that are taken from the work of Senese and Vasquez (2003, 2008). In their data, alliances are relevant if they include a major power or a state from the same region as the dyad under question. Alliance information is taken from Correlates of War alliance version 3.0 (Gibler and Sarkees 2004).

Mutual military buildups—the second main independent variable—are taken from Valeriano, Sample, and Kang (2011) data that include both major and minor power mutual military buildups. These data have been updated with a more inclusive measure of a military buildup that looks at the past three years of spending measures if two states interactively built up their military at a rate of 8 percent or more over that time; here this measure is simply called *mutual military buildups* (Valeriano, Sample, and Kang 2011). Territorial disputes are taken from the MID (Ghosn, Palmer, and Bremer 2004) coding of the territorial revision claim for disputes.

The main dependent variable in this analysis is taken from the Klein, Goertz, and Diehl (2006) coding of rivalry. This data set codes a rivalry as occurring if a pair of states has more than three disputes within ten years. Isolated conflicts represent the nonrivalry category in that these dyads have experienced between one or two MIDs. In this chapter, I also use Thompson's (2001) strategic rivalry coding as a dependent variable. Here, the dependent variable is a binary outcome between strategic rivalry and no strategic rivalry according to perceptions of rivalry. Both data sets are discussed in depth in Chapter 2.

TERRITORY AND RIVALRY

In this analysis the question is if territorial disputes are associated with rivalry. In other words, if a dyad has any territorial disputes during its history, is it more likely to become engaged in a rivalry than a dyad without any territorial disputes? This variable captures what may be the initial source of conflict for the dyad and allows the states in dispute to fight over many different issues during the life of that rivalry. Territory alone cannot drive the movement towards severe rivalry, but it does help the dyad along the path to rivalry.

Table 5.1 presents a basic two-by-two table of the relationship between territorial disputes and rivalry. In total, 46.51 percent of the territorial disputes occur during a rivalry, a high proportion given that there are only 331 rivalry cases. In fact, over 58 percent of the rival dyads have experienced territorial disputes. On the other hand, only 25.26 percent of the total number of isolated conflicts are involved in these conflicts. These results give us confidence to proceed to a multivariate model.

Table 5.1 Rivalry and Territorial Disputes 2x2

	No Terr	Territory	Total
Isolated Conflict	657	222	879
	74.74%	25.25%	
	82.64%	53.49%	
Rivalry	138	193	
	41.69%	58.31%	
	17.36%	46.51%	331
Total	795	415	1,210

Note: Percentages are calculated for row and column values.

Table 5.2 provides evidence to support the hypothesis that a pair of states whose relations involve territorial disputes are more apt to have recurring disputes and thus are likely to become rivalries. Even after controlling for contiguity, there is a statistically significant relationship between territorial disputes and rivalry.[1] The territory variable is statistically significant and positive for rivalry when compared to the base category, isolated conflicts. Contiguity is also positive and statistically significant in the model, as is the variable for major powers. In short, this analysis shows that territorial disputes are likely conditions that can predict when rivalries will be observed. The next analysis adds this factor to the variables previously investigated in Chapter 3.

Table 5.2 Territorial Disputes and Rivalry Coefficient Estimates, Logit Model for Rivalry Type

	Outcome			
	Rivalry			
Independent Variables	Coefficient	S.E.	ZScore	P>|z|
Territory	1.208	.141	8.55	0.000
Contiguity	0.998	.144	6.93	0.000
Major Powers	1.029	.285	3.61	0.000
Constant	-1.894	.109	-17.30	0.000

Notes: Isolated Conflict is the Reference Category.
N = 1210.
Prob > chi2 = 0.000.
Log likelihood = -624.691.

THE COMPLETE ADDITIVE MODEL

Multivariate Model

Table 5.3 presents results for a logit test of what we can call the complete additive steps-to-rivalry model. This table directly tests the additive hypothesis 5 from Chapter 2. All the factors previously investigated are included in one model. Here I consider the combined effects of military buildups, alliances, territorial disputes, contiguity, and major power status. This model does not test for interactive effects since it makes little sense to multiply one factor by another when the variables are binary in nature. More likely, these variables add up through time rather than combining for an effect. I envision a "pile on" model for rivalry development, where each issue adds another problem to help make the situation intractable.

The results support the proposition that states that form politically relevant alliances, participate in mutual military buildups, and fight territorial disputes are more likely to become involved in rivalries. The politically relevant alliance variable generates a coefficient of 0.819 and is statistically significant at the 0.001 level. The mutual military buildups variable produces a coefficient of 0.908 and is also statistically significant at the 0.001 level. Likewise, the territory variable produces a coefficient of 1.199 and is statistically significant at the 0.001 level. Contiguity has a positive impact on the model and is statistically significant, an important finding since this factor could account for positive results for the territory or alliance variable. Major power dyads generate a coefficient of 0.697, and this coefficient is statistically significant.

Table 5.3 Complete Rivalry Model Coefficient Estimates, Logit Model for Rivalry

	Outcome		
	Rivalry		
Independent Variables	Coefficient	S.E.	P>|z|
Military Buildup	0.908	.246	0.000
Alliance	0.819	.198	0.000
Territory	1.199	.145	0.000
Contiguity	1.059	.151	0.000
Major Power	0.697	.299	0.020
Constant	-2.645	.213	0.000

Notes: Isolated Conflict is the Reference Category.
N = 1209.
Prob > chi2 = 0.000.
Log likelihood = -606.353.

Probabilities of Rivalry for the Complete Model

Table 5.4 presents the predicted probability results for the complete rivalry model depending on the variables in question. The results are similar to those presented in earlier models in Chapter 3, and the values presented here take on the additive quality inherent in international politics.

The tables, sublabeled A through F, tell the full story of rivalry development. I start simple and build towards a more complex picture of the relationship between power politics strategies and rivalry development. For a mutual military buildup, observance of this factor predicts an increase in the probability of a rivalry relationship. When the factor is observed, the probability of rivalry more than doubles from the baseline model, where each factor is set at zero (model A). The same holds true for model B, which looks at how alliances affect the presence of a rivalry. In particular, the probability of isolated conflict declines and the probability of rivalry doubles as alliances are observed.

The relationship is even stronger when the values are set to one for politically relevant alliances, military buildups, and territory (model E). A positive observation for all these variables results in a probability of 0.570 for rivalry, and a zero observation for these variables results in a value of 0.066 (i.e., the baseline model). This is an increase in the probability of rivalry occurrence by a factor of over eight.

The final additive model shows a high probability for the combined factors of alliances, military buildups, territory, and major powers. For rivalry, the probability of occurrence is 0.884 if the values for the factors are set to one (model F). This represents an increase in probability by a factor of over thirteen. It is clear that as these types of events transpire, the probability of rivalry occurrence increases.

I next test hypothesis 5 using a multinomial logit model so as to investigate the impact of the variables on different types of rivalry. A prior study (Valeriano 2003) into the question of power politics and rivalry focused on the impact of these factors for different types of rivalry. Since then, the Klein, Goertz, and Diehl (2006) data set has largely jettisoned the concept of rivalry types, but there is enough information in the new data to construct the old rivalry levels in this new model. The basic level remains the isolated conflict stage with one or two disputes. The proto-rivalry stage is new to this analysis and counts those rivalries that engage in three to five disputes or those that include more than six disputes but do not occur for more than twenty years. The United States and Iraq would be an example of this. Finally, enduring rivals are those rivals that engage in more than six disputes over twenty years (Diehl and Goertz 2000).

Multinomial logit produces estimates of the probability of each outcome (isolated conflict, proto-rivalry, or enduring rivalry) occurring

Table 5.4 Predicted Probabilities for Complete Rivalry Model

A. Military Buildup and Rivalry

	Isolated Conflict	Rivalry
All Values = 0	0.933	0.066
MB = 1	0.850	0.149
Difference	-0.083	+0.083

B. Alliance and Rivalry

	Isolated Conflict	Rivalry
All Values = 0	0.933	0.066
Ally = 1	0.861	0.138
Difference	-0.072	+0.072

C. Territory and Rivalry

	Isolated Conflict	Rivalry
All Values = 0	0.933	0.066
Territory = 1	0.809	0.190
Difference	-0.124	+0.124

D. Alliance + Military Buildup and Rivalry

	Isolated Conflict	Rivalry
All Values = 0	0.933	0.066
Ally = 1 + MB = 1	0.714	0.285
Difference	-0.219	+0.219

E. Alliance, Military Buildup, and Territory

	Isolated Conflict	Rivalry
All Values = 0	0.933	0.066
Ally = 1 + MB = 1 + Terr = 1	0.430	0.570
Difference	-0.503	+0.503

F. Alliance, Military Buildup, Territory, Contiguity, and Major Powers

	Isolated Conflict	Rivalry
All Values = 0	0.933	0.066
Ally = 1 + MB = 1 + Terr = 1 + Maj = 1 + Contiguity = 1	0.115	0.884
Difference	-0.818	+0.818

given the independent variables and makes no assumption about the order of the outcomes. Ordered logit is not used because the results will not differ much from multinomial logit, and the ordering of rivals in the Diehl and Goertz (2000) data set does not assume a stepwise process towards the higher category of enduring rivalry. It also does not assume that each category is distinct. The dependent variable is rivalry type (defined as isolated conflict, proto-rivalry, and enduring rivalry).

As the multinomial model in Table 5.5 suggests, the results are largely consistent with the basic logic model presented in Table 5.3, but here we can be more specific about the impact of various factors for different rivalry categories. For the proto-rivalry category, the results largely hold, but the coefficients are not as large as they are in the prior model. Mutual military buildups and alliances are statistically significant and positive, as are the factors of territory, continuity, and major power states.

For enduring rivals, the main difference is that the variable for major powers fails to reach statistical significance, suggesting this factor may not have a consistent impact on the type of rivalry in which a dyad becomes involved. The other variables of alliances, buildups, territory, and contiguity still hold.

Table 5.5 Complete Rivalry Model by Rivalry Type Coefficient Estimates, Multinomial Logit Model for Rivalry Type

	Outcome					
	Proto-Rivalry			Enduring Rivalry		
Independent Variables	Coefficient	S.E.	P>|z|	Coefficient	S.E.	P>|z|
Military Buildup	0.569	.281	0.043	1.664	.334	0.000
Alliance	0.689	.209	0.001	1.343	.398	0.001
Territory	0.824	.157	0.000	3.062	.389	0.000
Contiguity	0.945	.161	0.000	1.534	.277	0.000
Major Power	0.704	.317	0.027	0.733	.467	0.117
Constant	-2.52	.221	0.000	-6.33	.550	0.000

Notes: Isolated Conflict is the Reference Category.
N = 1209.
Prob > chi2 = 0.000.
Log likelihood = -756.743.

FINDINGS BASED ON THOMPSON STRATEGIC RIVALS

Table 5.6 provides a breakdown of the results using Thompson's (2001) rivals. It is interesting and useful to compare the findings based on the coding of Thompson's rivals to the rivalries Klein, Goertz, and Diehl (2006) code. This provides an alternative test of the rivalry theory. If another rivalry data set can show evidence of the same process, even though this data set might be distinctly different in terms of cases investigated, we would have more confidence in the results presented here.

There are distinct differences in the coding of the data sets since the Thompson version does not rely on militarized conflict to code rivalry. Forty percent of Thompson's rivals would be coded as isolated conflicts under the Klein, Goertz, and Diehl (2006) coding. This means that a significant portion of Thompson's rivals had a low number of disputes through their life. Also captured in this measure is the fact that some of Thompson's rivals have multiple rivals under the Diehl and Goertz (2000) coding. The differences of the data sets are covered in Colaresi, Rasler, and Thompson (2008). Choosing which data set to use largely depends on intention and available data. I relied on the Klein, Goertz, and Diehl (2006) version because I wanted to focus on militarized rivalries with a real chance of war. No one data set is better than the other as each serves a distinct purpose.

Table 5.6 displays the results for a logit test of the basic steps-to-rivalry propositions when strategic rivalry (Thompson 2001) is used as the dependent variable. Here I control for war since this is not a dispute-level

Table 5.6 Complete Strategic Rivalry Model Coefficient Estimates, Logit Model for Rivalry

Independent Variables	Coefficient (S. Rivalry)	S.E.	P>|z|
Military Buildup	0.669	.203	0.001
Alliance	0.248	.095	0.009
Territory	1.004	.088	0.000
Contiguity	1.620	.083	0.000
War	-0.004	.145	0.976
Constant	-1.878	.107	0.000

Notes: N = 3320.
Prob > chi2 = 0.000.
Log likelihood = -1843.043.

Table 5.7 Predicted Probabilities for Thompson Model

| | Alliance, Military Buildup, and Territory ||
	Isolated Conflict	Rivalry
All Values = 0	0.761	0.238
Ally = 1 + MB = 1 + Terr = 1	0.318	0.681
Difference	−0.443	+0.443

investigation, and it would not be appropriate if war biased the results one way or the other. All the main variables of interest are positive and statistically significant. Mutual military buildups, alliances, and territorial disputes all contribute to the existence of strategic rivals and are statistically significant.

Table 5.7 presents the predicted probabilities for the Thompson model of rivalry. Much like the results in Table 5.4, models of rivalry occurrence tend to build to some conclusion. Here the factors of alliances, mutual military buildups, and territory combine to produce a probability of rivalry of .681, close to a threefold increase from the base probability. This finding also matches almost exactly with the same three factors for the Klein, Goertz, and Diehl (2006) coding of rivalry at .655.

PATHS TO RIVALRY

Table 5.8 presents the rank order probabilities of the occurrence of rivalry taken from Table 5.4. The presentation of data here allows one to look at the different paths to rivalry. There is an escalating probability of rivalry occurrence as the factors add up and pile on.

The basic probability of a rivalry is .066 if all values are set to zero. This probability increases to 0.138 if they have a politically relevant alliance. Territorial disputes or mutual military buildups increase the probability to .190 and .149, respectively. If a pair of states has a mutual military buildup, territorial disputes, and an alliance, the probability is .570. When the pair of states has an alliance, military buildup, territorial disputes, and both are major powers the probability jumps all the way to .884.

These probabilities would increase even more if variables were added for newly independent states and democracies. Space constraints preclude a case-by-case analysis of rivalry onset and the paths of development, but future work should explore the application of the theory to specific cases. There are many different paths to rivalry; this analysis demonstrates the power politics path.

Table 5.8 Paths to Rivalry: Rank Order of Predicted Probabilities

Rivalry Outcome:	
.884	Alliance, Military Buildup, Territory, and Major Powers
.570	Alliance, Military Buildup, and Territory
.285	Alliance and Military Buildup
.190	Territory
.149	Mutual Military Buildup
.138	Alliance
.066	No Factors Present

ASSESSMENT AND CONCLUSION OF THE COMPLETE ADDITIVE MODEL

It is clear that dyads that have territorial disputes are more likely to become rivals. While not every dispute in which a dyad fights has to be territorial to make the dyad dangerous, those dyads that have territorial disputes early on are likely to become rivals. I believe territory is the type of issue that triggers the rivalry process, but rivals can and will fight about anything and everything once the rivalry states. Regime type issues (the status of a leader) are likely to also trigger rivalries, but there are too few cases of this happening to build a statistical model predicting the impact.

Politically relevant alliances and mutual military buildups are important conditions for rivalry development. Each event makes the outcome of rivalry more likely to occur. The theory presented here is additive in that the factors of territorial disputes, major power involvement, mutual military buildups, and politically relevant alliances all combine to increase the probability of rivalry occurrence. In short, hypothesis 4 fails to be falsified, and I find strong support for the additive model of rivalry development.

From this study, a few typical paths to rivalry can be observed. The path with the highest probability of rivalry occurrence involves the use of politically relevant alliances, mutual military buildups, territorial conflict, and major power dyads. I hope others develop their own path to rivalry to add to the knowledge gathered through these empirical investigations. The next step is to analyze the theory as it applies to recent cases of rivalry, which will be the task of Chapter 6.

6 The Rivalry Story
Iraq and the United States

INTRODUCTION

The central question posed for the field of international relations is: why do states go to war? Scholars who conduct both empirical and qualitative analysis have demonstrated time and again that war is associated with the development of rivalry (Vasquez and Valeriano 2010; Diehl and Goertz 2000; Thompson 2001). More recently, scholars have focused on the war in Iraq (2003) and its ongoing security problems. What is lacking in these studies of the Iraq War is an examination of the preconditions for war that can be found through an analysis of the rivalry between the United States and Iraq prior to 2003. This chapter will seek to alleviate this confounding gap in research and also illustrates the mechanisms at work in the steps-to-rivalry theory as it pertains to the origins of war and rivalry. Fear, power politics behavior, and escalating tactics are all present in the buildup of this rivalry.

Thus far, this book has explored the origins of rivalry from a macro-investigative context. A drawback to this approach is that it may miss the broader context of the rivalry situation. The goal of this chapter is to tell the story of rivalry development and then add more contextual variables and policy analysis to the investigation. This chapter will not seek to test any specific arguments; the goal is only to elaborate and explain how causal processes work through the examination of a recent rivalry case. By skipping a contemporary application of a theoretical construct, other scholars may fail to place their research in a manner that is accessible and relevant to current international events and policy makers.

An important role this chapter will also fulfill is an examination of the applicability of the theory presented in this book to contemporary rivalry situations. A theory might be empirically accurate, but such a theory might be of little impact if it cannot be used to generate policy and procedural advice for decision-makers. Since all of the other chapters in this book examine the role of theory and events with scientific methods, this chapter will deviate from that practice and select a case based on its importance to the policy community and common discourse of the time. Here I will investigate the development of the rivalry through a structured and focused case study (George and

Bennett 2005). The focus will be on relations between the United States and Iraq from the end of the Cold War until the war in 2003. The structure will be determined by the theory utilized in this book to explain the onset of rivalry—the steps-to-rivalry model. Most of the sources used are first-person accounts, news stories from the time, and government documents. I took every effort to avoid secondhand academic analysis so as to focus on the facts of the rivalry rather than rhetoric. A clear limitation is that mostly Western sources were used due to language barriers.

This case is important because the Iraq War in 2003 will likely have a greater impact on the international environment than the terrorist attacks of September 11, 2001. The effects of the conflict will linger for decades in the United States, in Iraq, and in the Middle East. The encounter has shaped the world's perceptions about the United States; it had a direct impact on the economic policies throughout the world and the international course of political development in Iraq, the United States, and surrounding states and allies. The world has always been and continues to be an interdependent system. Conflict in Iraq has been the catalyst for great social and political change throughout the world; unfortunately, the question of why the conflict came about in relation to the historical and theoretical context is often ignored. The corresponding goal is to explain how one can prevent the onset of rivalry wars in the future. By explaining the development of the rivalry between the United States and Iraq, and also how that rivalry relationship developed into a war, we can hopefully identify the processes that interrupt the path to war. How did the rivalry between the U.S. and Iraq develop, and what role did rivalry play in leading to war?

RIVALRY DEVELOPMENT AND CONTEMPORARY HISTORY

A short review of the steps-to-rivalry theory is necessary before the case in question is examined. The theory relies on a negative notion of power politics factors. Power politics stratagems propel disputes forward until rivalry eventually develops. When threatened, states utilize the method of aggressive and coercive militarized diplomacy to achieve security and stability. Unfortunately the opposite almost always happens; the use of power politics strategies leads a pair of states towards long-standing rivalry rather than reconciliation and cooperation. This is due to the conflict spiral and the buildup in animosity, but more simply it operates through the mechanism of fear.

Fear is the true mechanism in operation in the steps-to-rivalry theory. Moves made to ensure your own security tend to ultimately threaten rather than secure the survival of the state and its people. What a state does to protect itself due to the influence of strategic culture actually ends up endangering the stability of a state. When cornered, most humans have a tendency to lash out and react through force rather than reason. This is how the rivalry situation develops. A state will feel cornered and threatened. It will then lash out. The opposing side, sometimes an innocent, will react to the use of force through countermoves that only rationalize the fear perceived on one side and also make this fear materialize in the form of aggressive actions. Once this happens, we end up in a situation that some call the security dilemma (Herz 1950), a concept that has a basic premise: moves made to ensure your own security end up threatening the security of others, provoking an equal or escalating action.

Outward signs of this process tend to be escalating bargain tactics; the development of grand strategies; the use and formation of alliance systems; military buildups; and the language and rhetoric both sides use in discussions, public comments, or private interviews. Any of these moves push states towards rivalry, and they are often a perverse self-fulfilling prophecy in that the original intention of such policies is designed to limit the likelihood of conflict, not increase it. This process is the true tragedy of international politics.

The story I tell through this theoretical process is ancient and repeats throughout history. Much like the first line in Disney's *Peter Pan* (1953), "All this has happened before, and it will happen again"—this is how the course of international politics works. This process is likely evident in the great majority of rivalry situations. Wars are different in that sparks can lead to total conflict; the rivalry situation represents more of a slow burn and a give-and-take endemic in human behavioral processes. Rivalries are not born out of sparks but through the slow process of building a relationship of hatred and mistrust. The following documents the rivalry process in a contemporary examination of a pressing policy problem.

BACKGROUND

> The coalition did not act in Iraq because we had discovered dramatic new evidence of Iraq's pursuit of weapons of mass murder. We acted because we saw the evidence in a new light, through the prism of our experience on September 11. (Secretary of Defense Donald Rumsfeld, July 9, 2003, at Senate Armed Services Hearing)

Many scholars have explored the rivalries between Pakistan and India or the United States and the Soviet Union. Unfortunately, very little work has been done on the theoretical significance of the interactions between the United States and Iraq from the end of the Cold War to the Iraq War in 2003. This chapter will make the case that the United States and Iraq had a rivalry from 1990 to 2003, and this rivalry was critical in determining who the United States went to war with after the invasion of Afghanistan in 2001. Due to rivalry, Iraq was chosen as a target despite the fact that there were more pressing problems, like nuclear proliferation in Iran and North Korea. The Iraq War of 2003 was certainly a war of misperception, but it was a war of misperception due to the context of rivalry. Without the presence of a rivalry it is unlikely there would have been war in 2003. At least there would not have been a war between the United States and Iraq.

First we must ask why there was a rivalry with Iraq. Why did the United States have a rivalry with a relatively weak minor power? These questions have dominated our recent reflection on the course of foreign policy events during the end of the Bush administration. Answers to these questions can be found in an examination of the recent historical events between the two states and others in the Middle East region. First we must take a step back and provide context for the relationship.

The Middle East has confounded Western governments for centuries. More recently the issue has been the failed promises after World War I. The British and the French failed to live up to their commitments when they encouraged the various Arab tribes in the region to rise up against the Axis powers, principally, the Ottoman Empire. They were promised independence if they took the necessary steps to upset the Axis powers during the time, and many Arab tribes used the opportunity to change the dynamics of colonial governance. The hope was for Arab sovereignty, but the reality would be much different.

The state that later became Iraq played a large part in this process. Hussain bin Ali Al-Hashemi and his son Faisal sided with the British against the Ottoman Caliphate at the urging of T. E. Lawrence.[1] While Lawrence intended to help create an Arab state, the British and French never considered this idea a reality because it had been apparent since at least 1908 that there was a strategic importance to the crude oil found in the region (Knightley 2003, 9).

From this perceived betrayal, the relationship between the West and Iraq would never be the same. Promises were quickly retracted. "The British Foreign Office thought that Lawrence was there to keep Faisal amenable and to calm him down when he learned the bitter truth—that Britain and France planned to divide the Middle East between them and turn Palestine into a national home for the Jews" (Knightley 2003, 7). While it is unclear if the British and French really planned to make Palestine a home for the Jews, the point still remains the same: promises from the West never became a reality or were never intended to become a reality.

While the United States did not have a direct role in this process, it remains that, for some, the West is seen as a monolithic group. The lesson learned by Middle Eastern states was that the West was not to be trusted. They have no honor or commitment and are only interested in the region in order to achieve strategic ends, whether that is to eliminate the Ottoman Empire or to ensure the free flow of oil.

Saddam Hussein's own personal history is another important event that must be examined to provide context. For Hussein, the Iraqi army was the centerpiece of the Iraqi state. It was the only strong institution able to hold the country together in the midst of intense sectarian divisions. "Between independence and Saddam's first breath of life, the Iraqi army had doubled in size. It saw itself at the embodiment of the new Iraqi state, 'the profession of death' that would forge a nation out of the competing religious, tribal, and ethnic factions tearing at one another's throat" (Miller and Mylroie 2003, 19).

Later, the Baath Party took the place of the military as the dominant institution in Iraq. "For all practical purposes, state and party are synonymous" (Miller and Mylroie 2003, 29). Its role proceeded in much the same way the military aided the creation of the state. Hussein argued that anyone striving to build the Iraq state was a member of the Baath Party.

Hussein learned to hate the West from the start. His mother never really provided a father for him except for Kheirallah Tilfah, his maternal uncle, who was later removed from the Iraqi army for supporting a Nationalist coup that had the support of the Axis powers (Nazi Germany). Psychologists can probably write reams of articles analyzing the deeper meaning of this event. For our purposes it must be remembered that the Iraqi army is the central institution of the state, at first, and Hussein's own relationship with this institution pivoted with its relationship with the West.

The Baath Party took control of Iraq in 1968, and Saddam Hussein had a direct role in its administration through his position in the Revolutionary Command Council and as deputy president. Hussein became president of Iraq on July 16, 1979, after Bakr resigned at the request of Hussein. From that point on, much of the initial problems he dealt with revolved around Iran. The United States sided with Hussein at first, hoping to both increase its influence in the region and also to moderate his behavior. "The U.S. backing of Saddam, including the covert arms sales, did not moderate the dictator's behavior; it only seemed to encourage more brutality" (Waas 2003, 39). Hussein engaged Iran in a long and devastating war of attrition. He also gassed the Kurds, Shiites, and Iranians at various times prior to the 1990s. His rule was not one of moderation but of extremes that many characterize as the worst practices of authoritarian dictators.

The seeds of the Iranian and Iraqi war and rivalry directly led to the rivalry between the U.S. and Iraq. Iran is a mostly Shiite state, while Iraq is about half or two-thirds Shiite, but ruled by those from the Sunni branch of Islam. The main issue under contention was the status of the Shatt al-Arab waterway, which constituted the primary access route to major ports and oil refineries of the Persian Gulf. Iranian provocations regarding the territorial question and the internal revolution Iran underwent in 1979 both scared and emboldened Saddam. The Iranians suggested the waterway should be split down the middle according to a 1975 treaty, while Saddam claimed the entire waterway as Iraq's.

Saddam Hussein saw the relationship as a simple case of constant violations by the Iranian side. He described the relationship in this way: "One day the neighbor's son beats up your son. The next day, the neighbor's son bothers your cows. Subsequently, neighbor's son damages your farmland by disturbing the irrigation system. If all these things occurred, eventually after enough incidents, you approach your neighbor, tell him each transgression by event and ask him to stop. Usually a warning or approach to the neighbor is enough to stop the behavior. With Iran, however, this approach by Iraq did not work."[2]

There was also the fear that a reassertive, revolutionary Iran would upset the internal sectarian imbalance within Iraq. Hussein did not want an emboldened Shiite group to take power from the Baath Party. "Iraq's Saddam Hussein decided to take advantage of Iran's turmoil [revolution] in order to resolve the border dispute and gain the entire waterway, remove the threat posed by Iran's Shiite government to the secular and Sunni regimes in the region, and gain access to Iranian oil and an Arab population that might welcome unification with predominantly Arab Iraq" (Sarkees and Wayman 2009, 172).

The war began on September 22, 1980, with Iraq's invasion of Iran and lasted until 1988. Estimates of deaths fall between 500,000 and 1.5 million dead when both side's casualties are included. The Correlates of War project codes 750,000 deaths on the Iranian side and 500,000 on the Iraqi side (Sarkees and Wayman 2009, 171). While Iraq did not win the conflict, it did not lose either, but it was a loser economically. What Hussein termed "aid" turned out to be loans that required repayment, as he recounted after the fact. "Iraq had received aid from Arab countries which Hussein believed to be aid and not loans. After the war, however, these countries 'changed their minds' and demanded repayment."[3] In 1980 Iraq had thirty billion in reserves. By 1988 Iraq owed over one hundred billion and the price of oil was falling drastically due to the end of the war and greater capacity in Kuwait.

The role the United States played during the conflict is generally characterized as a form of mutually assured destabilization. It was more convenient for the great powers of the time (the Soviet Union included) to foster an uncertain situation as long as oil supplies were not affected. Hussein tried to take advantage of Iran's split with the United States over the hostage situation so the Iranians could not resupply their U.S.-provided equipment. Late in the war, Iraq and Iran both started to harass shipping in a more concentrated manner by mining the waterway. In 1984 the United States reestablished diplomatic ties with Iraq, and in 1985 the United States also started to ship weapons to Iran under what became known as the Iran-Contra Scandal. In 1988, the United States retaliated after an Iranian mine hit a U.S. ship by attacking Iranian ports and shipping.

The perception of close ties between the United States and Iraq had a large influence on Hussein. The war ended in a stalemate as Iraq could not consolidate gains due to the larger amounts of manpower available to the Iranians. Later Hussein felt his close ties to the Americans might lead to U.S. approval of his plan to invade Kuwait, but he also maintained that there was a deep level of cooperation between Kuwait and the United States. He likely came to the conclusion that there was a link between the U.S. and Kuwait after the U.S. entered the war. The Gulf War and its run-up can be marked as the beginning of the rivalry, as will be covered next.

HOW DID THE RIVALRY BEGIN?

> Saddam vowed that Americans were the enemies of the Arab nation and the enemies of Iraq, swearing that he would destroy them. (Waas 2003, 38)

The great majority of rivalries in the system start due to power politics motivations, and this rivalry is no different in terms of process and origins. Saddam Hussein invaded Kuwait for a variety of reasons, but the main one was the idea of the efficacy of power and the notion that it could solve the various problems Iraq had at the time through a simple invasion. As Hussein put it, "The final decision to invade Kuwait was made in order to defend by attacking."[4] This reliance on a culture of violence and war triggered this rivalry. The Iraq–Iranian War had not gone well for Hussein, but it was not a complete disaster. Iran's advantage in manpower made it a tough target, and Hussein would not repeat the same mistake with his next conflict.

The development of the United States–Iraq rivalry is slightly atypical in that it started with a war first, then a long history of disputes, and then another, hopefully, final war in 2003. Most rivalries build towards war and endure depending on the outcome of the war. Here the unresolved issues prior to and from the Persian Gulf War in 1990–1991 led to a long period of contention between both sides. This period of animosity lasted for over a decade and terminated with the Iraq War in 2003. The main rivalry data set used in this book codes the rivalry as beginning in 1987 and continuing to the end of the data set in 2001 (Klein, Goertz, and Diehl 2006). There are eighteen militarized disputes during this period. Since the rivalry never reached a twenty-year threshold, it is not an "enduring" rivalry, but it is still a rivalry that matters in the international system, and we can draw lessons from its origins, endurance, and termination.

The Gulf War

Hussein's long mistrust of the West is rooted in the formative lessons of his early life. From the failed promises of the French and English after World War I to the turmoil Iraq experienced during World War II as factions picked sides in the battle between the Axis and Allies, Hussein always drew a negative lesson from the behavior of the West. All these lessons formed a culture of defiance in Iraq, and when mixed with a stagnating economy and territorial claim against a weak Kuwaiti neighbor, a war of conquest followed.

The Iran–Iraq War devastated Iraq in many ways. Generations of men were lost, the oil industry was ravaged, and development and education were secondary concerns to the war-fighting ethic. With debts due, a massive amount of the population geared towards war, and no other forthcoming outlet, Iraq invaded Kuwait in 1990. As Hussein described the situation, "When two individuals fight, the fight ends, and the two parties go their separate ways. Thereafter one of the previous disputing parties is bothered by someone else who also wants to fight. Then there is no choice but to fight again."[5] For Hussein, Kuwait was that other party just itching to join the fight. What is telling is that fighting seems to be the preferred option.

Iraq's claim to Kuwait was established legally by arguing that Kuwait was part of Iraq due to a supposed British mandate after World War I. In fact, the proposed statehood Iraq outlined to the League of Nations did not include the region of Kuwait. Yet, some in Iraq never really gave up claim to Kuwait, but Iraq also had little reason to invade until other outstanding circumstances motivated Hussein to act. These circumstances provided the opportunity: the massive amounts of trained military men and equipment left over from the Iranian war provided for the willingness (Most, Starr, and Siverson 1989).

In addition, the war between Kuwait and Iraq cannot be disconnected from the greater politics of pan-Arab Nationalism. "Hussein stated they [Kuwait leadership] were conspirators against Iraq, Kuwait, and all Arab countries."[6] Hussein thought an attack on Kuwait would serve the purpose of unifying the Arab people and hoped others in the region would support this goal. He dreamed of being able to unify the Arab world into an effective and powerful nation, with Hussein at the head of course.

One major issue was the price of oil. Due to a glut in the market, Iraq was only making ten billion per year, far from sufficient to run its economy and pay its debts. Iraq accused Kuwait of driving down the price of oil. They also accused Kuwait of slant drilling into Iraqi fields, much in a similar vein to an episode of the television show *The Simpsons* in 1995 when Mr. Burns slant drills into the town of Springfield's newly found oil, purely a fantasy on the part of the cartoon and Hussein. "Iraq could not possibility rebuild its infrastructure and economy with oil prices at this level. Kuwait was especially at fault regarding the low oil prices."[7]

While Kuwait did increase its oil production at the time, there was no evidence it did so maliciously to hurt the Iraqi economy. Nor could slant oil drilling be proved, no matter how sure Hussein was of the situation. As he noted, "When Kuwait was faced with the facts regarding stealing Iraqi oil using the practice of slant drilling, they admitted to having taken only two and half billion barrels. They stated this fact as if it was not significant."[8]

As a result of mounting losses, Iraq asked other Arab states to suspend payment of debt. The Arab League refused in the face of continued Iraqi aggression and the ill-tempered relations with Kuwait at the time. As Hussein noted, "It is difficult to avoid someone who is armed and standing outside your house unless you come out and shoot."[9] Hussein was backed into a corner and his only way out was to use war as a political and economic instrument. His target was Kuwait, but the United States became the real enemy in the process.

The Grand Conspiracy

For Hussein, there was a wider conspiracy at work during the Gulf War. "Iraq believed some other entity; some larger power was behind this conspiracy."[10] Hussein cited a visit by U.S. General Norman Schwarzkopf before the war as further proof of the conspiracy. "His visit included sand planning or wartime preparations for the invasion of Iraq confirming what Hussein and the leadership already believed."[11]

During his interrogation after the Iraq War in 2003, Hussein noted that he felt that the United States had been working with Kuwait well before the 1991 war. "America had a plan with Kuwait to attack Iraq. We had a copy of the plan in our hands. If I had the [prohibited] weapons, would I have let the United States forces stay in Kuwait without attacking? I wish the United States did not have the intention to attack Iraq."[12]

Enmity between the two sides dates to before the Gulf War in 1991, at least in Hussein's mind. "When did the United States stop shipments of grain to Iraq? In 1989. When did the United States contact European countries to boycott sales of technological equipment to Iraq? In 1989."[13]

When asked why the United States decided Iraq was its enemy, Hussein noted that it was a combination of Zionist plans, the desire of the U.S. to be the lone superpower and have no other country defy its wishes, and the weapons manufacturers within the United States who wanted war for financial profit. "After the collapse of the Soviet Union, all of these internal and external reasons combined to compel the United States to make Iraq its enemy."[14]

Hussein dates the start of the rivalry specifically after the passage of UNSCR 661 on August 6, 1990, after the invasion of Iraq.[15] As he related to his interviewer, it was the first resolution to contribute to the tension and the eventual war in 2003. While the first true resolution was UNSCR 660, passed on August 2, Hussein seems to remember UNSCR 661 as an important event. After the passage of UNSCR 662, Hussein stated, "the United States decided to attack Iraq, this action made the annexation of Kuwait the only solution . . . the United States forced our hand."[16] Due to the resolutions that were passed on U.S. and British initiative and Hussein's own comments, I date the start of the rivalry formally at August 1990.

Another important event in the "conspiracy" was UNSCR 687, which he claimed was passed at the insistence of the United States and "no such decision existed before in the history of the UN."[17] As to be discussed later, this resolution set the terms for the end of the Gulf War and placed a series of strenuous requirements on Iraq. Hussein further claimed that the United States had undertaken a series of "mistakes," including occupying Iraq, the no-fly zones, and bombing the country from 1991 until 2003, and questioned why the UN did not act against the United States over these issues.[18]

Hussein considers American hatred of Iraq to be born of a grand alliance with Israel. "The United States was planning to destroy Iraq, an intention pushed by Zionism and the effect of Zionism on elections in the United States."[19] For Hussein, the plan was a simple part of the grand conspiracy led by the Jewish people. It is clear that there is no evidence of conspiracy, but in his mind this was all true and fit a pattern, much in the same way Hitler saw a grand historical pattern. Misperceptions bred this rivalry, but actions dictated its course of action.

The Failure of Deterrence

Assumptions about deterrence suggest there was a failure on the part of the West to deter Iraqi aggression against Kuwait. The situation was not so simple. While the British did have a protectorate over Kuwait at the time, the British were in no position to solely launch a counterinvasion to protect Kuwait. NATO and the United States had no real connections to Kuwait beyond being economic consumers of their products, despite the ravings of Hussein detailed in the preceding.

The only real reason anyone would expect the United States to preempt an invasion of Kuwait is through its massive military power at the time. At the end of the Cold War, the United States came out on top militarily, economically, and culturally. Its influence was unparalleled, but its willingness to go to war during this time was limited due to the Vietnam hangover. Once the war did start, the Powell Doctrine was in effect, which committed overwhelming force to the situation to ensure a quick victory. The United States at the time had no lust for a military adventure.

On July 25, 1990, Saddam met American ambassador April Glaspie at her request. She had been tasked to improve relations between Iraq and the United States. She queried Hussein about the massive troop buildup on the southern border, and Hussein took this as a cue to explain the long history between Iraq and Kuwait. Hussein explained that the loss of the Shatt al-Arab waterway could be dealt with if Iraq could press its claims on Kuwait.

Hussein then asked the opinion of the United States regarding the border dispute between Kuwait and Iraq. Glaspie's answer lives in infamy, "We have no opinion on the Arab–Arab conflicts, like your border dispute with Kuwait. I was in the American embassy in Kuwait during the late 60s. The instruction we had during this period was that we should express no opinion on the issue and that the issue is not associated with America" (Sifry and Cerf 2003, 68). She went on to say, in reference to the perceived unfair borders drawn up by the British, "I clearly understand your message. We studied history at school." These colossal mistakes of diplomacy will live on as one of the greatest mistakes ever committed by a diplomat. While there is a dispute as to what the actual correct transcript of the events is, Glaspie did confirm that the current account is largely correct.

Saddam Hussein understood the message communicated by Glaspie as a green light to invade. Other statements by various U.S. policy makers reinforcing the point only made things clearer for him. Unfortunately for Hussein, no green light was forthcoming. The United States would never condone unprovoked aggression during the height of what George Bush called the "New World Order," and the gist of the statements at the time only reflected a general policy of quasi isolationism at the time, articulated very poorly.

Different leaders have differing conceptions of the usefulness of force. Some leaders, actors, and states find force, conflict, and aggression to be the preferred methods to settle political disagreements. Others would rather work within a tight global system that constrains violence in most forms. Hussein underestimated the systemic norms of the time. The period at the end of the Cold War was not a period when states enforcing the global order would allow, condone, and accept conquest. The reaction against this move by Iraq was met with global revulsion once the relevant actors really figured out what was at stake in the conflict.

While Bush wavered in response to the situation at first, the British were firm in their demands that Iraq return the situation to the status quo, and they pushed the United States to change its tone on the conflict. United States did as its faithful ally asked and demanded that Iraq reverse course.

The Invasion and the International Reaction

On August 2, 1990, Iraq invaded and quickly overran Kuwait, mostly over a few hours. The fear was that Saudi Arabia was next, and the United States immediately sent troops to the region to prevent this development. Combined, Iraq and Kuwait controlled 15 percent of the world's oil supply; add the contribution of Saudi Arabia to the equation and all of a sudden Iraq and Hussein could control as much as 25 percent of the world's total oil production capabilities, making it instantly the largest oil-producing country in the world.

The United Nations acted swiftly. UN Security Council Resolution 660 demanded withdrawal hours after the invasion was launched. By November the United States decided to use its troops in the region to force Iraq out of Kuwait (Sarkees and Wayman 2009, 176). On November 29, the UN passed Security Council Resolution 678, authorizing the use of force if Iraq did not leave Kuwait by January 15, 1991.

Initial reluctance to go to war over the situation was quickly countered by the global disgust at the invasion of Kuwait. Although largely untrue, the story circulating at the time was that Iraqi forces were killing innocent civilians and particularly babies. The revulsion against the acts by the Iraqi military was widely spread. This conflict was directly linked to the long-term rivalry between Iraq and the British. American reluctance to go to war could not withstand British pressure on the matter, an issue of honor for some. In 1961, the British guaranteed Kuwaiti sovereignty against Iraq. "President Bush was initially cautious about possible responses; however, his support for a military option was considerably bolstered by the intervention of Britain's Margaret Thatcher who wanted a tough response" (Finlan 2003, 27). In fact, Bush and Thatcher announced together in Aspen, Colorado, that the invasion would not stand.

On January 16, UN coalition forces led by the United States started an aerial bombardment of Iraq called Operation Desert Storm. At first it was thought this attack had a devastating effect on the Iraqi military, but subsequent analysis found it made little impact. Iraq even attacked the Saudi Arabian border town of Khafji on January 29, to disastrous results (Sarkees and Wayman 2009, 176). While the aerial campaign did not decimate Iraqi capabilities, it did destroy its ability to respond, organize counterattacks, and unify command once the invasion did start.

The coalition launched a ground offensive on February 24, 1991, and quickly took control of Kuwait and pressed into southern Iraq. Iraq gave up and signed a cease-fire on February 29, even as Saddam claimed victory in what he called the "mother of all battles." Previously, they had agreed to a cease-fire with the Soviet Union, but the international community would not accept anything short of full withdrawal from Kuwait.

The UN Coalition did not record Iraqi fatalities in a comprehensive manner to avoid negative public opinion during the war. At the time, the slogan "No War for Oil" became popular; it was not in the West's interests to celebrate the massive loss of life on the Iraqi side. The Correlates of War project estimates casualties at 40,000 on the Iraq side, 1,000 on the Kuwaiti side, 376 for the United States, and around 100 causalities total for other allied powers (Sarkees and Wayman 2009).

War Termination and Rivalry Initiation

The UN coalition forces won a quick and comprehensive victory in Kuwait. Modern warfare advances such as GPS satellites made it easier for the Americans to maneuver when Iraq should have had the advantage as the defender. Decades of Cold War military capability development bore fruit in this conflict. American tanks and various "smart weapons" dominated the battlefield. The Iraqi forces deserted in the tens of thousands, and the coalition forces were barely able to contain all the prisoners.

Iraq did not put up much of a fight in Kuwait and instead reserved the majority of its more capable forces for the defense of the homeland and Baghdad itself. Due to this fact, Hussein could claim some sort of minor victory in that his military was not totally decimated by UN forces. The failure to reign in and humiliate Hussein would come back to haunt the United States in the future.

The question often asked is: why didn't the United States invade Iraq in 1991 and remove Hussein? Some forces crossed the border, but the great majority of forces were kept in Kuwait or in Saudi Arabia. On February 27, 1991, George Bush announced that Kuwait was liberated and ordered a cease-fire. The UN resolution authorizing the attack only defined the liberation of Kuwait as the goal, so it is unclear if the coalition forces had a mandate to launch a war of regime change. The Gulf War turned out to be really a war to return the world to the status quo. Unfortunately, the status quo was no longer tenable. Hussein's ability to keep the majority of his forces and withstand an attack by UN forces that did not penetrate the homeland was helpful for his long-term prospects as the leader of the country.

The other issue was that an invasion of Iraq would likely not have been supported by the Arab members of the coalition. This was a primary concern for the United States in that they wanted global public opinion on their side in this conflict; if the other Arab members of the coalition deserted, the mandate for action would be compromised. There was little desire for a unilateral conflict in a region the United States had little engagement with beyond the demand for oil and the preference for strategic imbalance. The U.S. spent a great amount of effort holding the Israelis back from entering the conflict after Iraq launched a series of Scud missiles at the country. It could not contain the wider revolt that would occur if the great power deemed regime change a necessary policy outcome.

It is also slightly astounding to find that many of the leaders for the invasion of Iraq in 2003 articulated reasons for not invading Iraq in 1991 that would later prove prescient and largely correct. Various American policy makers expressed the lack of desire to invade Iraq because they did not want the responsibility of an occupation and election process. Unfortunately, they failed to follow their own advice years later.

The coalition partners, particularly the United States, hoped that Saddam would eventually fall through his own mistakes without external forces helping him along. The case for the assumption of internal regime change was strong, but it also failed to recognize the political skill and devious nature of Saddam Hussein. Bush took it upon himself to tell "the Iraqi military and the Iraqi people to take matters into their own hands and force Saddam Hussein the dictator to step down."[20]

A coup was assumed and encouraged due to the poor showing of the Iraqi military. This strong institution should have reacted negatively to the errors of Hussein. Hussein succeeded in launching a bloody series of preemptive strikes against disloyal regime members, and the United States looked on helplessly as any hope of internal regime change was lost. Things got even worse when Hussein turned from political reprisals to ethnic reprisals against the Kurds and Shiites. The coalition forces failed to protect the people from these moves, and Hussein proved to be virtually untouchable internally. These human rights violations would later serve as central issues of contention in the rivalry as the coalition instituted no-fly zones in the regions to protect civilians.

Weapons of Mass Destruction (WMDs) also became an important issue that resonated much later in the conflict. Due to the use of WMDs against the Kurds and Shiites within Iraq and against the Iranians to push back waves of human attacks, Iraq was deemed a threat to the international order. Another active norm since World War II was the rejection of the use of WMDs against military or civilian targets. Since Iraq had used the tactic in the past, it was thought it was likely to do so again. While Hussein was careful externally about what weapons he used and against whom, rationality was not a trait the West projected on Iraq's leader, and they feared his continued reliance on WMDs.

UN Security Council Resolution 687 was passed on April 3, 1991, after the termination of the war. This document set the stage for a decade of defiance by Saddam Hussein and can be seen as the motivating force for the rivalry in terms of policy provocations. The resolution enfranchised the idea of a Middle East free of WMDs. "Iraq shall reaffirm unconditionally agree not to acquire or develop nuclear weapons or nuclear-usable material or any subsystems or components or any research, develop, support, or manufacturing facilities related to the above." This requirement was used as a justification for war by the United States and also placed an undue burden on Iraq, as the country saw it. Their right to develop and maintain advanced weaponry was constricted by an external power that did not occupy the country. Much the way a petulant child would react to a similar situation, the prevention of Iraq's WMDs programs only made these programs more likely to exist.

The positive outcome was that Iraq could not maintain a program of WMDs in the face of a global blockade, restriction of scientific research, and likely activities of American and Israeli spies, who sabotaged various programs. Unfortunately, this was of little value to the external community because Iraq could not publicize this development for fear that it would look weak internally and externally. The power situation within the state and balance of forces in the Middle East made it virtually impossible that Hussein would ever forswear WMDs programs publically. This form of a military buildup, both real and imagined, became a central issue for rivalry between the United States and Iraq.

Other confounding problems remained. Since Iraq's forces were largely intact, it still posed a security threat to both Kuwait and Saudi Arabia, not to mention to the Kurdish population in the north. The threat posed to Saudi Arabia was the most pressing issue since Saudi Arabia controls a massive amount of the world's oil supply and has been a longtime friend of the United States. Hussein felt Saudi Arabia was under the influence of the United States and not truly committed to the greater pan-Arab struggle. Due to these alignments, Iraq remained a threat to peace in the region, from the American perspective.

The final reason that the rivalry was set to ignite and persist was the fear of terrorism, the main post–Cold War security problem in the region. UN Security Council Resolution 687 stated firmly that Iraq "will not commit or support any act of international terrorism or allow any organization directed towards commission of such acts to operate within its territory and to condemn unequivocally and renounce all acts, methods, and practices of terrorism." This requirement was a tough restriction on Iraq in that Hussein liked to foment rebellion since he considered himself a revolutionary, not a politician. He also invoked the sense of Arab hospitality towards the enemies of his enemies. While Iraq did not actively support terrorism, this issue did reassert itself and became a prominent question after 9/11.

Equality and Rivalry

Starting with Vasquez (1993), most rivalry scholars assume equality is a central assumption of a rivalry process. This view is incorrect both historically and theoretically. There have been many rivalries between unequal powers for various reasons. In the past, distance was the central reason that some great powers failed to wipe out small powers that became a nuisance or obstructed plans and ideas. For some, distance brought safety. When coupled with more relevant and pressing threats in a region, some long-standing disputes between unequal powers can fester for decades with no resolution.

The rivalry between the United States and the United Kingdom from independence until about 1903 is an example of this situation. While the U.S. was able to defeat the British with French help during the Revolution, it was not so lucky during the War of 1812. The British succeeded in burning Washington, D.C., and after some initial setbacks, were able to virtually confine American shipping to port. The only reason the UK did not press its advantages was because of the distance involved in tackling the American problem once and for all and the more the pressing issue of Napoleon and the French threat.

The United States and Britain agreed to peace in 1815, and the rivalry continued over various issues such as shipping concerns and the border between the United States and Canada at least into the 1890s. Towards the end of the rivalry, American power started to come close to equaling British power, but the British by far outmatched the United States for the majority of the time the rivalry was in existence.

In the case between Iraq and the United States, distance did play a role in the sustained rivalry after 1990; the more important issue was international norms and diplomacy. The United States had no desire to invade Iraq directly during the Gulf War because it was not in the mandate of the war and could also upset various Arab allies. The most critical issue was norms; after World War II it no longer became acceptable for a great power to invade and conquer a small power. Conquest is dead (Simons 2003). The death of conquest removes the most central option for a large state to deal with a pestering minor power. Without the option of conquest, some major powers had to live with the proverbial thorn in the side until other systemic situations allowed for the termination of the rivalry through formal conflict. The systemic situation important in this case was the attacks on 9/11 and the changing security situation thereafter, to be detailed in the following.

Issues at Stake the Rivalry

The original issue at stake in the rivalry is clearly territorial. The claim Iraq held on Kuwait started the entire process of rivalry. Such a claim was not really strategic, but it was a colonial-ethnic claim to the region. Hussein claimed that Kuwait was the nineteenth providence of Iraq, and that the people wanted him to invade on their behalf. When asked what evidence of this desire he had, Hussein replied, "We felt they were asking."[21]

Background to the claim extends to the era of Mesopotamia and ancient history. Kuwait was an administrative region of the United Kingdom from 1899. To keep what later became Iraq from having open access to the Persian Gulf, the British split the Kuwaiti area off and administered it as a separate territory. This humiliation became a symbol of Arab nationalism and Western arrogance in the region.

In 1961, Kuwait became an independent country after it formed an official government. The acceleration of the oil industry in the region transformed Kuwait into a rich and modern country. Iraq recognized Kuwait's boundary in 1963 and Kuwait helped Iraq fund the Iran–Iraq War, so they managed to cooperate before the 1990 invasion. Resistance to the status quo in the region was mainly a function of the nature of the debt Iraq owed to Kuwait, fears that Kuwait was driving down the price of oil by flooding the market, and the notion of a U.S.–Kuwait alliance against Iraq, outlined as a conspiracy earlier.

This claim demonstrates the ability of a territorial issue thought resolved to lay dormant only to be revived by a situation later. The perspectives or claims did not change; what did was the situation within Iraq and the idea that Hussein could claim leadership of the Arab national movement by combining Kuwait and Saudi Arabia into a grand coalition. This was a new development since Hussein originally took power in Iraq partly because Bakr was planning on forming a unified state with Syria, pushing Hussein out of the leadership structure.

Another facet of a territorial claim is its heavy influence on other disputes. A territorial claim can be thought to be resolved, but it can also be the starting point for other disputes. In a rivalry, anything and everything can be an issue under contention if a territorial question starts the process. This rivalry is one such rivalry; the territorial claim between Kuwait and Iraq triggered the rivalry when the United States defended Kuwait, but other issues quickly became more important.

One other such issue at stake in the conflict between the United States and Iraq was the imbalance of power in the region. The idea of a balance of power is a key concept in international relations (Morgenthau 1948), but it mostly fails to explain behavior since it's inadequate, tough to measure, and unrealistic. What does have meaning is the idea of a permanent imbalance. The situation in foreign policy relates to the instance when a state decides it is advantageous to put those who can cause problems for a state's foreign policy prerogatives on unsure footing. This seems to have been the goal of the United States and the West during the post–Cold War era.

During the Cold War, the Soviets and the United States played at influence in the region, claiming one space or another as its ally when it was politically or economically convenient. With the dormancy of Russian power after the fall of the Soviet Union, the United States had the prerogative to control the Middle East and played a part in Iranian, Iraqi, and Kuwaiti internal politics. While the actions of the Americans in the region were minimal at first, the fear that these actions engendered in the region was very real. Hussein remembers the quote from Secretary of State James Baker vividly. "[The U.S. would] take Iraq back to the preindustrial age."[22] Hussein stated that Iraq would not be intimidated by threats. Iraq was determined to not accept operating from a weak position and giving in to threats. Threats beget threats and rivalry.

The main issue at stake after the failed invasion of Kuwait was one of regime change. This issue is the second most war-prone issue after a territorial dispute (Vasquez and Valeriano 2010). During the disputes over the level of economic sanctions placed on Iraq after Gulf War, insiders remarked that the issue really was not Iraq's behavior, but the continued presence of Saddam Hussein. Until this issue was solved, there could be no cooperation between the United States and Iraq.

In fact, this relationship was really predetermined. Either prior to or during the Gulf War, Hussein convinced himself that the United States was involved in a conspiracy to bring down Iraq. What really was likely is a policy of imbalance was perceived as a directed and targeted policy of regime change in Iraq. The United States had taken this step in the past, condoning activities in Cuba, Chili, and Guatemala. It did not take a large logical leap for Hussein to extend this practice to his backyard. While it is unlikely that the United States put this policy in operation before 1991, it became a reality after 1991 when they supported revolts and coups internally. These moves did not succeed and only reinforced the idea that Hussein was a targeted man. The tragic set of circumstances in the region made it so that a paranoid dream became the perceived reality.

After 2001, the central issue in the rivalry revolved around the question of WMDs and terrorism. These are two issues that should not be connected but were, according to the time period, and dominated the course of foreign policy at the time. The attacks on the United States on 9/11 confirmed for some that a small group of terrorists could harm a great power. This lesson, reinforced and learned from a single data point, became a national policy enfranchised by the Bush Doctrine.

The Bush Doctrine laid out the foundation for the use of American power during the Bush administration (White House 2002). It only ended with the election of Barack Obama, and the quagmire that became Afghanistan sapped the impulse to promote democracy in the region. The main premise of the Bush Doctrine was that small powers can now harm great powers through the use of WMDs (later termed weapons of mass murder when no WMDs were found in Iraq) or support of terrorist organizations. These two concepts became linked in the imagination in that a terrorist group could use WMDs to achieve their ends. The action prescribed in the Bush Doctrine suggested that preemptive action was necessary when these foreign policy issues arose and these problems should be tackled early, during the pre-crises period.

The Bush Doctrine was conceived after the war with Afghanistan began, but it is clear that the document was directed towards Iraq and other "rogue states." These actors were thought to be irrational and sought to destroy America because they hated its freedom. In reality, these states were perfectly content to harass the United States but offered little direct evidence of proactive offensive operations against the United States. What became clear was that the United States would no longer tolerate states that skirted the global agenda of peace and sought a policy of regime change, canonized in neoconservative thought, that suggested that some states were good and some were evil. What these states offered as policy was inconsequential in the face of the true hidden and evil intentions of these actors. Iraq was the prime example of this sort of state, a state caught up in the post-9/11 fervor to ensure security through offensive action.

While Iraq had little direct connection to terrorist groups, it did try to establish tenuous connections to various groups. For the United States, the main concern after 9/11 was any links with Osama bin Laden. Bin Laden was willing to "explore possibilities for cooperation with Iraq," but he also supported anti-Hussein actions in the Kurdish north (National Commission on Terrorist Attacks upon the United States 2004, 61). In late 1994 or early 1995, bin Laden asked to establish training camps within Iraq and was rejected (National Commission on Terrorist Attacks upon the United States 2004, 61). By 1998, the tone had changed, and Iraq was open to starting a relationship with al-Qaeda because of the intensifying conflict with the United States and frayed relations with Saudi Arabia. In 1999, "According to reporting, Iraqi officials offered bin Laden safe haven in Iraq. Bin Linden declined, apparently judging that his circumstances in Afghanistan remained more favorable than the Iraqi alternative" (National Commission on Terrorist Attacks upon the United States 2004, 66).

Iraq is a traditional and secular state and works under the typical constrictions of a state in the international system. The interrogation of Saddam is filled with overtures to international law and the Geneva Conventions. Many may have doubted Iraq's intentions—the past actions of Hussein certainly gave credibility to the idea that he was a dangerous rouge actor—but the reality of the situation was that he was a humbled leader clinging to power after at least 1998.

THE REPEATED DISPUTE PHASE

Dispute Accumulation

Iraq entered into what some term a decade of defiance after the Gulf War. Issues piled upon issues to push the United States and Iraq on a collision course for conflict. Issue accumulation (Dreyer 2010) is a key problem in the rivalry field and the concept is underutilized as an explanation for why conflict erupts. For most wars and rivalries, there is not one single issue that pushes the states towards conflict but an accumulation and interaction of various minor and major issues that motivate the leaders in each state to act in a conflict prone manner.

After the Gulf War, a series of issues dragged the United States and Iraq into periods of crises or near crises. This level of tension was sustained and is typical for the dysfunctional relationship that is really the foundation of rivalry. Besides the disgust over Iraq's burning of oil and oil wells during the pullout of Kuwait, the first dispute to arise was over the no-fly zones that the UN Coalition, led by the United States, placed on Iraq after the Gulf War. The West enforced a no-fly zone in the north and south of Iraq to protect the Kurds in the north and the Shiites in the south. After that, economic sanctions crippled Iraq and were enforced by the United States; violations of these sanctions and the hatred they engendered led to tense relations. The issue of an assassination attempt on former president George H. W. Bush; Iraq troop movements; and, finally, weapons inspections all became militarized and increased hostility levels within the developing rivalry.

Throughout this process of issue accumulation, the demands and level of violence at first was extreme, dropped off for a short of time, and then ramped up until there was a near war during Operation Desert Fox in 1998 and total war for regime change during the Iraq War in 2003. It is clear that the escalating demands from 1990 until 1991 triggered the rivalry, and, thereafter, the demands placed on Iraq (due to their own actions) sustained the rivalry.

No-Fly Zones

The main issue in the aftermath of the Gulf War in 1991 was the status of Kurdish and Shiite peoples in the north and south of Iraq. Some were openly rebelling against Hussein in the face of his disastrous loss to the coalition forces and promises by the United States. Unfortunately, the rest of the county either was unaware of the struggle or chose to continue to support the Baath Party. Hussein decided to utilize his remaining forces to brutally strike down the revolting portions of his country. As he noted, "Within a day of the cease-fire of 1991, some elements had initiated sabotage operations in the southern Iraq cities of Basra, Nasiriyyah, and Amarah. Later, this activity spread to the northern cities of Suleimaniyyah, Erbil, and Kirkuk."[23] Hussein also noted that sixty-eight Iranian intelligence officers were captured. Refugees and freedom fighters alike had to be protected from Iraqi reprisals after the war.

No-fly zones are a relatively new tactic in the system. The Iraq situations appear to be the first use of the idea, with no-fly zones instituted in Bosnia-Herzegovina in 1993 and Libya in 2011. Since then they have become a common tactic thought to be effective in fighting repression within a state.

The first no-fly zone operation was to protect the Kurds in the north. In the past Hussein had attacked and gassed the Kurds, who were a separate nation seeking an independent state. The Kurds operate on the border of Iraq, Iran, and Turkey. Iran also attacked Kurds in the region during the period between 1991 and 2003. Hatred of the breakaway national group is likely the one thing Iraq and Iran agreed on at the time.

Code-named Operation Provide Comfort and later, Operation Northern Watch, the no-fly zones were in effect from 1991 until 2003 and were justified as part of the UN resolution terminating the Gulf War (UNSCR 688). Although they were not directly authorized by the UN, the coalition forces felt they had proper clearance according to Resolution 688, which states that Hussein had to stop the repression and attacks against the Iraqi people.

The consequence of the northern no-fly zone was to establish a virtual autonomous Kurdish state in the north and to increase tensions between Iraq and the United States after the Gulf War. Initially the no-fly zone was instituted on April 8, 1991, to protect the Kurds after Hussein launched reprisals weeks after the Gulf War, but they later became de facto forms of occupation in the region north of the thirty-sixth parallel. There were a constant flow of incidents as coalition forces shot down Iraqi planes and helicopters, targeted radar facilities, and were harassed by Iraqi forces. Several of the militarized disputes between Iraq and the United States can be attributed to no-fly zone incidents. Operation Desert Fox in 2001 was launched after Iraq increased the amount of no-fly zone violations after a drawdown for years.

The southern no-fly zone was meant to protect the Iraq Shiites, or Marsh Arabs as some call the group. The southern zone was instituted on August 26, 1992, south of the thirty-second parallel. On September 3, 1996, the southern no-fly zone was extended north just to Bagdad at the thirty-third parallel.

Casualties during these operations were limited on the coalition side mainly to friendly fire incidents. The 1994 mistaken attack against two Black Hawk helicopters killed twenty-six service members. While the no-fly zones may have moderated the behavior of Hussein at the time and limited his ability to pursue WMDs programs, it seems clear that these incidents provided the context for continued rivalry. Without the engagement of Iraq in such a concentrated manner after the Gulf War, the United States is unlikely to have been as active as it was in the region.

ECONOMIC SANCTIONS

Scholars have continuously debated the efficacy of sanctions for decades, coming to the general conclusion that sanctions do not achieve the policy ends they desire. What is more critical is that sanctions also tend to harm the poor, children, and women disproportionately. During the Gulf War, sanctions were placed on Iraq, and these sanctions were in effect from 1991 until 2010 with the major trade, economic, and political sanctions being lifted after 2003.[24] The only sanction that remains is the 5 percent tax on oil revenues Iraq has to maintain to pay Kuwait for reparations from the 1990–1991 invasion.

The sanctions clearly were an economic and humanitarian disaster for the country. Politically the goal was to first punish Iraq for invading Kuwait; then the goal became to compel Iraq to follow UN Security Council resolutions and moderate behavior. The sanctions were clearly linked to the continued power of Hussein's regime. Although sanctions were lifted against Libya once they renounced their nuclear weapons program, calling into question whether the sanctions were directed solely against Hussein.

Unfortunately, the brunt of the costs of sanctions was felt by the normal, everyday Iraqi citizen. Limiting or eliminating food supplies, medical supplies, and agricultural products harmed the capacity of the Iraqi state to deal with basic subsistence needs. The decline in revenue for the state is an obvious result of the sanctions, but more critically the loss of health supplies, educational materials, and farming materials directly hurt the underclass unable to pay the rising costs of goods during this time. The Iraqi government estimated that there were 1.5 million deaths that could be attributed to the costs of the sanctions. While this figure is likely in dispute, even cutting the figure in half demonstrates the massive impact of the sanctions.

For the purposes of rivalry, the sanctions only entrenched Hussein's position and emboldened his perspective that the West wanted to destroy Iraq. The leadership class was able to skirt the major effects of the sanctions. The main effect was that sanctions increased threat perceptions and contributed to a significant amount of disputes between the two countries from 1991 to 2003. In 1995 Iraq threatened to end cooperation with UN inspectors unless sanctions were lifted. This threat was empty, but it demonstrates the salience of the sanctions issue. At various times throughout the period, ships and cargo were seized as they tried to skirt the embargo.

If the point of sanctions was to moderate the behavior of Hussein, the sanctions clearly did fail. While they did reduce his ability to marshal an effective fighting force and resupply his forces, the sanctions had the perverse effect of helping those close to Hussein make even more money as they skirted the regulations and were rewarded with even more profit (Mazaheri 2010).

UN Security Council Resolution 986, passed in 1995, was designed to allow Iraq to sell one billion (in U.S. dollars) in oil supplies every month for food and humanitarian assistance. Iraq accepted the resolution in 1996 after severe economic decline. Originally a similar scheme was offered in 1991, and the delay Iraq took in accepting the resolution certainly contributed to the massive loss of life during this period.

The oil for food program caused a scandal itself when it was found that members of the Iraqi regime were skimming money from the program. It was found that the regime was underpricing oil and taking the resulting savings through direct payments, skirting the program (Baram 2000). Later, the Iraqi government traded oil directly for influence or opportunities with various government forces. Russia was the biggest beneficiary of this program, but even some people in the United States were indicted under the scheme.

The Assassination Attempt

In the buildup to the war in Iraq in 2003, George W. Bush invoked the past twice. "This is a man who continually lies ... After all, this is the guy who tried to kill my dad."[25] The incident Bush was referring to was the purported assassination attempt against George H. W. Bush during a visit to Kuwait in 1992. At the time, Bill Clinton responded with a missile strike directed against an intelligence facility in Iraq on June 26, 1993. "The Iraqi attack against President Bush was an attack against our country and against all Americans" (Hersh 2003, 146).

Hersh (2003) conducted an intensive investigation of the incident and was unable to come up with any firm conclusions. It is likely that Iraqi intelligence forces tried to assassinate former president Bush during a visit in Kuwait in 1992, but it is unclear if Hussein knew of the plot and ordered the hit. Hersh (2003, 141) concluded, "But my own investigations have uncovered circumstantial evidence, at least as compelling as the Administration's that suggest that the American government's case against Iraq—as it has been outlined to the public anyway—is seriously flawed." It is likely that the process became politicized and intentions were projected on Hussein during the investigation.

Nonetheless, it is perceptions that truly matter, and here it is clear that this event lives in the memory of the leadership of the United States. Whether true or false, it makes no difference, what is important is that both Bill Clinton and George W. Bush believed Saddam Hussein ordered the assassination of George H. W. Bush. Perceptions are important, and here the perception was that Hussein would do anything to attack his enemies. This attempt fed directly into perception of the rivalry and was revived almost ten years later as a justification for the war.

Troop Movements

If the intention of the Gulf War and the various displays of force the coalition demonstrated after 1991 were to moderate Hussein's behavior, these moves clearly failed. Instead Saddam Hussein showed a tendency to use his one big resource left, massive amounts of troops, to achieve his political ends. Through the rivalry from 1991 to 2003, Hussein massed his troops and mobilized forces to harass the United States.

After the withdrawal from Kuwait in 1991, Hussein continued to threaten the state. The Kuwait–Iraq rivalry did not end with the 1991 war; they continued to engage in militarized disputes and came to the brink of renewed war at least three times during the interwar period, conflicts that likely would have dragged the United States into the picture. In 1994, Hussein rejected UN movements to monitor weapons activity and threatened to stop cooperating with UN inspectors. At the same time, to make sure his threats were taken seriously, he moved troops to Kuwait's border region.

To resolve the dispute, on October 15, 1994, the UN Security Council passed Resolution 949, demanding that Iraq withdraw all military units from southern Iraq and return to their original positions. While Hussein did withdraw his troops, he also demonstrated that he still had military capabilities and the ability to threaten the coalition forces. Defeat in Kuwait in 1991 clearly did not reduce the capacity of Iraq to utilize its military to achieve foreign policy goals. Although rarely successful in achieving his ends, Hussein did demonstrate he was a real threat in the region.

In 1996, Hussein attacked the Kurdish region covered by the no-fly zone. He massed thirty to forty thousand troops outside of Erbil. This militarized incident was just another in the series of threats that materialized against the coalition. Although Hussein backed down, the legacy of human rights violations in the region is stifling. Mass graves continue to be found and investigated; the Iraqi government believes there are five hundred thousand missing in the region.[26] In August of 2001, Iraq also crossed into Saudi Arabia, triggering another militarized dispute.

UN Weapons Inspections

The pivotal issue between the United States and Iraq late in the 1990s was over the status of weapons inspections within Iraq. The UN Security Council resolutions that terminated the Gulf War made Iraq give up any ambition to pursue WMDs. The goal of the inspections was to root out and destroy any nuclear, biological, or chemical weapons programs left in the country. Since Hussein had used WMDs in the past, it was reasoned that he would be likely to do so in the future.

Section C in UNSCR 687 states, "Iraq shall unconditionally accept, under international supervision, the destruction, removal or rendering harmless of its WMDs, ballistic missiles with a range over 150 kilometers, and related production facilities and equipment. It also provides for establishment of a system of ongoing monitoring and verification of Iraq's compliance with the ban on these weapons and missiles."[27]

On April 18, 1991, Hussein declared the location of some chemical weapons stockpiles and Scud missiles. No biological weapons programs were ever admitted at first, but on August 2, 1991, Iraq admitted it had some biological programs aimed at defense only. On June 9, 1991, the first inspection took place. The UN inspection program under the United Nations Special Commission (USCOM) revealed that Iraq might have obtained nuclear weapons by 1992, but this capability was destroyed during the Gulf War. Huge stockpiles of chemical and biological weapons were destroyed under the resolution.

On August 15, 1991, UN Security Council Resolution 707 demanded that Iraq complete a full and final review of weapons activates. After this, Iraq became increasingly defiant, refusing to accept Resolution 707 and denying entry of later weapons inspections groups. Resolution 715 later authorized continuing monitoring activities by the group. Iraq defied these resolutions because, as Hussein noted, "a country that accepts being violated will bring dishonor to its people."[28]

Most of the 1990s were marked by new resolutions, denials by the Iraqis, and then subsequent disclosures, only to repeat the process over and over again. Each time Iraq admitted to the scope of various weapons operations, it was found that Iraq was not truly forthcoming about their activities. The reason for Iraq's reluctance to admit the full scope of weapons development activities is due to the external and internal threats it faced, and also false claims by Hussein's own scientists. Hussein did not want to admit to weapons programs and have them eliminated because he would appear weak and his capabilities would be degraded. Hussein noted, "If Iraq had given up its principles, we would have been worthless."[29] It is also likely that Hussein thought he had more capabilities than he actually had, with his own scientists lying to him to save their jobs and perhaps lives. Evidence of this is nonexistent at this point.

After the mid-1990s, Iraq gave up the pursuit of WMDs. Iraq could barely feed its people, let alone pursue advanced weapons programs in the face of inspections and foreign intelligence activities. The paradox was that Iraq could not admit this was the situation. "Saddam stated he was more concerned about Iran discovering Iraq's weaknesses and vulnerabilities than the repercussions of the United States for his refusal to allow UN inspectors back into Iraq."[30]

One central issue of dispute during the inspections were the Presidential Palaces, which were off-limits since they were residency buildings but generally were large compounds that could facilitate weapons research. Hussein's foreign minister and later deputy prime minister, Tariq Aziz, was the main combatant with the UNSCOM group. "Aziz got right to the point: Iraq was fed up. The country was disarmed he said, and the information we were seeking was of no importance" (Butler 2003, 182).

On October 29, 1997, Aziz sent a letter to UNSCOM demanding that all U.S. government personnel working with UNSCOM leave Iraq and withdraw cover for a spy plane the commission was using to monitor Iraqi activities. These actions led to a stalemate.

To end the four-month standoff, UN Secretary-General Kofi Annan signed an agreement with Iraq on February 23, 1998, to allow full inspections, including the previously off-limits Presidential Palaces. Prior to signing the new agreement the United States sent an "armada" to Iraq with twenty-five thousand troops available to help launch strikes.[31]

The Iraqi position on the weapons inspections was that they were politically motivated to push Iraq towards war. Some contend that the inspections teams were compromised and utilized by the American and Israeli intelligence services to gather information inside the county.[32] The controversy over this issue will never likely die down as the United States is unlikely to admit complacency in the operations and those that have supported the Iraqi view, Scott Ritter chief among them, have been compromised over other issues and could be looking to stir up notice for their public appearances, books, and other endeavors.

All these events, plus near constant no-fly zone violations, led to Operation Desert Fox from December 16 to December 19 in 1998. This was a four-day attack and bombing of Baghdad to force Iraq to comply with UN Security Council resolutions. The other goal was to destroy or degrade Iraq's ability to produce WMDs. It has become clear after the fact that Iraq was not producing WMDs and any attacks during Operation Desert Fox were deliberate attempts to constrain and modify the behavior of Hussein. There was also the issue that some contend that the attacks were meant to distract the American public from Bill Clinton's scandals, but evidence of this is flimsy since there is a long history of conflict between Iraq and the U.S. prior to this event. After Operation Desert Fox, Hussein made no attempt to behave according to American dictates and offered rewards for shooting down coalition forces in the region, escalating the stalemate. As Byman (2000–2001, 510) notes, "In 1999, Iraqi forces made over 400 separate attacks on coalition aircraft, and over 140 violations of the no-fly zones; the figures for 2000 are similar."

9/11 and the Changing Security Situation

As pundits are apt to say, 9/11 changed everything. The event did not change everything in the grand sense of updating our preferences or ideas about who a state's threats were. What 9/11 did was change the systemic structure of how international relations are conducted. Instead of 9/11 making it so the world realizes a small power can be a threat to the global order, as the Bush administration claimed, the event instead offered license to states to use extreme measures to tackle relatively minor nuisances. In fact, most argue that Hussein, while an annoyance, was well contained by 2001 (Byman 2000–2001; Harvey and James 2009).

Seeing the threat of Iraq through a new prism, as suggested by various American government officials, is a false statement that betrays the real motives behind the post-9/11 security apparatus. The goal was really to clean up old threats that could, possibly, become greater threats. Al-Qaeda and terrorism has been a thorn in the side of the international community for decades, if not centuries. The 9/11 attacks did nothing to change estimates of their capabilities or ability to do damage to the state; it only showed that some actors had devised new methods to attack targets, and these terrorists could possibly combine with traditional states to become greater threats.

The United States claimed Iraq was continuing to seek WMDs. Iraq maintained that it had no such weapons ambitions or capabilities. As Hussein claimed, "By God, if I had such weapons, I would have used them in the fight against the United States."[33] Iraq's hindrance of the weapons inspection regime convinced many they were in breach of UN regulations. In hindsight, it is tough to find the trigger for the 2003 war beyond the events of 9/11 and the global War on Terror. At the time, a majority of Americans believed that Saddam Hussein was working with al-Qaeda.[34] Hussein commented during this interrogation that he wanted to have a relationship with the United States but was never given the chance. He remarked that the U.S. was not listening to anything that Iraq had to say.[35]

This imaginary link between Hussein and WMDs was the trigger for the war and the last series of disputes between the countries. Iraq was ordered to finally come clean about the status of their weapons programs. Although they did produce a report that detailed many events, others claimed they were not completely truthful and this claim turned out to be true, as Hussein admitted. Hussein noted, "Iraqi leaders made decisions which gave the United States an opening and the reasons for the most recent war."[36]

The conjecture was that if Hussein gained nuclear weapons, he would use them or give them to terrorists. There was no evidence that Hussein had access to nuclear weapons, nor was there any real reason to believe that he would cooperate with terrorists, having only harbored but not materially supported them in the past. As Condoleezza Rice said, "The problem here is that there will always be some uncertainty about how quickly he can acquire nuclear weapons. But we don't want the smoking gun to be a mushroom cloud."[37] It was during the situation of rivalry that uncertainty became certainty. Assumptions became fact. Rivalry changes the context of the situation, and the war in Iraq in 2003 was a result of the negative perceptions both sides articulated about each other.

In the end, the United States was able to gain wide support for the plan to attack Iraq. As Hussein noted, "The United States was looking for a reason to do something."[38] Since the 2003 war, it has become clear that for many in the U.S. administration this might be true. Donald Rumsfeld, secretary of defense, famously wrote about Iraq during a 9/11 briefing, "Go massive. Sweep it all up, related or unrelated."[39] Due to the rivalry, unwarranted connections were made and war became inevitable because of the changing systemic structure.

VARIABLES OF INTEREST

Alliances

The actions by Iraq and the United States during this rivalry and during its inception were clearly influenced by a long history of alliances in the region and throughout the world. The main driving factor was the linkage between Britain's security interests and the interests of the United States, formalized through the North Atlantic Treaty Organization (NATO). As the conflict ramped up, a coalition of willing partners was organized through the United Nations. Iraq even had a few alliances of its own, although its aggression was not motivated by alliance politics; these issues did play a role and gave Iraq a free hand to plan its operations in 1990.

The NATO alliance was signed on April 4, 1949, and remains in effect to this day (Gibler 2009, 385). Twelve states originally signed the alliance, including the United States, the United Kingdom, France, Italy, and Iceland. The alliance was later expanded to include West Germany, a reunited Germany, Greece, Turkey, Poland, and former Soviet states in 2004. It will likely continue to expand and demonstrate its use of coordinated military power in the face of any challenge to a member state.

NATO was originally formed to counter the Soviet threat, prior to the signing of the Warsaw Pact. The alliance coordinated defense in Europe to prevent overrun by Soviet forces. Built on strong foundations of cooperation and institutionalization, the alliance endured long past the end of the Soviet Union and later became a force for conflict outside of Europe after the end of the Cold War. This enduring alliance remains one of the most effective security institutions in the world and considers an attack on one an attack on all. The central link between the United Kingdom and the United States, through NATO, is the key to understanding how the alliance pushed the states towards rivalry. This linkage through the alliance was a central reason the United States became so involved in the events of 1990.

While NATO was not invoked during the Gulf War in 1991, the foundations of the alliance are clear to see in the eventual coalition arrayed against Iraq. After Iraq defied UN resolutions to withdraw from Kuwait, the United States assembled a coalition to oppose Iraq. This coalition comprised thirty-four states, including most members of NATO and many Arab states (including Syria, the UAE, Saudi Arabia, and Kuwait). Norman Schwarzkopf of the United States was named the commander of coalition forces in the Persian Gulf.

The alliance between the United Kingdom and the United States deserves special mention. Tony Blair felt intimately close to Bill Clinton, and these ties carried over to George W. Bush. By 1997, Blair himself was appalled by Hussein's behavior and brought the issue up during unrelated matters (Shawcross 2004, 47).

It is likely that Blair and Britain joined the bandwagon to push for war in 2003 for two reasons. One is the need to respect the support the United States offered Blair during the Kosovo crises in 1997–1998 and the eventual war the United States supported. The other is Blair's desire to moderate Bush's behavior and force the United States to go through the UN. Unfortunately this plan failed, likely because Blair overestimated his influence and underestimated the influence of neoconservatives in the Bush administration (McHugh 2010). In any case, Blair's unwavering support served to embolden the United States and also provided a valuable link to European security partners. "He not only wanted to offer unconditional support to the United States and to reaffirm the 'special relationship' that successive British prime ministers had cultivated. He also wanted to forge agreement with his European partners" (Shawcross 2004, 50).

Prior to the entrenchment of the rivalry and the Gulf War in 1990, Iraq was an ally with Saudi Arabia and signed a nonaggression pact on March 27, 1989 (Gibler 2009, 517). The goal of this defense pact was clearly to ease Saudi Arabia's concerns about Iraq's aggression in the region. From Iraq's perspective, they gained with this alliance some assurance that Saudi Arabia was not prepared for a threat that Iraq might pose on its border, and Saudi Arabia also promised to help Iraq develop a nuclear plant. This alliance only lasted until the onset of the Gulf War in 1991 with Saudi Arabia participating on the side of the coalition. It was also attacked by Iraq on the border during the conflict.

It is unclear what the purpose of this alliance was for Hussein beyond maintaining the element of surprise. It is a matter of debate if Iraq was really prepared to invade Saudi Arabia, and Hussein's ambitions could have stopped at Kuwait if the international community had allowed his actions to stand. Likely this alliance allowed for Hussein to have some piece of mind that the Saudis would not be prepared for conflict and could support Iraq as long as they were not targeted.

One prior alliance and one post–Gulf War alliance also played a part in the political calculations in the region. Iraq had an alliance with the Soviet Union that was signed in 1972 and in effect until September 12, 1990 (Gibler 2009, 456). This alliance was intended to counteract the support the United States gave to Iran at the time. The Soviets provided military assistance and equipment to Iraq. The alliance went through its up and downs when the Soviets invaded Afghanistan, a Muslim state, an act condemned by Iraq and when Iraq invaded Iran, an act condemned by the Soviets. The alliance was only terminated once Iraq invaded Kuwait. The Soviets had no interest in supporting Iraq as it was condemned by the great majority of the world.

On December 31, 2000, Bahrain, Kuwait, Oman, Qatar, Saudi Arabia, and the United Arab Emirates formed a defense pact as part of the

Gulf Cooperation Council (Gibler 2009, 536). While this alliance did not include any members of the rivalry under discussion, the purpose of the alliance was clearly to support cooperation in the case of another war in the region involving Iraq. The real goal to make a unified army to support prior defense pacts signed by Gulf states.

The total impact of the various alliances in the region reinforced the decision-making process of Iraq and the United States. The United States had support of allies and coalition members in the region, giving it license to conduct operations in the Middle East, and Iraq had security partners that would at least not complicate its initial plans to invade Kuwait. It is unclear if the United States would have ever become rivals or fought wars with Iraq without the support of its NATO allies or the UN coalition in 1991. By 2003, the alliances were irrelevant for the process of war, but, as dictated by the theory presented here, it is the power politics tactics that happen early that have an impact on the probability of rivalry, and this relationship is clear. Despite the Middle East being relatively short of alliances during the time period, Iraq and the United States managed to utilize alliances in an effective manner, and these alliances helped trigger the rivalry.

Military Buildups

Both Iraq and the United States participated in military buildups at different times. Although there was no conventional arms race as most scholars measure the practice (Sample 1998), there is clearly a pattern of high levels of military spending that was accelerated at different times during the rivalry.

For the United States, the Cold War was a period of an almost uninterrupted military buildup. "The long Cold War had produced a massive build-up of conventional and nuclear forces, particularly based in Europe" (Finlan 2003, 10). This Cold War buildup then translated into a peacetime buildup as the United States sought to modernize its forces and prepare to face new enemies and threats.

The data on the military spending process within the United States are clear.[40] Table 6.1 displays the levels of military spending in Iraq and the United States from 1985 until 2003 (2001 and 2002 for Iraq are excluded due to missing data). If one uses the 8 percent military buildup rate conventional in the field (Sample 1997), the United States has a monadic military buildup from 1986, 1992, 2002, and 2003. While the buildups in 2002 and 2003 can be attributed to the looming war, the buildup in 1986 occurred prior to the rivalry with Iraq, and the buildup in 1992 occurred early in the rivalry but after the first war. This demonstrates the typical pattern of military buildups in the system as explored previously in Chapter 4. The military buildup on the U.S. side came before the rivalry, early in the life of rivalry, and before war in 2003. Certainly a more fine-tuned measure of military spending data allows for a closer examination of how military spending can feed into a rivalry.

132   Becoming Rivals

Table 6.1   Military Expenditures in Iraq and the United States, 1985–2003

Iraq	Year	Mil Exp	% Change	USA	Year	Mil Exp	% Change
	1985	12,870,000			1985	245,154,000	
	1986	11,579,000	-0.1	MB	1986	265,480,000	0.083
MB	1987	13,990,000	0.208		1987	273,966,000	0.032
	1988	12,870,000	-0.08		1988	281,935,000	0.029
	1989	11,000,000	-0.145		1989	294,880,000	0.046
	1990	8,610,000	-0.217		1990	289,755,000	-0.017
MB	1991	12,900,000	0.498		1991	262,389,000	-0.094
	1992	2,500,000	-0.806	MB	1992	286,892,000	0.093
	1993	2,600,000	0.04		1993	297,600,000	0.037
	1994	2,748,000	0.057		1994	293,214,000	-0.015
	1995	1,250,000	-0.545		1995	277,834,000	-0.052
	1996	1,277,000	0.022		1996	277,254,000	-0.002
	1997	1,250,000	-0.021		1997	276,324,000	-0.003
	1998	1,428,000	0.142		1998	279,702,000	0.012
	1999	1,500,000	0.05		1999	292,147,000	0.044
	2000	1,400,000	-0.067		2000	303,136,000	0.038
	2001	1,372,000	-0.02		2001	322,365,000	0.063
	2002	N/A		MB	2002	348,555,000	0.081
	2003	N/A		MB	2003	404,920,000	0.162

Here the issue is not the threats that this spending pattern directs toward Iraq, but really how it signals the willingness of the U.S. to use force against its competitors when possible. The military spending pattern, exasperated by fear that the Middle East would be the next battleground, drove both military spending and foreign policy dynamics in the region. As the *New York Times* noted at the time, "The entire process of trying to avert war through inspections and negotiations was undercut by the military buildup that the United States said was necessary to force Iraq to comply."[41] This military buildup was not simply a spending program but a program meant to modernize and reorganize American forces towards new threats to be found in the Middle East. Once the process starts, it is tough to resolve the situation in a peaceful manner without suffering some form of strategic defeat.

Iraq did experience a military buildup prior to the rivalry in 1987, but the general pattern is one of a decline of military spending for one simple reason. Spending during the Iran–Iraq War reached astronomical levels and virtually bankrupted the country. It was unable to rapidly build up the military because it did not have the funds to do so; this lack of economic capacity was a central reason there was a conflict with Kuwait. In 1991 Iraq increased spending by close to 50 percent. During the rivalry, Iraq deceased spending drastically as a consequence of the embargo and inability to sell oil. Table 6.1 displays these patterns.

What Iraq did have was a large military force ready for conflict. Prior to the Gulf War, Iraq had the fourth largest military in the world. There was full conscription for all men from eighteen to thirty-four. The country was simply massively mobilized and prepared to use its military might to achieve its foreign policy ends. On top of this, Iraq had a large military that had nothing really to do. These men were trained to kill, experienced in battle, and lacked the skills necessary to enter the civilian population. With so much military power ready to be utilized, it is little wonder that Hussein picked a fight and was prepared for war.

Rivalry Linkages

Like many rivalries, the origins of the rivalry between the United States and Iraq can be found through the linkages between this dyad and others in the region. This factor tends to be overlooked in the field, and there are few treatments of how interactions between rivalries lead to new rivalries (Valeriano 2003, chap. 7). The data work I did on the problem before still stands as relevant but it is tough to present as a simple causal process. Empirically the finding basically holds that the more rivalries a state engages in, the more likely it is for a state to engage in a new rivalry (Valeriano 2003). This finding flies in the face of the war weariness hypothesis. States that engage in conflict are more likely to engage in more conflict because they likely break the taboo of the use of force early and learn that militarized diplomacy can be an effective tactic.

The empirical finding that suggests an overutilization of rivalry as a method of foreign policy that predicts future rivalry holds true, but it is only interesting if put in the proper context. Here I hope to demonstrate that the linkages between the Iraq and United States rivalry and other rivalries were important to the origins of the main rivalry of interest.

Iraq is one of the most disputatious states in the system. They have rivalries with just about every neighbor in their region and even some unexpected relationships (e.g., a rivalry between the Netherlands and Iraq due to multiple disputes). For our purposes, the main linkage rivalry of interest is likely the rivalry between the UK and Iraq. This rivalry began in 1958 and continued until the Iraq War in 2003 with nineteen total militarized disputes. The main issue of contention was the status of Kuwait, but other regional issues provided grounds for competition. What is important here is that the security interests of Britain transferred to the United States due to their "special relationship." A relevant counterfactual would ask if there would be a rivalry between the United States and Iraq if there had never been a rivalry between Iraq and the United Kingdom. This is unlikely.

The other important rivalry linkage is the relationship between Iraq and Kuwait. This was a rivalry from 1961 until 2003. Over this time, there were twenty-five disputes, including an invasion in 1990. It is unquestionable that if Iraq did not have a rivalry with Kuwait, it would never have been in competition with the United States. This pivot dyad drew in the United Kingdom and the United States as actors in the region. Without these disputes, there never would have been a war in 2003.

The next rivalry of consequence was the relationship between Saudi Arabia and Iraq. This rivalry began in 1961 and also continued until the 2003 war with seven disputes over its lifetime. The fear that Iraq would invade Saudi Arabia to control its oil and create a greater pan-Arab state was on the forefront of the reasons why it was important that the international community stop Iraq after it attacked Kuwait. These power politics games directly fed into the situation that created hostility between the U.S. and Iraq.

The final rivalry of consequence is the rivalry between Iraq and Iran. This rivalry lasted from 1934 to 1999. There were thirty-one disputes over this long period of time, but the most important was the Iran–Iraq War. As documented in the preceding, the Iran–Iraq War directly led to the war between Iraq and Kuwait because of the economic devastation that Iraq experienced after its failed military adventure. This rivalry spurred on other conflicts in the region and remains an issue of concern even after the 2003 war. The American fear is that Iranian influence and Shiite political alignments will push Iraq away from the path of cooperation with the West and back towards belligerence.

Grand Strategy

The initiation of a grand strategy is a clear indicator of the development of a rivalry. A grand strategy is a total political, military, economic, and social plan to deal with a potential threat. Unfortunately, time and space preclude me from doing an in-depth examination of the factor as it relates to all cases of rivalry development. Future studies should not ignore the factor as an important indicator of when a rivalry is brewing.

There are elements of grand strategy active in this case. One example is the quest to democratize authoritarian governments according to the neoconservative project. The *New York Times* notes "Mr. Bush's efforts to paint a grand vision of democracy in the Arab world."[42] Here, the grand strategy for the United States represents an effort to counter those governments opposed to the policies of the United States and disrespectful of democratic values. Elements of a grand good versus evil battle are clear; here the hidden intentions of Saddam Hussein influenced American domestic actors to quest for his fall. Regime change is clearly the goal in this conflict after the Gulf War, and the goal of regime change is based on the feeling that Hussein is detrimental for peace and stability within his own state and the region, fostered through the idea that some leaders are just not suitable for some states. This form of judgmental international politics is quite new in the American experience since the guiding principle during the Cold War was alignments, not support for democracy.

The other element of grand strategy results from the Bush administration's "National Security Strategy" document released in September 2002. This document outlines the vision of American foreign policy in the future and makes the action of preemptive attack a doctrine of action. In no other potential case is the notion of preemptive attack more relevant than in Iraq. It is almost as if the National Security Strategy was written to deal with Iraq and North Korea rather than the problem of terrorism.

While Iraq has not directly threatened the national security interests of the United States, it does represent a potential threat to the nation, and thus it must be dealt with preemptively. The American "National Security Strategy" is little more than a justification and plan to attack Iraq before it is capable of attacking the interests of the United States. According to this plan, the United States would act alone if necessary to secure its interests. This is exactly what happened during the Iraq War in 2003, when the United States attacked preemptively without any new evidence of Iraq's intentions. The United States also acted unilaterally despite the creation of a flimsy "Coalition of the Willing" including the United Kingdom, Poland, and Togo.

Domestic Actors

The situation of hard-liners in power proves another element at work consistent with the steps-to-war theory (Vasquez 1993). While domestic attributes were not a part of theoretical underpinnings of this project, it is an important aspect that should not be left out of the story. The problem is that there are little data or hard evidence about the foreign policy preferences of each member of government for all states preventing a suitable examination of the hard-line actors from the macro standpoint (Valeriano and Marin 2010). In this case, it is clear that hard-liners were at work in both the United States and Iraq during the development of the rivalry.

In the United States government, the dividing line between hawks and doves is apparent. Colin Powell, U.S. secretary of state, is the dove in this case since he advocated using the United Nations to disarm Iraq and consistently tried diplomatic efforts to quell the dispute. On the other side are Secretary of Defense Donald Rumsfeld, National Security Advisor Condoleezza Rice, Vice President Dick Cheney, and President Bush. Each of these members supported the use of force in Iraq, regardless of disarmament. Before them were Bill Clinton and Madeline Albright, secretary of state, who used force in 1993 and 1998 in response to various actions by the Iraqi government.

While the hard-liners did concede some points to Colin Powell and used the UN at first, the ultimate failure of diplomacy can be pointed to the hard-line stance of the administration. Right or wrong, Iraq felt that nothing they could do would satisfy American demands. The fear Iraq caused in the American foreign policy apparatus was extreme. "The prospect of a nuclear-armed Saddam is so worrisome that it requires drastic action . . . The United Sates should invade Iraq, eliminate the present regime, and pave the way for a successor prepared to abide by its international commitments and live in peace with its neighbors" (Pollack 2002, 33).

Placing the burden of proof on Iraq and not on the United States left little area for compromise since Iraq operated under the same hard-line stance. This rivalry and its enduring quality developed from the interaction between two hard-line governments. Saddam Hussein was clearly a dangerous and troubling hard-liner on the Iraqi side. As Kenneth Pollack noted, "Saddam Hussein is one of the most reckless, aggressive, violence-prone, risk-tolerant, and damage-tolerant leaders of modern history" (2003, 403). Hussein had confidence in his own abilities and strengths, so much so that he ignored every piece of evidence and insisted that the United States would never invade Iraq. During the run–up to the 2003 war, he believed that at worst the United States would bomb Iraq for a few days as it had done in 1998.[43] No amount of evidence could convince him that coming clean to the United States and following its example would be a beneficial strategy for Iraq. When Iraq did bargain, it worked with the Soviet Union and later Russia, preferring to never engage the Americans.

With hard-liners usually comes bullying and realpolitik tactics. The central focus of this project has been to demonstrate how realpolitik tactics can lead to rivalry. This is the case here, where the demands placed on Iraq only increase as time goes by. The Iraq and United States rivalry shows how the steps-to-rivalry theory can explain the course of contemporary rivalries.

LESSONS AND CONCLUSION

The rivalry between the United States and Iraq serves as an illustrative lesson for many reasons. The pattern uncovered here is likely typical of the rivalry process in modern-day state-to-state interactions. Power politics is the driving force of this conflict and the wars experienced during the rivalry's lifetime. The willingness to use militarized diplomacy to solve international questions increases the probability a state will launch aggressive military operations and sustain a rivalry. The opportunity for war lies in the circumstances of the time when a dispute arises, the systemic condition, linkages to other rivalries, alliances, and military buildups.

The Gulf War from 1990 to 1991 was born out of the depression in Iraq after the Iran–Iraq War and the rigid international system after the Cold War. The Iraq War of 2003 was a war born of the loose systemic norms after 9/11 and the allowance for the use of force to deter the acquisition of WMDs and state support of terrorist groups. While the era of loose norms during 9/11 seems to have ended, the situation where the system can allow conflicts like this to fester and revert back to war endures.

Territorial questions clearly triggered this rivalry early on. The question was the status of Kuwait, which was an ally of the British. The transfer of security of interests between the United States and the United Kingdom is a common practice; the interests of the two countries go hand in hand, and the Kuwait issue was no different. It was in the interest of the United States to enforce the promises of its ally, to support the stability of the territorial status quo in the region, and to ensure the free flow of oil and avoid large monopolies in the region. This early question triggered the Persian Gulf War in 1991 and later fed into other issues that promoted rivalry.

After the initial issue, the steps-to-rivalry theory is largely confirmed. Territory set off the rivalry, but the rivalry continued over issues of the status of the strategic balance in the region and later fears of WMDs and terrorism. The initial rivalry in 1990 was triggered at a time when both countries were continuing large military buildups. Iraq sought to rebuild its forces after the Iran–Iraq War, and the United States continued momentum from the Cold War as the military transformed itself into a modern digital force. Late 1980s and 1990s weapons development was focused on fighting smaller targets in different locations, exactly like Iraq.

In this rivalry, alliances were a key motivating factor for enduring conflict. The link between the United Kingdom and its support of Kuwait was central in pushing the United States to support Kuwait from the start of Iraq's aggression against Kuwait. The linkage between the United Kingdom and the United States was critical in the process of rivalry development. Iraq even had its own alliances that helped provoke its early belligerent moves in 1990.

In the end, the key for this rivalry was the fear each progressing move engendered in the other side. At first, Hussein acted in Kuwait over predatory impulses, but later he displayed the fear common in a cornered animal. The United States itself was not immune to fear, especially after the 9/11 attacks. This fear fed its way into the U.S. foreign policy apparatus, and virtually every decision-maker in the United States had a hard-line stance against Iraq. The additive quality of each factor—territorial disputes, rivalry linkages, hard-liners in government, escalating bargaining tactics, alliances, and military buildups—would predict that rivalry would develop in this case. The goal in the future is to stop this tendency and push states away from the use of militarized diplomacy and escalating bargaining tactics.

7 What Do We Know about Rivalry Now?

WHAT HAVE WE UNCOVERED?

Despite over a century of research into the causes of war, international relations scholars have generally failed to indentify rivalry as a central factor that can cause war. This missing or omitted variable can simply be called historical animosity. The failure of the field to recognize the importance of this issue highlights failings within the field. Instead scholars focus on concepts such as power, balance, or bargaining. While these concepts are important, there is very little about rivalry that they can help explain. Rivalry is essentially an irrational project that defies normal power or balance considerations. It is a path to war, and it should be studied as such.

This study is the first comprehensive macrohistorical investigation of the development of rivalry and ideally will spur future scholars to investigate why states become long-term enemies. The idea of the enemy image, how it is created, and how it is sustained, should be a central question for all social and behavioral scholars since the implications of the question are wide-ranging within the field of political science and beyond. Do we need rivals or competitors to thrive as social actors? Do rivals harm the growth prospects of a state? How can the situation of rivalry, built on misperceptions and faculty perceptions, be controlled in the system?

The central premise of this book is that power politics strategies such as escalating tactics, alliances, and military buildups help initiate the rivalry process. When these tactics, part of the strategic culture of foreign policy, are utilized, states tend to end up in long-term conflictual relationships. Sometimes decades pass and the initial motivation for conflict falls out of collective memory, but conflict persists. It seems clear that it is the behavior of states, modeled as the steps-to-rivalry, on the road to conflict that leads them to become long-term enemies. Becoming locked in the death grip of rivalry only leads to more devastation, trauma, and perpetual underdevelopment until the issues are settled and each side can move on to deal with more pressing internal or external problems. The international system can only get to this peaceful situation once we understand why rivalry develops in the first place.

POWER POLITICS STRATEGIES

The Theory

The steps-to-rivalry theory predicts that the onset of rivalry will occur through a series of steps. These steps usually take the form of power politics foreign policy strategies. States rely on a version of the realist folklore, envisioned as demonstrating strength, to deal with potential enemies. Once threatened, states react the way folklore dictates, usually with force and militarized threats. The use of force and militarized threats pushes states towards rivalry.

Once an initial issue arises, states must determine how they will handle the relationship with a potential rival. By not responding with militarized force, pairs of states are unlikely to become rivals (Hensel and Diehl 1994). Using power politics strategies, however, increases the likelihood that states will become rivals due to the security dilemma. When one state increases its security through alliances and military buildups, the opposing state perceives a decline in their own security. That state then responds in kind, and the situation develops into a zero-sum game that dictates the course of the rivalry relationship.

There are a series of factors that signify that this dynamic is an ongoing and additive process. The general notion of power politics strategies leading to rivalry has to provide actual empirical evidence as measured by the existence of certain factors on the road to rivalry. These factors are a contentious issue—usually territorial, alliances, and military buildups.

Territory

States fight over issues. A disagreement over the preferences over certain issues is how conflicts erupt. Issues vary according to their contentiousness; symbolic and transcendent issues tend to lead to disagreements because it is tough to settle these disputes through bargaining (Mansbach and Vasquez 1981). These types of issues usually become winner take all and thus divisive. Territorial issues are the main example of issues that are transcendent of typical rational calculations due to their symbolic nature; regime leadership issues can also take on these qualities.

Territorial disputes are the primary cause of war and help explain the motivation behind a great majority of wars (Vasquez and Valeriano 2009). What is even more critical is the discovery that territorial disputes contribute to the onset of rivalry (Tir and Diehl 2002; Vasquez and Leskiw 2001). With this finding, we can better understand a path to war. This path likely includes a territorial dispute early in the process, and this can lead states toward rivalry and later war. The basic probability of rivalry in the absence of a territorial dispute is 0.066. When territorial disputes are observed, the probability jumps to 0.190 (Chapter 5).

In this analysis, I have found that in combination with other factors, territorial disputes increase the probability of rivalry. Through an analysis of the rivalry between the United States and Iraq, it is also clear that territorial disputes can come early in the rivalry and trigger other disputes. Without the territorial dispute between Iraq and Kuwait since these countries were born, rivalry and war would have been unlikely. Without these events, war in 2003 is almost unimaginable. Territory is part of the path to both war and peace, but more likely it is the key to rivalry and an important issue that must be included in any analysis of the rivalry process.

Alliances

Alliances are a typical power politics response to a perceived security threat. A state will try to find alliance partners to ensure its security. Alliance formation in turn provokes an equal response in the other state or the escalation of tensions through other means. When states feel targeted, these moves signal a change in relations for the pair of states. Once this move is made, repeated disputes and rivalry become likely. Alliances embolden states to act; they can remove pressing threats from the security agenda (such as Iraq's alliance with Saudi Arabia before the invasion of Kuwait), and they draw states into conflicts they otherwise might avoid (the United States during the Gulf War). Alliances are troubling in the realm of international politics and a key factor in the path to rivalry.

The facts about alliances are clear, the combined additive model (Chapter 5): simply observing a relevant alliance increases the probability of rivalry from 0.066 to 0.138. What is more, relevant alliances observed decrease the probability of isolated conflicts or quick fights. Alliances provoke a long-term hostile relationship when one side feels threatened by an alliance. When combined with the factors of mutual military buildups, and territorial disputes, the probability of rivalry jumps from 0.066 all the way to 0.570.

Alliances generally occur early in the life of a rivalry, and, by increasing the capabilities of one side of the rivalry, they make recurring disputes more likely. The threatening nature of alliances and other power politics strategies increase the likelihood that historic animosity will develop and a long-standing conflict between the two states will result. How a dispute is handled early in its development determines the probability of rivalry occurrence. Using power politics increases the salience of disputes between a rival pair and leads to the serial nature of crises between the pair of states.

Modern alliances are changing in shape and scope. Some states utilize alliances to settle past disputes. Others avoid alliances and instead add security clauses to trade pacts. Often they are not formalized, so a state can avoid involving the legislature and public opinion in the security discourse. Yet NATO endures, and it is a dangerous alliance that can draw states into conflict and embolden others to start fights they might not be prepared to fight alone. It is almost assumed that NATO is an important pillar of the security interests of the United States, but why?

Alliances must end; they are needless, antiquated, and defy the normal dynamics of cooperation. Multilateral cooperation agreements that include security clauses, trade exchanges, and the enfranchisement of international law should take the place of alliances in the system. States can guarantee the security of other states, but acting in coordination or combining power is a move towards rivalry. Alliances lead to rivalry, they lead to war, and they draw states into situations they otherwise might avoid.

Military Buildups

Rapidly building up the military is the typical state response to a threatening security issue. The hope is that by building up the military the opposing side will be deterred from attacking or challenging the state. Unfortunately, the path from military buildups to peace is nonexistent. Military buildups engender conflict. They are steps toward conflict, not peace.

The same is true for military buildups in the context of a rivalry. Mutual military buildups increase the probability of rivalry. Observing a mutual military buildup during a dispute results in doubling the probability of rivalry. When combined with other factors, such as an alliance and a territorial dispute, the probably of rivalry increases by a factor of six (Chapter 5).

Military buildups are the likely response to a threatening enemy. In principle, states build up their military to increase their security; in practice military buildups increase the chances for unprompted belligerence because building up the military makes it more likely those capabilities will be used. Spending more on guns as opposed to butter (public goods) is a tough choice. Those that make this choice are more apt to use force. Building up the military can also provoke an equal response in the other state, leading to an arms race. Arms races also signify that a pair of states is engaged in a rivalry and more likely to fight a war.

Mutual military buildups do not occur solely in rivalries. There are a significant amount of mutual military buildups cases that occur in dyads that have had few disputes. What likely happens is that the early existence of mutual military buildups leads to war. Chapter 4 found that close to half of the cases of early mutual military buildups went to war quickly. A future task would be to recalculate the mutual military buildup measure into a monadic variable. I believe if one side builds up its military, rivalry will likely result. The opposing side might not need to respond in kind (it could be a major power that has enough weapons, not requiring a buildup). It could also be that increases in military weapons procurement might not meet the criteria for a mutual military buildup because the timing might be delayed on one side as it calculates its response and finds the money needed to fund weapons programs.

Buildups are dangerous; I look forward to others pushing research progressively forward on this front. Whether a buildup is mutual, interactive, or monadic, the point is still the same: they contribute to rivalries because they are part of the power politics response to a threatening situation. Buildups may not come early, but when they do occur they tend to lock states into rivalry.

Timing

The timing of events is critical in any causal process. In terms of the steps-to-rivalry theory, it is clear that power politics moves must come early to trigger a rivalry based on simple notions of how the causal process works. Chapter 6 outlined this process clearly in the Iraq–United States rivalry case. Early on, the United States used extreme force to push Iraq out of Kuwait and continued this level of threat through disputes over the treatment of civilians (no-fly zones); the embargo; and, finally, the quest for WMDs. Hussein and Iraq did the same, attacking Kuwait, Saudi Arabia, and threatening Kuwait, Saudi Arabia, and the north and south of Hussein's own country in response to American actions. Rivalry is a tic-for-tat process, and this case clearly outlines the sequence of events.

In terms of specific variables, alliances come early in the process of rivalry development (Chapters 4 and 6). They embolden both sides to act, clear potential troubling problems from the security agenda, and drag states into conflict they might otherwise avoid. Alliances can be one of the triggers for rivalry.

The relationship between mutual military buildups and rivalry is more complicated. Used as a measure of an arms race, a mutual military buildup increases the probability of a rivalry. When these events occur varies by case. When mutual military buildups do occur, war sometimes results, and this process can terminate a rivalry before it can really become entrenched in the system (Chapter 4). In other cases, mutual military buildups come early and push the states towards rivalry. The norm seems to be that mutual military buildups occur after the initial few disputes and help lock the rivalry system in place.

A more fine-tuned measure of a military buildup specific to individual states without an interactive element helps tell the story of military buildups and rivalry development better (Chapter 6). Requiring a buildup to occur at the same time betrays the fundamental dynamics of the military spending process. It does not happen all at once, at the same time; when it does it usually leads to war (Sample 1998).

The central contribution of this work is to specify how rivalries develop, but also to put sequencing on the forefront of the process of the steps-to-war theory (Vasquez 1993). War occurs through certain paths, and the timing of events on this path is key to determining when conflict will occur. The same is true for rivalry, which occurs according to certain dominant paths. Understanding how and when these paths are in operation should be a key concern for the conflict studies community.

Combinations

In combination, the steps-to-rivalry model delineates the road to rivalry. Pairs of states that form alliances against each other, participate in mutual military buildups, have territorial disputes, and have extensive rivalry linkages are likely to become rivals. Each step increases the probability that rivalry will occur. Furthermore, states can do little to avoid a rivalry outcome once the steps-to-rivalry process is started. The key is to stop the process before it becomes locked in and intractable.

Linkages are tough to account for empirically, but a past investigation (Valeriano 2003) does show that when a state becomes involved in one rivalry, it is likely to become involved in more. This finding counters the war weariness hypothesis and demonstrates that rivalries beget other rivalries. This is likely because the power politics tactics used during the onset of a rivalry result in other rivalries. States learn to use militarized diplomacy to settle disputes.

Unfortunately, this leads to more disputes and rivalry. It also leads to other rivalries when the same tactics are directed towards other states. In foreign policy, states as units often learn the wrong lessons, and this is very true of the power politics path to rivalry. This path happens over and over again and shows no signs of ebbing in the system.

The other issue for rivalry linkages is that security ties can drag one state into a rivalry. Who would have predicted that after 1990, the United States would engage Iraq in a twenty-three-year battle resulting in two wars, the loss of tens of thousands of lives, and increased perceptions of hatred in the Middle East towards the United States, all due to the linkage between British security interests and American interests? Chapter 6 demonstrates this process well, and linkages are likely a key part of the explanation for why some rivalries exist.

Once a rivalry becomes locked in, it becomes part of the national security culture of a state. The culture of rivalry endures and is tough to terminate when the entire security apparatus is directed towards a rival, public opinion is fixated on the problem, and real grievances become tough to dislodge through reason. Rivalry then becomes part of the normal foreign policy of a state, an assumed process that should never be assumed.

It should also be clear that all social processes are either additive or interactive. No single event can cause an outcome to occur. In social reality, events mix and combine to produce outcomes. Here I have laid out the most likely path to rivalry for a specific set of states, those states that utilized power politics processes. Table 5.8 in Chapter 5 is important in that it shows how each event on the road to rivalry adds to the probability the rivalry outcome will occur. When alliances, mutual military buildups, territorial disputes, and major powers are present, the probability of rivalry for this path is 0.884. There are likely other paths to rivalry and other variables that are important in explaining the event; it is hoped that others suggest their own paths towards rivalry so the problem can be minimized in the system.

SUMMARY

In explaining the origins of rivalries, the steps-to-rivalry theory is more precise than Diehl and Goertz's (2000) political shock explanation since political shocks are too general to account for the development of rivalry in most cases. The steps-to-rivalry theory builds on Hensel's (1996) model of evolutionary development within rivalries in that rivalry is a process born out of an accumulation of events and tactics to lead states into the situation. This theory represents both a refinement of the Vasquez (1993) steps-to-war theory and an extension of the rivalry as an evolutionary process idea that Hensel (1996) developed early on. Rivals do not really evolve for their entire life span; likely the main developmental influences occur early in the life of a rivalry, and then these states lock into a long-term hostile relationship.

Chapter 3 determined that politically relevant alliances are probabilistic conditions that predict rivalry. Relevant alliances are "almost always" sufficient conditions of for rivalry. They come early and also increase the probability of rivalry. Mutual military buildups are probabilistic sufficient conditions of rivalry, but the timing of the event is unclear and buildups may not come early in the process. Some mutual military buildups are observed in pairs of states with few disputes (one or two). It is likely that these mutual military buildups drive the pair of states to war, settling any outstanding issues and preventing the occurrence of rivalry.

Chapter 5 outlined how territorial disputes increase the probability of rivalry outcomes. More importantly, in combination, the factors of relevant alliances, mutual military buildups, major powers, and territorial disputes dramatically increase the probability rivalry. Each of these factors can now be added to what we know about rivalry to this point. The following lists the factors that are now known to be associated with rivalry.

Factors Associated with Rivalry Development including the Steps-to-Rivalry

1. Absence of a Democratic Dyad (Hensel, Goertz, and Diehl 2000).
2. Participation of Newly Independent States (DiCicco 2002; Goertz and Diehl 1995).
3. Territorial Disputes (Vasquez and Leskiw 2001; Chapter 5).

What Do We Know about Rivalry Now? 145

4. Escalating Bargaining Demands (Hensel 1996; Leng 2000; Chapter 6).
5. Rival Dyads are Dissatisfied Powers (Maoz and Mor 2002; Chapter 6).
6. Militarized Response to Initial Dispute (Hensel and Diehl 1994; Chapter 6).
7. Stalemate Outcomes during a Rivalry Are Likely to Make Rivalries "Endure" (Goertz, Jones, and Diehl 2005).
8. Politically Relevant Alliances Increase the Probability of Rivalry (Chapter 3 and 5).
9. Mutual Military Buildups Increase the Probability of Rivalry (Chapter 3 and 5).
10. Politically Relevant Alliances Occur Early in the Life of a Rivalry (Chapter 4).
11. Military Buildups Tend to Occur during the Middle Stages of Rivalry (Chapter 4).
12. Linkages between Different Rivalries Can Spark New Rivalries (Chapter 6).
13. In Combination, the Factors of Relevant Alliances, Mutual Military Buildups, Major Powers, and Territorial Disputes Increase the Probability of Rivalry (Chapter 5).

POLICY OPTIONS

This project demonstrates that power politics strategies lead a state down a path to rivalry, which is the most deadly form of relations between states. The relations between a rivalry pair are always contentious and almost always dangerous. There are very few stable and managed rivalries with a low probability of war. The relevant policy advice would be to avoid a power politics response towards a potential rival so that a state is not sucked into this situation. Rivalry situations are counterproductive to the natural course of state politics; cooperation is the norm, and the concerns coming from internal situations should override external concerns.

There is a path to rivalry and a path out of rivalry. By avoiding the typical responses to threatening situations, one can avoid the more drastic situation of rivalry. At first, I thought policy advice for this project was limited, but time has since proven me wrong due to the continued development of rivalry in situations like Iraq versus the United States or Sudan versus South Sudan. Chapter 6 is a response to this dilemma. In the post-9/11 world, it seemed that terrorism reduction and low-intensity conflict would be the norm. Instead, the international system is still dominated by state-to-state interactions. Rivalry matters and will continue to matter in the system as long as states behave as traditional states.

The concept of rivalry can be extended to many different forms of analysis and political thought. Thies (2005) uses the concept to uncover how in

146 *Becoming Rivals*

the absence of war, violence still leads to the development of states in Latin America. Rivalry can increase state capacity, but it is clear that this is not the best path of development. There are better ways for a state to build. Competition might work in some cases, but in general it is counterproductive to the mission of a state as it develops, grows, or tries to sustain its existence in the system.

It makes little use to analyze threats in the international system without utilizing the concept of rivalry. Empirically the United States and China might be in a rivalry, but qualitatively it is difficult to argue that these states have serious issue disagreements or show a tendency of escalating bargaining tactics. The United States and China are not engaged in a rivalry at the moment, and the security focus on this problem is misguided.

Rivalry is also useful as a case selection device. In understanding how cyberwar works in the system, it makes little sense to analyze the entire system of state-to-state interactions. Instead it makes more sense to focus on how cyberwar works in a rivalry situation (Valeriano and Maness 2012a). In focusing on regional security interests, it is advantageous to focus on rivalry dynamics because of the linkages between rivalries in regions. A key example might be the war between Argentina and the United Kingdom. Instead of focusing on the threat from the British, the Argentines had to first worry about the threat from their rivals, Chile, and thus did not devote the necessary amount of resources to the conduct of an ongoing war. The situation in Iraq during the weapons inspection regime shows a similar dynamic. One reason Hussein was not so forthcoming about weapons technology is because he did not want to appear weak to the Iranians.

Policy makers should be more cognizant of the factor of rivalry. It will hone analysis and provide the context under which conflict, cooperation, and reconciliation should really be discussed. I have done this in other work examining the process of Russia's post–Cold War foreign policy choices, in the examination of cyberwar, and in the examination of the Latin American state system. Rivalry as an outcome to be explained, as a process to examine, or as a case selection device should be a critical part of the study of international relations, security studies, and foreign policy.

FUTURE RESEARCH

This book is meant to provide a comprehensive guide to research on the development of rivalry. Unfortunately, research on the origins of rivalry is still in an early phase. There is much to do and much to accomplish in the field of rivalry studies. Here I have outlined the power politics path to rivalry, and, as I have written in a different place (Vasquez and Valeriano

2010), there are many paths to outcomes, the power politics path being the most common. Here I explain a specific path to rivalry, but there are other paths that need to be investigated.

The path outlined here includes states that use typical foreign policy practices outlined by power politics scholars. When threatened, they fight back and attempt to scare the enemy off. This almost never works in reality, and instead the outcome tends to be prolonged rivalry rather that satiability and peace. When a state is challenged with a territorial dispute, the most likely outcome is the development of alliance systems, explosions in military budgets, linkages with other partners, and escalating threats to achieve the necessary ends. All these factors promote rivalry rather than reduce its occurrence.

Other paths to rivalry might include the cultural perspective, economic rivalry, and rivalries born fighting at statehood. These are likely rivalries that have been developing since the start of civilizations. These ancient cultural rivalries transform into state-to-state rivalries with few specific reasons beyond ancient enmity. The dispute between Iraq and Iran is an example of this. While they did have a territorial dispute, it is more likely that the real trigger to the rivalry lies in the dispute between the Persians and Shiites, on one hand, and the Arabs and Sunnis on the other. Another example is the dispute between the Hutu and Tutsi in Rwanda, now extending to the Democratic Republic of the Congo versus Rwanda. Cultural hatreds can be just as dangerous as power politics tactics. Territorial issues are clearly present, but the trigger to the events can come from cultural differences.

Another path might be rivalry that develops due to clashes in economic policies or systems. The clash between Capitalism and Communism is an example of this type of dispute. Yet, recent examples of this type of rivalry are truly just territorial or influence rivalries and not clearly about the types of economic system in use. The future might bring more policy rivalries due to such factors as disputes over how to tackle global warming or conflicts that erupt due to constrained energy supplies. It could also be that a new round of global depression will spark a new battle between socialist-populist regimes and Capitalist systems.

The final path to rivalry might be rivalries just born fighting. It is the placement of the states as they become states in the first place that leads to conflict because it upsets the status quo and territorial balance of power. Power politics tactics do not engender rivalry here, but simple location dynamics might explain these cases more than any sort of theory presented in this volume. The question that could be asked is: are Sudan and South Sudan developing rivals in a power politics sense or rivals because where South Sudan is located and the problems this causes for Sudan?

There might be other critical paths to rivalry. I hope others are encouraged by this volume to investigate and outline their own proposed path to rivalry. No single theory of action can explain the entire range of a process, and there is much more to be uncovered about the rivalry process.

LESSONS LEARNED

The predominant lesson I want the reader, scholar, or student to take away from this project is that power politics strategies are detrimental to the state in many ways. Conventionally, these actions represent the course of action a leader should take when encountering a foe in the international system. I find that this path, the path that follows the dictates of a power politics strategic culture, is detrimental to the health of a state. Power politics considerations become self-fulfilling prophecies in that they do not lead to security, but insecurity. Actions taken to ensure a state's security usually end up endangering a state rather than making it more secure.

Power politics considerations, whether they be through the use of escalating bargaining tactics, hostile demands, shows of force, the institution of alliances, or building up the military, lead to rivalry situations. They are prescriptions for constant conflict. They are also prescriptions to war. This path is tough to avoid since it is so easy to counter a threat with another threat or a display of force. It is only natural, according to learned behavior. Bad practices should be replaced with better options, but just what are those options?

Compromise, concessions, and cooperation are the true path to security. A state should be able to defend itself and also conduct offensive operations when necessary. However, a state should not use its last-resort options as the first-resort option when they encounter a foe in the system. When a bully manifests, it is best not to antagonize or enrage that actor. Rather it is important to find a way to come to some mutual agreement as to the course of security in a region. If an actor is uncooperative, work with other states to set up a system of norms that will punish offenders and ensure others do not learn positive lessons from the aggressor. Time and time again, the leaders of states fail to learn this lesson, and thus we are doomed to a constant system full of rivalries and aggressive actors who learn the wrong lessons and continue to spread those lessons to others.

Rivalry herein has been presented as a process. The stages of rivalry development need to be taken into account in any analysis of formation of rivals. One cannot look at severe or famous rivals alone but must also investigate the factors present in developing rivals and isolated conflicts to understand the process, or the disease.

I have argued that power politics strategies are dangerous precedents in international interactions. Those pairs of states that use power politics practices against each other are likely to become dangerous rivals. States should avoid threatening actions because they are likely to lead to the security dilemma and rivalry. Those states that are involved in rivalry are the most likely dyads to become involved in war. According to the research presented here, to avoid war, one must avoid rivalry in the first place. Suppressing the urge to use power politics to respond to threatening situations is the path towards nonviolent conflict in the international system.

Notes

NOTES TO CHAPTER 1

1. David E. Sanger and Choe Sang-Hun, "North Korea Cuts All Ties with South Korea," *New York Times*, May 25, 2010.
2. There are few international situations that cannot be explained by rivalry or lack the influence of rivalry. Most terrorist or colonial-type conflicts tend to lack the direct influence of interstate rivalry, yet these processes are influenced by internal or ethnic rivalries. This research will not attempt to explain the onset of internal or nonstate actor rivalries, yet many of theories and ideas presented herein can be applied to these processes.
3. Rivalry cannot explain why conflicts occur without examining the issues that caused escalation and initiation of the rivalry in the first place.
4. The existence of national plans, or grand strategy, may be a critical element of rivalry, yet this factor is left for future investigations. It is difficult to quantify or even qualify the existence of a grand strategy (see Valeriano 2003 for more on this topic). Most grand strategies are either secret or publicly benign so as to not provoke reactions.
5. Levels of analysis concerns are important in terms of understanding where solutions to the problems or causes might come from, but in terms of specifying agendas the construct should be replaced with different ideas.

NOTES TO CHAPTER 2

1. There does not appear to be a stable pattern for all rivals. Some experience war early and settle into a managed period of conflict; others continue to experience frequent wars and serious disputes long after onset (Klein, Goertz, and Diehl 2006).
2. Bennett (1997) identifies rivalry according to a connection of issues at stake. While this might be important for identifying early rivals, most of international history demonstrates that hatred during a rivalry runs so deep that even settling the issue might not terminate a rivalry.
3. An MID is a threat, display, or use of force (Ghosn, Palmer, and Bremer 2004) condoned by government actors. Past efforts to code and categorize MIDs (Gochman and Maoz 1984; Jones, Bremer, and Singer 1996) have had a large impact on the study of rivalry as a field. Without the existence of the MID data set scholars would be hard-pressed to identify who fights so often in the system.
4. Early efforts to code and specify rivals or protracted conflicts include efforts by Brecher and colleagues, Wayman, and Maoz (Brecher 1984; Brecher and Wilkenfeld 2000; Gochman and Maoz 1984; Wayman and Jones 1991).

5. The remaining criticism would be how does one know when a dispute is not part of the rivalry context? Would not all disputes during a rivalry be folded into the greater issue of us versus them? While the elimination of certain cases is certainly justified, these changes do mean that it is now virtually impossible to replicate the data set completely.
6. Another unfortunate consequence of the new data set the scholars are right to point out is that the prior data sets lead others to focus only on enduring rivals and not proto-rivals, which are just as important. This change also does simplify analysis since the dependent variable is now binary.
7. Disputes must come within eleven years of the first dispute to be connected to a "rivalry." Later disputes much come within twelve years after the second dispute and up to fifteen years after the fifth.
8. The rivalry between Vietnam and the Republic of Vietnam (1960–1975) is included as a rivalry because of the long war between the two parties.
9. Unfortunately, at the time of writing the ICOW data set that codes issues and their salience outside of disputes is incomplete and only restricted Western Europe and the Americas (Hensel 2001; Hensel et al. 2008).
10. This is in reference to various restaurants in the United States changing the name of French fries to Freedom fries during the French opposition to a potential war in Iraq in 2003.
11. Multiple issues are likely to make rivalries endure and persist, but it is unclear if the number of issues at stake has an impact on the development of a rivalry.
12. This is not to say that alliances cannot also come after the activation of a rivalry. Alliances tend to be short-lived according to treaty provisions. They need new consultations and ratification to remain active so new alliances or reformulated alliances after the development of rivalry can also account for the onset of war. Alliances likely cause both rivalry and war.
13. Some scholars (Diehl and Crescenzi 1998; Goertz and Diehl 1993) suggest that arms races can only occur after the onset of rivalry. This is a question that needs more investigation. Later chapters will conduct this experiment to find the impact of arms-racing behavior on conflict processes.
14. Diehl and Goertz (2000) also investigate rivalry linkages, but they study how rivals are linked to other parties through alliances or mutual engagement in the same dispute. Not how some disputes will influence new disputes.
15. In general, rivals should only develop between near equals (Vasquez 1993). Others find that this is not universally true (Colaresi, Rasler, and Thompson 2008; Diehl and Goertz 2000). There will be some rivals that develop dispute vast inequalities in terms of military capabilities, but these rivalries will not occur with great frequency and, when they do, they tend to be driven by the demands of domestic political concerns (as will be shown in the case examination of the U.S.–Iraq rivalry).

NOTES TO CHAPTER 3

1. All probabilities in this manuscript were generated using the SPost command set in Stata 11.

NOTES TO CHAPTER 5

1. Contiguity is used as a control variable to rule out the possibility that the occurrence of rivalries is better predicted by measures of contiguity. It is also used to

show that territorial disputes, even when controlling for the location of a pair of states, are more apt to lead a state to become involved in rivalry and war.

NOTES TO CHAPTER 6

1. Faisal later became King Faisal I, who at first was given Syria, which was later claimed by the French, and who was then given Iraq by the British.
2. Department of Justice (DOJ), February 8, 2004, Interview Session 2—Saddam Hussein. The DOJ interviews of Hussein are used throughout this chapter. For the sake of readability, the statements are taken as first-person direct statements rather than the transcribed and translated accounts they likely are.
3. Ibid.
4. DOJ, February 24, 2004, Interview Session 9—Saddam Hussein.
5. Ibid.
6. Ibid.
7. Ibid.
8. Ibid.
9. DOJ, February 13, 2004, Interview Session 4—Saddam Hussein.
10. DOJ, February 24, 2004, Interview Session 9—Saddam Hussein.
11. Ibid.
12. DOJ, February 13, 2004, Interview Session 4—Saddam Hussein.
13. Ibid.
14. DOJ, February 24, 2004, Interview Session 9—Saddam Hussein.
15. DOJ, February 13, 2004, Interview Session 4—Saddam Hussein.
16. DOJ, February 27, 2004, Interview Session 10—Saddam Hussein.
17. DOJ, February 13, 2004, Interview Session 4—Saddam Hussein.
18. Ibid.
19. Ibid.
20. See http://www.pbs.org/frontlineworld/stories/iraq501/events_uprising.html (accessed 7/19/2012).
21. DOJ, March 3, 2004, Interview Session 11—Saddam Hussein.
22. DOJ, March 11, 2004, Interview Session 13—Saddam Hussein.
23. DOJ, March 13, 2004, Interview Session 14—Saddam Hussein.
24. See http://www.bbc.co.uk/news/world-middle-east-12004115 (accessed 7/11/2012).
25. See http://articles.cnn.com/2002-09-27/politics/bush.war.talk_1_homeland-security-senators-from-both-parties-republican-phil-gramm?_s=PM: ALLPOLITICS (accessed 7/11/2012).
26. See http://www.egyptindependent.com/news/iraq-faces-painful-legacy-mass-graves (accessed 7/14/2012).
27. See http://www.un.org/Depts/unscom/Chronology/chronologyframe.htm (accessed 7/11/2012).
28. DOJ, February 13, 2004, Interview Session 4—Saddam Hussein.
29. Ibid.
30. DOJ, June 11, 2004, Interview Session Reflections—Saddam Hussein.
31. See http://www.cnn.com/WORLD/9802/23/iraq.deal.update.4am/index.html (accessed 7/11/2012).
32. See http://news.bbc.co.uk/2/hi/middle_east/2544691.stm (accessed 7/11/2012).
33. DOJ, February 13, 2004, Interview Session 4—Saddam Hussein.
34. See http://articles.philly.com/2004-04-23/news/25364015_1_weapons-inspector-international-policy-attitudes-new-poll (accessed 7/13/2012).

35. DOJ, June 11, 2004, Interview Session Reflections—Saddam Hussein.
36. DOJ, February 13, 2004, Interview Session 4—Saddam Hussein.
37. See http://articles.cnn.com/2003-01-10/us/wbr.smoking.gun_1_smoking-gun-nuclear-weapons-hans-blix?_s=PM:US (accessed 7/12/2012).
38. DOJ, February 13, 2004, Interview Session 4—Saddam Hussein.
39. See http://www.cbsnews.com/2100-500249_162-520830.html (accessed 7/13/2012).
40. Data on military expenditures come from the Correlates of War project's National Material Capabilities data set, updated (Singer, Bremer, and Stuckey 1972; Singer 1987). A conventional military buildup is an 8 percent increase over three years. Here I just use the 8 percent figure since the data are not sustained for a long period of time.
41. See http://www.nytimes.com/2003/03/17/world/threats-responses-foreign-policy-long-winding-road-diplomatic-dead-end.html?pagewanted=all&src=pm (accessed 7/19/2012).
42. See http://www.nytimes.com/2003/03/17/world/threats-responses-foreign-policy-long-winding-road-diplomatic-dead-end.html?pagewanted=all&src=pm (accessed 7/19/2012).
43. See http://www.washingtonpost.com/wp-dyn/content/article/2008/01/25/AR2008012503052.html (accessed 7/14/2012).

References

Baram, Amatzia. (2000) "The Effect of Iraqi Sanctions: Statistical Pitfalls and Responsibility." *Middle East Journal* 54 (2). 194–223

Bennett, D. Scott. (1997) "Democracy, Regime Change and Rivalry Termination." *International Interactions* 22 (4): 369–397.

Bennett, D. Scott, Christopher Baker, and Allan C. Stam. (2002) "The Extent of Selection Effects in the Study of International Conflict." Paper presented at annual meeting of Peace Science Society International, Tucson, Arizona, November 1–3.

Bennett, D. Scott, and Allan C. Stam. (2004) *The Behavioral Origins of War*. Ann Arbor: University of Michigan Press.

Berger, Peter L., and Thomas Luckmann. (1966) *The Social Construction of Reality*. New York: Doubleday.

Brecher, Michael. (1984) "International Crises and Protracted Conflicts." *International Interactions* 11 (3–4): 237–297.

Brecher, Michael, and Jonathan Wilkenfeld. (1997) *A Study of Crisis*. Ann Arbor: University of Michigan Press.

———. (2000) *A Study of Crisis*. Ann Arbor: University of Michigan Press.

Brecher, Michael, Jonathan Wilkenfeld, and Sheila Moser. (1988a) *Crises in the Twentieth Century*. 1st ed. Oxford: Pergamon Press.

———. (1988b) *Handbook of International Crises*. 1st ed. Oxford Pergamon Press.

Bremer, Stuart A. (1992) "Dangerous Dyads: Conditions Affecting the Likelihood of Interstate War." *Journal of Conflict Resolution* 36:178–197.

———. (2000) "Who Fights Whom, When, Where, and Why?" in *What Do We Know about War?* ed. John A. Vasquez. Lanham, MD: Rowman and Littlefield.

Bremer, Stuart A., and Thomas Cusack. (1995) *The Process of War*. Amsterdam: Gordon.

Butler, Richard. (2003) "The Inspections and the U.N.: The Blackest of Comedies." In *The Iraq War Reader*, ed. M. L. Sifry and C. Cerf. New York: Transaction.

Byman, Daniel. (2000–2001) "After the Storm: U.S. Policy toward Iraq Since 1991." *Political Science Quarterly* 115 (4): 493–516.

Colaresi, Michael P. (2001) "Shocks to the System: Great Power Rivalry and the Leadership Long Cycle." *Journal of Conflict Resolution* 45 (5): 569–593.

———. (2005) *Scare Tactics: The Politics of International Rivalry*. Syracuse: Syracuse University Press.

Colaresi, Michael P., K. Rasler, and W. R. Thompson. (2008) *Strategic Rivalries in World Politics: Position, Space, and Conflict Escalation*. Cambridge: Cambridge University Press.

References

Colaresi, Michael, and William R. Thompson. (2002) "Strategic Rivals, Protracted Conflict, and Crisis Behavior." *Journal of Peace Research* 39 (3): 263–287.

Cornwell, Derekh, and Michael Colaresi. (2002) "Holy Trinities, Rivalry Termination, and Conflict." *International Interactions* 29 (1): 325–353.

Cusack, Thomas, and Wolf-Dieter Eberwein. (1982) "Prelude to War: Incidence, Escalation, and Intervention in International Disputes." *International Interactions* 9 (1): 9–28.

DiCicco, Johnathan M. (2002) "Born under a Bad Sign: State Independence and the Origins of Persistent International Rivalries." Paper presented at the Annual Meeting of the International Studies Association, March, 2002. New Orleans, LA.

Diehl, Paul. (1985) "Contiguity and Military Escalation in Major Power Rivalries, 1816–1980." *Journal of Politics* 47:1203–1211.

Diehl, Paul, and Mark Crescenzi. (1998) "Reconfiguring the Arms Race–War Debate." *Journal of Peace Research* 35 (1): 111–118.

Diehl, Paul, and Gary Goertz. (2000) *War and Peace in International Rivalry*. Ann Arbor: University of Michigan Press.

Dreyer, David R. (2010) "Issue Conflict Accumulation and the Dynamics of Strategic Rivalry." *International Studies Quarterly* 54 (3): 779–795.

Finlan, Alastair. (2003) *The Gulf War 1991*. London: Routledge.

Gartzke, Erik, and Michael Simon. (1999) "Hot Hand: A Critical Analysis of Enduring Rivalries." *Journal of Politics* 61 (3): 777–798.

Geller, Daniel S., and J. David Singer. (1998) *Nations at War: A Scientific Study of International Conflict*. Cambridge: Cambridge University Press.

George, Alexander L., and Andrew Bennett. (2005) *Case Studies and Theory Development in the Social Sciences, BCSIA Studies in International Security*. Cambridge, MA: MIT Press.

Ghosn, Faten, Glenn Palmer, and Stuart Bremer. (2004) "The MID3 Data Set, 1993–2001: Procedures, Coding Rules, and Description." *Conflict Management and Peace Science* (21): 133–154.

Gibler, Douglas. (1996) "Alliances That Never Balance: The Territorial Settlement Treaty." *Conflict Management and Peace Science* 15 (1): 75–97.

———. (1997) "Control the Issues, Control the Conflict: The Effects of Alliances That Settle Territorial Issues on Interstate Rivalries." *International Interactions* 22 (4): 341–368.

———. (2000) "Why Some Alliances Cause War, and Why Other Alliances Cause Peace: An Investigation into the Multiple Effects of Alliance Formation." In *What Do We Know About War?* ed. J. Vasquez. Lanham, MD: Rowan and Littlefield Press.

———. (2007) "Bordering on Peace: Democracy, Territorial Issues, and Conflict." *International Studies Quarterly* 51 (3): 509–532.

———. (2009) *International Military Alliances from 1648 to 2000*. Washington, DC: Congressional Quarterly Press.

Gibler, Douglas M., Toby Rider, and Marc Hutchinson. (2005) "Taking Arms Against a Sea of Troubles: Interdependent Racing and the Likelihood of Conflict in Rival States." *Journal of Peace Research* 42 (2):131–147.

Gibler, Douglas M., and Meredith Sarkees. (2004) "Measuring Alliances: The Correlates of War Formal interstate Alliance Data set, 1816–2000." *Jounral of Peace Research* 41(2): 211–222.

Gibler, Douglas, and John Vasquez. (1998) "Uncovering the Dangerous Alliances, 1495–1980." *International Studies Quarterly* 42:785–807.

Gochman, Charles, and Zeev Maoz. (1984) "Militarized Interstate Disputes, 1816–1976: Procedures, Patterns, and Insights." *Journal of Conflict Resolution* 28 (December): 585–616.

Goertz, G., and Paul Diehl. (1992) "The Empirical Importance of Enduring Rivalries." *International Interactions* 18 (2): 151–163.

———. (1993) "Enduring Rivalries: Theoretical Constraints and Empirical Patterns." *International Studies Quarterly* 37:147–171.

———. (1995) "The Initiation and Termination of Enduring Rivalries: The Impact of Political Shocks." *American Journal of Political Science* 39:30–52.

Goertz, G., Bradford Jones, and P. Diehl. (2005) "Maintenance Processes in International Rivalries." *Journal of Conflict Resolution* 49 (5): 742–769.

Guetzkow, Harold. (1950) "Long Range Research in International Relations." *American Perspective* 4:421–440.

Harvey, Frank P., and Patrick James. (2009) "Deterrence and Compellence in Iraq, 1991–2003." In *Complex Deterrence: Strategy in a Global Age*, ed. T. V. Paul, P. Morgan and J. J. Wirtz. Chicago: University of Chicago Press.

Hensel, Paul. (1996) "The Evolution of Interstate Rivalry." PhD dissertation, University of Illinois at Urbana-Champaign.

———. (1998a) "The Evolution of the Franco-German Rivalry." In *Great Power Rivalries*, ed. W. Thompson. Columbia: University of South Carolina Press.

———. (1998b) "Interstate Rivalry and the Study of Militarized Conflict." In *Conflict in World Politics: Advances in the Study of Crisis, War and Peace*, ed. F. Harvey and B. Mor. New York: St. Martin's Press.

———. (1999) "An Evolutionary Approach to the Study of Interstate Rivalry." *Conflict Management and Peace Science* 17 (Fall): 175–206.

———. (2000) "Territory: Theory and Evidence on Geography and Conflict." In *What Do We Know about War?* ed. J. Vasquez. Lanham, MD: Rowman and Littlefield.

———. (2001) "Contentious Issues and World Politics: The Management of Territorial Claims in the Americas, 1816–1992." *International Studies Quarterly* 45 (1): 81–109.

Hensel, Paul, and P. Diehl. (1994) "It Takes Two to Tango: Nonmilitarized Response in International Disputes." *Journal of Conflict Resolution* 38 (3): 479–506.

Hensel, Paul, Gary Goertz, and Paul Diehl. (2000) "The Democratic Peace and Rivalries." *Journal of Politics* 62 (4): 1173–1188.

Hensel, Paul R., Sara McLaughlin Mitchell, Thomas E. Sowers II, and Clayton L. Thyne. (2008) "Bones of Contention: Comparing Territorial, Maritime, and River Issues." *Journal of Conflict Resolution* 52 (1): 117–143.

Hersh, Seymour M. (2003) "Did Iraq Try to Assassinate Ex-President Bush in 1993? A Case Not Closed." In *The Iraq War Reader*, ed. M. L. Sifry and C. Cerf. New York: Touchstone.

Herz, John. (1950) "Idealist Internationalism and the Security Dilemma." *World Politics* 2 (2): 157–180.

Hewitt, J. Joseph. (2005) "A Crises-Density Formulation for Identifying Rivalries." *Journal of Peace Research* 42 (2): 183–200.

Horn, Michael Dean. (1987) "Arms Races and the International System." PhD dissertation, University of Rochester.

Huth, Paul. (1996a) "Enduring Rivalries and Territorial Disputes, 1950–1990." *Conflict Management and Peace Science* 15 (1): 7–41.

———. (1996b) *Standing Your Ground: Territorial Disputes and International Conflict*. Ann Arbor: University of Michigan Press.

James, Patrick. (1988) *Crisis and War*. Kingston: McGill-Queen's University Press.

Jervis, Robert. (1978) "Cooperation under the Security Dilemma." *World Politics* 30 (January): 167–214.

Johnston, Alastair Iain. (1995) *Cultural Realism: Strategic Culture and Grand Strategy in Chinese History*: Princeton, NJ: Princeton University Press.

Jones, Daniel, Stuart Bremer, and J. David Singer. (1996) "Militarized Interstate Disputes, 1816–1992: Rationale, Coding Rules, and Empirical Patterns." *Conflict Management and Peace Science* 15 (2): 163–213.

Klein, James P., G. Goertz, and P. Diehl. (2006) "The New Rivalry Dataset: Procedures and Patterns." *Journal of Peace Research* 43 (3): 331–348.

Knightley, Phillip. (2003) "Imperial Legacy." In *The Iraq War Reader*, ed. M. L. Sifry and C. Cerf. New York: Touchstone.

Leng, Russell. (1983) "When Will They Ever Learn? Coercive Bargaining in Recurrent Crises." *Journal of Conflict Resolution* 27 (3): 379–419.

———. (1993) *Interstate Crisis Behavior, 1816–1980: Realism Versus Reciprocity.* Cambridge: Cambridge University Press.

———. (2000) *Bargaining and Learning in Recurring Crises: The Soviet–American, Egyptian–Israeli, and Indo–Pakistani Rivalries.* Ann Arbor: University of Michigan Press.

Levy, Jack. (1989) "The Diversionary Theory of War: A Critique." In *Handbook of War Studies*, ed. M. I. Midlarsky. London: Unwin-Hyman.

———. (1981) "Alliance Formation and War Behavior: An Analysis of the Great Powers, 1495–1975." *Journal of Conflict Resolution* 25 (December): 581–613.

———. (1983) *War in the Modern Great Power System, 1495–1975.* Lexington: University Press of Kentucky.

Mansbach, Richard W., and John A. Vasquez. (1981) *In Search of Theory: A New Paradigm for Global Politics.* New York: Columbia University Press.

Maoz, Z. (2004) "Pacifism and Fightaholism in International Politics: A Structural History of National and Dyadic Conflict, 1816–1992." *International Studies Review* 6 (2): 107–133.

Maoz, Zeev, and Ben Mor. (2002) *Bound by Struggle: The Strategic Evolution of Enduring International Rivalries.* Ann Arbor: University of Michigan Press.

Mazaheri, Nimah. (2010) "Iraq and the Domestic Political Effects of Econmic Sanctions." *Middle East Journal* 64 (2): 253–268.

Mearsheimer, John. (2001) *Tragedy of Great Power Politics.* New York: W. W. Norton.

McHugh, Kelly. (2010) "Bush, Blair, and the War in Iraq: Alliance Politics and the Limits of Influence." *Political Science Quarterly* 125 (3): 465–491.

Miller, Judith, and Laurie Mylroie. (2003) "The Rise of Saddam Hussein." In *The Iraq War Reader*, ed. M. L. Sifry and C. Cerf. New York: Touchstone.

Mitchell, Sara McLaughlin, and Brandon Prins. (2004) "Rivalry and Diversionary Uses of Force." *Journal of Conflict Resolution* 48 (6): 937–961.

Mor, Ben. (1997) "Peace Initiatives and Public Opinion: The Domestic Context of Conflict Resolution." *Journal of Peace Research* 34 (2):197–215.

Morgenthau, Hans J. (1948) *Politics among Nations.* New York: Knopf.

———. (1960) *Politics among Nations: The Struggle for Power and Peace.* 3rd ed. New York: Knopf.

Most, Benjamin, and Harvey Starr. (1989) *Inquiry, Logic, and International Politics.* Columbia: University of South Carolina Press.

Most, Benjamin, Harvey Starr, and Randolph Siverson. (1989) "The Logic and Study of the Diffusion of International Conflict." In *Handbook of War Studies*, ed. M. Midlarsky. Boston: Unwin Hyman.

National Commission on Terrorist Attacks upon the United States (Philip Zelikow, executive director; Bonnie D. Jenkins, counsel; Ernest R. May, senior advisor). (2004) *The 9/11 Commission Report.* New York: W. W. Norton.

Prins, Brandon, and Ursula Daxecker. (2007) "Committed to Peace: Liberal Institutions and the Termination of Rivalry." *British Journal of Political Science* 38:17–43.

Pollack, Kenneth. (2002) "Next Stop Baghdad?" *Foreign Affairs*, March/April, 32–47.

———. (2003) "Can We Really Deter a Nuclear-Armed Saddam?" In *The Iraq War Reader*, ed. M. L. Sifry and C. Cerf. New York: Touchstone.

Putnam, Robert. (1988) "Diplomacy and Domestic Politics: The Logic of Two-Level Games." *International Organization* 42 (3): 427–460.

Reed, William. (2000) "A Unified Statistical Model of Conflict Onset and Escalation." *American Journal of Political Science* 44 (1): 84–93.

———. (2002) "Selection Effects and World Politics Research." *International Interactions* 28 (1): 1–3.

Richardson, Lewis F. (1960) *Arms and Insecurity*. Pacific Grove, CA: Boxwood Press.

Ruggie, John Gerard. (1993) "Territoriality and Beyond: Problematizing Modernity in International Relations." *International Organization* 47:139–174.

———. (1998) *Constructing the World Polity: Essays on International Institutionalization*. New York: Routledge.

Saideman, Stephan, and R. William Ayres. (2008) *For Kin or Country: Xenophobia, Nationalism, and War*. New York: Columbia University Press.

Sample, Susan. (1996) "Arms Races and the Escalation of Disputes to War." PhD dissertation, Vanderbilt University.

———. (1997) "Arms Races and Dispute Escalation: Resolving the Debate." *Journal of Peace Research* 34 (1): 7–22.

———. (1998) "Military Buildups, War, and Realpolitik: A Multivariate Model." *Journal of Conflict Resolution* 42 (2): 156–175.

———. (2002) "The Outcomes of Military Buildups: Minor States vs. Major Powers." *Journal of Peace Research* 39 (6): 669–692.

Sarkees, Meredieth R., and Frank W. Wayman. (2009) *Resort to War 1816–2007*. New York: CQ Press.

Schroeder, Paul. (1994) *The Transformation of European Politics, 1763–1848*. New York: Oxford University Press.

Senese, Paul D. (2005) "Territory, Contiguity, and International Conflict: Assessing a New Joint Explanation." *American Journal of Political Science* 49 (4): 769–779.

Senese, Paul D., and John Vasquez. (2003) "A Unified Explanation of Territorial Conflict: Testing the Impact of Sampling Bias, 1919–1992." *International Studies Quarterly* 47 (2): 275–298.

———. (2005) "Assessing the Steps to War." *British Journal of Political Science* 35:607–633.

———. (2008) *The Steps to War: An Empirical Analysis*. Princeton: Princeton University Press.

Shawcross, William. (2004) *Allies: The U.S., Britain, Europe, and the War in Iraq*. New York: Public Affairs.

Sifry, Micah L., and Christopher Cerf. (2003) "The Glaspie Transcript: Saddam Meets the U.S. Ambassador." In *The Iraq War Reader*, ed. M. L. Sifry and C. Cerf. New York: Touchstone.

Signorino, C. S. (1999) "Strategic Interaction and the Statistical Analysis of International Conflict." *American Political Science Review* 93:279–298.

Simons, Anna. (2003) "The Death of Conquest." *National Interest* 3 (Spring): 41–49.

Singer, J. David. (1961) "The Level of Analysis Problem in International Relations." *World Politics* 14 (1): 77–92.

Singer, J. David. (1987) "Reconstructing the Correlates of War Dataset on Material Capabilities of States, 1816–1985." *International Interactions* 14:115–32.

Singer, J. David, Stuart A. Bremer, and John Stuckey. (1972) "Capability Distribution, Uncertainty, and Major Power War, 1820–1965." In *Peace, War, and Numbers*, ed. Bruce Russett. Beverly Hills, CA: Sage Publications.

Singer, J. David, and Melvin Small. (1968) "Alliance Aggregation and the Onset of War, 1815–1945." In *Quantative Politics: Insights and Evidence*, ed. J. D. Singer. New York: Free Press.
Small, Melvin, and J. David Singer. (1982) *Resort to Arms: International and Civil Wars, 1816–1980.* 2nd ed. Beverly Hills, CA: Sage.
Snyder, Glenn Herald. (1997) *Alliance Politics, Cornell Studies in Security Affairs.* Ithaca, NY: Cornell University Press.
Stevenson, D. (1988) *The First World War and International Politics.* Oxford: Oxford University Press.
———. (1996) *Armaments and the Coming of War: Europe, 1904–1914.* Oxford: Oxford University Press.
Stinnett, Douglas, and Paul Diehl. (2001) "The Path(s) to Rivalry: Behavioral and Structural Explanations of Rivalry Development." *Journal of Politics* 63 (3): 717–740.
Strange, Susan. (1996) *The Retreat of the State: The Diffusion of Power in the World Economy.* Cambridge: Cambridge University Press.
Thies, Cameron G. (2005) "War, Rivalry, and State Building in Latin America." *American Journal of Political Science* 49 (3): 451–465.
———. (2008) "The Construction of a Latin American Interstate Culture of Rivalry." *International Interactions* 34:231–257.
Thompson, William. (1995) "Principal Rivalries." *Journal of Conflict Resolution* 39 (2): 195–223.
———. (2001) "Identifying Rivals and Rivalries in World Politics." *International Studies Quarterly* 45:557–586.
Tilly, Charles. (1985) "War Making and State Making as Organized Crime." In *Bringing the State Back In*, ed. P. Evans, D. Rueschemeyer, and T. Skocpol. Cambridge: Cambridge University Press.
Tir, Jaroslav, and Paul Diehl. (2002) "Geographic Dimensions of Enduring Rivalries." *Political Geography* 21:263–286.
Valeriano, Brandon. (2003) "Steps-to-Rivalry: Power Politics and Rivalry Formation." PhD dissertation, Vanderbilt University.
———. (2009) "The Tragedy of Offensive Realism: Testing Aggressive Power Politics Models." *International Interactions* 35 (2): 179–206.
Valeriano, Brandon, and Christopher Leskiw. (2010) "Concerts of Action: Intergovernmental Organizations and the Dynamics of Interstate Rivalry." Unpublished Manuscript.
Valeriano, Brandon, and Ryan Maness. (2012a). "Persistent Enemies and Cybersecurity: The Future of Rivalry in an Age of Information Warfare." In *Cyber Challenges and National Security*, ed. D. Reveron. Washington, DC: Georgetown University Press.
———. (2012b) "Why Won't It Die? Rivalry Persistence and the Case of the United States and Russia." Presented at the Annual Meeting of the *International Studies Association*. March, San Diego, CA.
Valeriano, Brandon, and Victor Marin. (2010) "Causal Pathways to Interstate War: A Qualitative Comparative Analysis of the Steps to War Theory." *Josef Korbel Journal of Advanced International Studies* 2 (Summer): 1–26.
Valeriano, Brandon, and Matt Powers. (2010) "Complex Rivalries in World Politics." Unpublished Manuscript.
Valeriano, Brandon, Susan Sample, and Choong-Nam Kang. (2011) "What Motivates the Arming Process? The Internal and External Mechanisms for Military Buildups." Presented at the Annual meeting of the *International Studies Association*. March, Montreal, Canada.
Valeriano, Brandon, and John A. Vasquez. (2010) "Identifying and Classifying Complex Interstate Wars." *International Studies Quarterly.* 54: 561–582

Van Evera, Stephen. (1999) *Causes of war : power and the roots of conflict, Cornell studies in security affairs*. Ithaca: Cornell University Press.
Vasquez, John. (1983) *The Power of Power Politics: A Critique*. New Brunswick, NJ: Rutgers University Press.
———. (1998) *The Power of Power Politics: From Classical Realism to Neotraditionalism*. Cambridge: Cambridge University Press.
———. (1993) *The War Puzzle, Cambridge Studies in International Relations; 27*. Cambridge: Cambridge University Press.
———. (2000) "What Do We Know About War?" In *What Do We Know About War?*, edited by J. Vasquez. Lanham, Maryland: Rowan and Littlefield Press.
———. (2004) "The Probability of War, 1816–1992." *International Studies Quarterly* 48 (1): 1–27.
———. (2009) *The War Puzzle Revisited*. Cambridge: Cambridge University Press.
Vasquez, John, and Christopher S. Leskiw. (2001) "The Origins and War-Proneness of International Rivalries." *Annual Review of Political Science* 4:295–316.
Vasquez, John, and Brandon Valeriano. (2009) "Territory as a Source of Conflict and a Road to Peace." In *Sage Handbook on Conflict Resolution*, ed. J. Bercovitch, V. Kremenyuk, and I. W. Zartman. Beverly Hills: Sage Publications.
———. (2010) "Classification of Interstate Wars." *Journal of Politics* 72 (2): 292–309.
Waas, Murray. (2003) "What Washington Gave Saddam for Christmas." In *The Iraq War Reader*, ed. M. L. Sifry and C. Cerf. New York: Touchstone.
Walker, Thomas. (2001) "Hitting the Target: Alliances, Specific Threats and the Spiral to War." Paper presented at the Annual Meeting of the International Studies Associated, Chicago, IL, February 21–24.
Waltz, Kenneth. (1959) *Man, the State, and War: A Theoretical Analysis*. New York: Columbia University Press.
———. (1979) *Theory of International Politics*: Reading, MA: Addison-Wesley.
Wayman, Frank, and Daniel Jones. (1991) "Evolution of Conflict in Enduring Rivalries." Paper presented at Annual Meeting of International Studies Association, March, Vancouver, BC.
White House. (2002) *The National Security Strategy of the United States of America*. Washington, DC: White House.
Wendt, Alexander. (1999) *Social Theory of International Politics, Cambridge Studies in International Relations; 67*. Cambridge: Cambridge University Press.
Zizzo, D.J., and A.J. Oswald. (2001) "Are People Willing to Pay to Reduce Others' Incomes?" *Annales d'Economie et de Statistique* 63–64 (July–December): 39–62.

Index

9/11, 104–105, 118, 120, 127–129, 137

A
Addicted, 13
Afghanistan, 17, 18, 19, 21, 23, 105, 130
Amarah, 122
Albright, Madeline, 135
Albania, 17, 21, 22, 25
Algeria, 20
Al-Qaeda, 120, 128
Anan, Kofi, 127
Angola, 23, 26
Arab League, 110
Arab nationalism, 110
Argentina, 16, 18, 22, 24, 36, 146
Armenia, 17, 22, 23
Aspen, 114
Austria, 25
Austria-Hungry, 21, 22, 24, 25, 76, 84
Australia, 26, 76
Ayers, W., 6
Axis, 107, 109
Azerbaijan, 17, 22
Aziz, Tariq, 126–127

B
Baath, 107–108, 121
Bahrain, 23, 130
Baghdad, 114, 127
Baker, C., 49
Baker, J., 119
Bakr, 107
Balance of power, 66
Bangladesh, 17
Baram, A., 124
Basra, 122
Belize, 18
Belgium, 18, 19, 24

Bennett, A., 104
Bennett, S., 7, 49, 151
Berger, S., 31
Berlin, 76
Biology,
  Biological theory, 3
Blair, Tony, 129–130
Bolivia, 16, 20
Bosnia and Herzegovina, 20, 22, 122
Botswana, 19, 21
Brazil, 20, 24
Brecher, M., 27, 151
Bremer, S., 8, 34, 39, 43, 55, 94, 151, 154
Bulgaria, 18, 21, 22, 25, 74, 84
Burkina Faso, 25
Burns, Mr., 110
Burundi, 20, 26
Bush Administration, 106, 135
Bush Doctrine, 119–120
Bush, G.W., 124, 130
Bush, G.H., 113–115, 121, 124
Byman, D., 127

C
Capitalism, 147
Cambodia, 16, 18, 23
Cameroon, 17
Canada, 18, 19, 21, 117
Cerf, C., 112
Chad, 19, 25
Cheney, Dick, 135
Chile, 16, 18, 20, 24, 119, 146
China, 16, 17, 18, 19, 20, 21, 24, 25, 26, 74, 76–77, 80, 82, 84, 87, 146
Climate change, 2
Clinton, Bill, 124, 127, 129, 135
Coalition of the Willing, 135

164 Index

Colaresi, M., 6, 14, 26–29, 36, 43, 44, 100, 152
Cold War, 2, 12, 50, 56, 80, 89, 104, 105, 119, 131, 136, 146
  Post-, 117
Colorado, 114
Columbia, 17, 19, 22, 24
Communism, 147
Congo, 17, 23
Constructivist, 6, 30–33,
Correlates of War, 54, 94, 108, 114, 154
Costa Rica, 18, 22, 32
Cornwell, D., 29
Crescenzi, M., 73, 152
Croatia, 18, 20
Cuba, 16, 23, 119
Cusack, T., 8, 42
Cyberwar, 146
Cyprus, 17
Czech Republic, 20
Czechoslovakia, 24, 25

D

Deterrence, 12
Democratic Republic of Congo, 17, 18, 20, 23, 24, 26, 147
Denmark, 20
Deterrence, 37
Dexecker, U., 29
DiCicco, 144
Diehl, P., 2, 3, 5, 8, 14, 15, 26–29, 36, 48, 55, 59, 67, 69, 73, 93–94, 97, 99, 100–101, 103, 109, 139, 144–145, 151, 152
Disney, 105
Djibouti, 23
Dominican Republic, 21
Dreyer, D., 121

E

Eberwein, W., 42
Economic Rivalry, 147
Economic Sanctions, 123–124
Ecuador, 16, 17, 18, 24
Egypt, 16, 18, 19
El Salvador, 19, 21, 24
Endogeneity, 48–49
Erbil, 122, 125
Eritrea, 20, 23
Ethiopia, 2, 17, 20
Egypt, 20, 26
Europe, 39
Evolutionary, 28

F

Faisal, 106
Falklands, 36
Fear, 7
Finlan, A., 114
Finland, 74, 80, 131
France, 16, 17, 18, 19, 20, 21, 22, 24, 49, 76, 84–86, 129
  French, 106, 109, 117

G

Garztke, E., 45
Genetic, 7
Georgia, 19
George, A., 103
Germany, 16, 18, 19, 21, 24, 25, 49, 76, 78, 80, 83–86, 107, 129
German Democratic Republic, 22
German Federal Republic, 21, 22, 25, 129
Ghana, 17, 25
Ghosn, F., 34, 94, 151
Gibler, D., 37–40, 54, 55, 69, 73, 94, 129–131
Glaspie, A., 112–113
Globalization, 2
Gochman, C., 151
Goetz, G., 2, 5, 8, 14, 15, 26–29, 48, 55, 59, 67, 69, 93–94, 97, 99, 100–101, 103, 109, 144–145, 151, 152
Grand Strategy, 134–135, 151
Greece, 16, 18, 19, 22, 24, 25, 129
Guatemala, 18, 21, 24, 119
Guetzkow, H., 6
Gulf Cooperation Council, 131
Guinea, 22, 23, 25
Guyana, 18, 19

H

Haiti, 18, 21, 24
Harvey, F., 127
Hashemi, Ali Al, 106
Hatfields, 56
Hensel, P., 3, 28, 29, 31, 36, 139, 144–145, 152
Hersh, S., 124
Herz, J., 32, 39, 53, 105
Hewitt, J., 2, 27
Hitler, Adolf, 49
Hobbesian, 3
Honduras, 16, 19
Horn, M., 55, 60, 62–63
Hungary, 17, 22, 25, 74

Hussein, Saddam, 106–137, 142, 146, 153–154
Hutchinson, M., 39–40, 55
Huth, P., 36, 42

I

Iceland, 20, 22, 129
ICOW, 152
India, 2, 16, 17, 23, 24, 36, 41, 56, 105
Indonesia, 19, 23, 24, 26
Interstate Crises Behavior data set, 27
Intergovernmental Organizations (IGOs), 29
Iraq, 2, 16, 18, 19, 21, 23, 24, 25, 26, 42, 47, 97, 103–137, 140, 142–143, 145–147
Iraq-Iranian War, 109–110, 118, 132, 136–137
Iraq War, 8, 103–105, 106, 109, 111, 133, 135–136
Iran, 16, 17, 18, 19, 22, 24, 25, 42, 106–108, 122, 147
  Iranians, 107, 119, 146
Iran Contra Scandal, 108
Islands of Theory, 6–7
Israel, 16, 17, 18, 20, 112
  Israeli spies, 116, 127
Italy, 17, 19, 20, 21, 22, 24, 25, 76, 83–84, 129

J

James, P., 42, 127
Japan, 16, 17, 19, 20, 21, 23, 24, 76, 80, 81, 87
Jervis, R., 39, 53
Jones, B., 28, 145
Jones, D., 151
Johnston, A., 31
Jordan, 17, 18, 20

K

Kang, C., 39, 55, 60–63, 90, 94
Kashmir, 36
Kenya, 17, 23
Kosovo, 130
Kyrgyzstan, 23
Klein, J., 15, 26, 29, 48, 55, 59, 67, 94, 97, 100–101, 109, 151
Kirkuk, 122
Knightly, P., 106
Kosovo, 56
Kurds, 107, 115, 121–122
  Kurdish region, 125

Kuwait, 16, 108–116, 118–125, 129–135, 137, 140, 142

L

Laden, Osama bin, 120
Laos, 17, 23, 26
Latin America, 146
Latvia, 22
Lawrence, T.E., 106
Lebanon, 18, 26
Leng, R., 28, 40, 48, 145
Leskiw, C., 6, 29, 37, 93, 139, 144
Lesotho, 23
Levels of analysis, 7, 151
Levy, J., 31, 37
Liberia, 21, 23, 25
Libya, 17, 18, 19, 20, 23, 122
Lithuania, 22
Luckmann, T., 31

M

Macedonia, 21, 22
Machiavellian, 32
Malaysia, 21
Maldives, 36
Mali, 25
Maness, R., 56, 146
Mansbach, R., 31, 139
Maoz, Z., 13, 145, 151
Marin, V., 135
Marsh Arabs, 122
Mauritania, 25
Malaysia, 26
Mazaheri, N., 124
McCoys, 56
McHugh, K., 130
Mearsheimer, J., 40
Mexico, 16, 19
Miller, J., 107
Militarized Interstate Disputes (MIDs), 14–15, 26, 34, 48, 55, 74, 93–94, 151
Mitchell, S., 28
Moaz, Z., 28
Moldova, 25
Mongolia, 23
Mor, B., 28, 29, 145
Morgenthau, H., 8, 31, 32, 40
Morocco, 18, 20, 24, 25
Moser, S., 27
Most, B., 5
Mozambique, 26
Myanmar, 26
Mylroie, L., 107

N

Napoleon, 34, 117
Nasiriyyah, 122
National interest, 31
National Security Strategy, 135
Nazi, 107
Nepal, 23, 26
Netherlands, 19, 22, 24, 133
New World Order, 113
New York Times, 132
New Zealand, 26
Nicaragua, 16, 18, 19, 22, 23, 24
Nigeria, 17, 25
North Atlantic Treaty Organization (NATO), 37, 74, 76, 80, 112, 129, 131, 141
North Korea, 1, 16, 17, 20, 106, 135, 151
Norway, 16, 20, 25

O

Obama, Barack, 120
Oman, 23, 26, 130
Operation Desert Fox, 121–122, 127
Operation Desert Storm, 114
Operation Provide Comfort, 122
Operation Northern Watch, 122
Ottoman Caliphate, 106
Ottoman Empire, 106

P

Pakistan, 2, 16, 17, 41, 56, 105
Palmer, G., 34, 94
Papal States, 25
Papua New Guinea, 23
Paraguay, 16, 20
Philippines, 17, 21, 23, 76
Peter Pan, 105
Persian Gulf, 118, 129
 War, 107, 109, 111–112, 116, 119, 121–123, 125–126, 130, 133, 136, 137, 140
Peru, 16, 17, 18, 19, 22, 24
Poland, 20, 22, 25, 74, 129, 135
Political shock, 28
Pollack, K., 136
Portugal, 20, 21, 22, 24, 84
Powers, M., 35
Powell, Colin, 135–136
Powell Doctrine, 112
Prins, B., 28, 29
Prussia, 78, 84
Putnam, B., 29

Q

Qatar, 26, 130

R

Rasler, K., 6, 14, 26–29, 36, 43, 44, 100, 152
Reed, W., 48–49
Republic of China, 76
Republic of Vietnam, 18, 19, 26, 152
Revolutionary Command Council, 107
Rice, Condoleezza, 128, 135
Richardson, L., 38
Rider, T., 39–40, 55
Ritter, Scott, 127
Rivalry linkages, 41–43
Romania, 22, 24, 25, 74
Ruggie, J., 30
Rumsfeld, Donald, 105, 128, 135
Russia, 16, 17, 18, 19, 20, 21, 22, 24, 25, 75, 76, 79, 80–82, 84, 88, 124, 146
Russians, 56
Rwanda, 19, 23, 25, 26, 147

S

Saideman, S., 6
Sample, S., 38, 39–40, 55, 60–63, 70, 73, 90–91, 94, 131, 142
Sang-Hun, C, 151
Sanger, D., 151
Sarkees, M., 37, 54, 69, 94, 108, 113–114
Saudi Arabia, 19, 20, 21, 23, 26, 113–116, 120, 129–130, 140, 142
Saxony, 25
Scandinavian, 32
Schroeder, G., 37
Schwarzkopf, Norman, 129
Scud missiles, 115, 126
Security Dilemma, 12, 29, 31–33, 39, 53
Selection Effects, 48–49
Senegal, 21
Senese, P., 33, 36, 49, 66, 94
Sequencing, 8
Shatt al Arab waterway, 107
Shawcross, W., 130
Shiite, 107–108, 115, 121–122, 134, 147
Sierra Leone, 21, 23
Signorino, C., 48
Sifry, M., 112
Simon, M., 45

Simons, A., 117
Simpsons, 110
Singer, J.D., 7, 34, 37, 55, 154
Small, M., 34, 37
Snyder, G., 38
Solomon Islands, 23
Somalia, 2, 17, 23
South Africa, 18, 21, 23, 26
South Korea, 1, 16, 17, 21, 80, 151
South Sudan, 145, 147
Soviet Union, 12, 56, 105, 108
  Soviet, 80, 119, 129
Sri Lanka, 23
Spain, 17, 18, 19, 22, 24, 84
Sports, 11
Stam, A., 7, 49
Starr, H., 5
Stata, 152
Steps-to-rivalry model, 33–45
Steps-to-war theory, 33
Stevenson, D., 39
Stinnett, D., 29
Strange, S., 34
Stuckey, J., 55, 154
Sudan, 17, 18, 20, 23, 145, 147
Suleimaniyyah, 122
Sunni, 107, 147
Suriname, 19
Sweden, 21, 25
Syria, 16, 17, 18, 20, 23, 26, 56, 129

T

Taiwan, 16, 20, 21, 23, 26, 76
Tajikistan, 19
Tanzania, 20, 21
Territorial disputes, 6
Terror, War on, 56
Terrorist, 151
Thailand, 16, 17, 18, 21, 22
Thatcher, Margaret, 114
Theoretical incest, 50
Thies, C., 31, 145
Thompson, W., 5, 6, 13, 14, 26–29,
  34, 36, 39, 43–44, 47, 48, 67,
  93–94, 100, 103, 152
Tilfah, K., 107
Tilly, C., 34
Time, 5
Tir, J., 36, 139
Togo, 17, 135
Trinidad and Tobago, 20
Tunisia, 21, 23
Turkey, 16, 17, 18, 20, 21, 22, 23, 24,
  25, 84, 89, 122, 129

U

Uganda, 17, 19, 20, 21
Ukraine, 21
Union of Soviet Socialist Republics
  (USSR), 74, 76, 79, 80–82
United Arab Emirates, 21, 129–130
United Kingdom, 16, 17, 18, 19, 20,
  22, 24, 49, 76, 78–79, 80, 84,
  88, 89, 117, 129, 133–135, 137,
  146
  British, 106, 112–114, 118, 137, 143,
    146
  English, 109
United Nations, 43, 111–11, 115,
  126–128, 135–136
  Coalition, 114, 121
  United Nations Security Council, 43,
    123, 125–127
  UNSCR 660, 113
  UNSCR 661, 111
  UNSCR, 662, 111
  UNSCR 678, 113
  UNSCR 687, 111, 116–117, 125
  UNSCR 688, 122
  UNSCR 707, 126
  UNSCR 715, 126
  UNSCR 949, 125
  UNSCR 986, 124
United States, 2, 12, 16, 17, 18, 19,
  20, 21, 23, 24, 37, 42, 47, 56,
  74–77, 80, 97, 103–137, 140,
  142–143, 145–146
Uzbekistan, 18

V

Valeriano, B., 6–7, 29, 35, 36, 37, 39,
  40, 41, 55–56, 60–63, 67, 90,
  94, 97, 103, 119, 133, 135, 139,
  143, 146, 151
Van Evera, S., 39
Venezuela, 17, 18, 20, 22
Vietnam, 16, 18, 21, 23, 26, 56, 112,
  152
Vasquez, J., 5, 6–7, 13, 31, 32, 33, 35,
  36, 37, 39, 41, 44, 49, 53, 54,
  66–67, 73, 93, 94, 103, 117, 119,
  135, 139, 143–144, 146, 152

W

Walker, T., 38
Waltz, K, 3, 66
War of 1812, 117
War weariness, 42
Warsaw Pact, 80, 129

168 Index

Washington, G., 37
Wayman, F., 108, 113–114, 151
Weapons of Mass Destruction
 (WMDs), 116, 120, 122, 126,
 128, 137–142
Wendt, A., 30
Wilkenfeld, J., 27, 151
World War I, 38, 84, 89, 106
World War II, 76, 80, 84, 89, 109,
 116
 Allies, 109

Y

Yemen, 20, 23, 26
Yemen Arab Republic, 20, 21
Yemen People's Republic, 23
Yugoslavia, 17, 18, 19, 20, 21, 22, 25,
 74, 80

Z

Zambia, 18, 19, 24
Zimbabwe, 19
Zionist, 111–112

CPSIA information can be obtained
at www.ICGtesting.com
Printed in the USA
JSHW011454201219
3107JS00006B/150